Gaelic in Contemporary Scotland

GAELIC IN CONTEMPORARY SCOTLAND

The Revitalisation of an Endangered Language

Edited by Marsaili MacLeod and Cassie Smith-Christmas

EDINBURGH
University Press

Edinburgh University Press is one of the leading university presses in the UK. We publish academic books and journals in our selected subject areas across the humanities and social sciences, combining cutting-edge scholarship with high editorial and production values to produce academic works of lasting importance. For more information visit our website: edinburghuniversitypress.com

Edinburgh University Press Ltd
The Tun – Holyrood Road
12(2f) Jackson's Entry
Edinburgh EH8 8PJ

Typeset in 10/12 Ehrhardt by
Servis Filmsetting Ltd, Stockport, Cheshire, and
printed and bound in Great Britain by
CPI Group (UK) Ltd, Croydon, CR0 4YY.

A CIP record for this book is available from the British Library

ISBN 978 1 4744 2065 5 (hardback)
ISBN 978 1 4744 2066 2 (webready PDF)
ISBN 978 1 4744 2067 9 (epub)

Contents

List of Figures

List of Tables

Notes on Contributors

Timothy C. Armstrong is a Senior Lecturer in Gaelic and Communication at *Sabhal Mòr Ostaig*, where he was previously a Soillse Research Fellow. Originally from Seattle in the United States, he has a BA from *Sabhal Mòr Ostaig* and a PhD in sociolinguistics from UHI/University of Aberdeen. His thesis explored the circulation of linguistic ideology in the Irish language revival in Ireland. His research has been published in the *International Journal of Bilingual Education and Bilingualism*, *Language Policy* and *Current Issues in Language Planning* and on topics of linguistic ideology, adult language learning, family language policy, and language revival movements. He is co-editor, with Richard Cox, of *Cleachadh na Gàidhlig* (Using Gaelic), published by *Clò Ostaig* in 2011.

Nicola Carty is the Postdoctoral Research Assistant on the project *Comasan Labhairt ann an Gàidhlig/Gaelic Adult Proficiency* at the University of Glasgow. Her major research interests lie in the acquisition of Gaelic as a second language by adults. She gained her PhD, which was funded by Soillse, from the University of Glasgow in 2015. She has conducted research in this area from a range of perspectives, including language processing, language testing and assessment, learner motivation, and language in education policy. Her current research project, in collaboration with colleagues from the Universities of Glasgow and Aberdeen, takes a corpus-based approach to the development of a framework for the teaching and learning of Scottish Gaelic.

Ingeborg Birnie is a Lecturer in Gaelic Teacher Education at the University of Strathclyde. She gained her PhD, which was funded by Soillse, from the University of Aberdeen in 2018. Her doctoral research examined the management, ideologies and usage of the Gaelic language in public domains. Inge is former Administrator and Research Assistant of the Scottish Deans of Education (SCDE) language group. She has a BSc in Applied Physics from the Robert Gordon University in Aberdeen, a PGCE (secondary) teaching qualification in physics and science from the University of Aberdeen, and a BA (Hons) degree in Gaelic and Development from Sabhal Mòr Ostaig (2013).

Robert Dunbar is Chair of Celtic Languages, Literature, History and Antiquities at the University of Edinburgh. Previously, he was a Senior Research Professor at the University of the Highlands and Islands and Research Director of the Soillse project. He has written extensively on language legislation and language policy and planning for minoritised languages, particularly Scottish Gaelic and other Celtic languages. He is a former board member of Bòrd na Gàidhlig and MG Alba, and he played a significant role in the development of the Gaelic Language (Scotland) Act 2005 and the Statutory Guidance for the preparation of Gaelic language plans under the 2005 Act. He is an expert of the Council of Europe and has regularly advised the Secretariat and the Committee of Experts of the European Charter for Regional or Minority Languages on matters relating to law and policy for minoritised languages. He has also worked with a variety of international organisations in relation to language policy.

Stuart Dunmore is British Academy Postdoctoral Fellow at the University of Edinburgh and is currently investigating new Gaelic speakers' linguistic practices and ideologies in Scotland and Nova Scotia, Canada. Stuart obtained his MA in Celtic and Linguistics in 2008, before graduating from the University of Oxford with a postgraduate MSt degree in 2010. Stuart's doctorate, which was funded by Soillse, examined long-term outcomes of Gaelic-medium education in Scotland. He has held postdoctoral positions at the University of Glasgow and the University of Edinburgh. His principal research interests are in the sociolinguistics of minority language use and speakers' ideological perceptions of their varieties. He has also published research on the Cornish language and 'new speakers' of minority languages.

Mark McConville is a researcher and project manager in Celtic and Gaelic at Glasgow University, with particular responsibility for the Digital Archive of Scottish Gaelic (DASG), the Bòrd na Gàidhlig-funded Leasachadh Corpas na Gàidhlig (LEACAG) project, and the technical aspects of the inter-university historical dictionary Faclair na Gàidhlig. He has degrees in modern languages, linguistics and artificial intelligence, as well as a PhD in Informatics from Edinburgh University, and he worked as the Soillse research fellow at Glasgow University from 2010 to 2015.

Kirstie MacLeod is a Teaching Fellow in Celtic Studies and Soillse PhD candidate at the University of Edinburgh. Her PhD research examines Gaelic in families with young children in Edinburgh and in Barra. Her research adopts an anthropological approach to understanding parental language and education choices. Kirstie earned her MA and MPhil in Celtic from the University of Glasgow. Her additional research interests include kinship and language, anthropology of education, bilingual pre-school education, and additional support for learning in bilingual education.

Marsaili MacLeod lectures in Gaelic Studies at the University of Aberdeen, where she also did her PhD. Prior to joining the University of Aberdeen, she held appointments at the SRUC (Scotland) and Queen's University Belfast. She has conducted extensive research and policy analysis on issues relating to community development, Gaelic revitalisation and cultural heritage at the national and European level. Her ongoing research examines the use of Gaelic in public service delivery, the effectiveness of Gaelic in adult education policy, and the language practices and identities of young Gaelic speakers. She is co-editor of the journal *Scottish Gaelic Studies*.

Michelle Macleod is a Senior Lecturer in Gaelic Studies at the University of Aberdeen, where she is also co-director of Soillse. Previous posts have included Language Planning Manager for Bòrd na Gàidhlig, Director of the Columba Centre and Lecturer in Scottish Gaelic at the National University of Ireland, Galway. She has published extensively on a range of topics relating to Gaelic language and society and is co-editor, with Moray Watson, of Edinburgh University Press's *The Edinburgh Companion to Gaelic Scotland*.

Wilson McLeod is Professor of Gaelic at the University of Edinburgh. He was previously a Course Leader at Sabhal Mòr Ostaig. He earned his BA from Haverford College, his JD degree from Harvard Law School, and his MSc and PhD from the University of Edinburgh. He has published extensively on various aspects of Gaelic language policy in Scotland and minority languages more generally, as well as Gaelic literature and culture in Scotland and Ireland from the Middle Ages to the present.

Gillian Munro is the Deputy Director for Education at Sabhal Mòr Ostaig; prior to that she was a Research Fellow, Arkleton Centre for Rural Development, University of Aberdeen. She has recently led research into language usage in the Western Isles and into the training needs of Gaelic development workers. She has published widely on language use in the community and is co-editor, with Iain Taylor, of *Coimhearsnachdan na Gàidhlig / Gaelic Communities Today*.

Sìleas L. NicLeòid is a Soillse Research Fellow based at Sabhal Mòr Ostaig. She has degrees in German and English linguistics and literature and pedagogics, as well as a PhD in sociolinguistics from Sabhal Mòr Ostaig, which she gained in 2013. Her doctoral research, funded by Soillse, examined the link between language and culture in Gaelic-medium education (GME) and the influence of the input the children receive on their abilities and attitudes towards the language. Her first book, *A' Ghàidhlig agus beachdan nan sgoilearan: cothroman leasachaidh ann am foghlam tro mheadhan na Gàidhlig* (*Gaelic and Pupil Attitudes: Development Opportunities in Gaelic-medium Education*), which is based on the results from her doctoral research, was published by Clò Ostaig in 2016.

Susan Bell was awarded her PhD from the University of Glasgow on modern Scottish Gaelic orthography in 2016. She was Research Assistant on the Soillse project Dlùth is Inneach, which carried out ideological clarification within the Gaelic-speaking community in order to inform corpus planning approaches. Her other research interests include Gaelic drama and language planning. She is currently based at the National Library of Scotland in her position as Gaelic Wikipedian (Uicipeidiche na Gàidhlig).

Cassie Smith-Christmas is a Research Fellow at the National University of Ireland, Galway, where she is conducting a comparative study of Family Language Policy (FLP) in Scotland and Ireland. From 2012–2016 Cassie was a Research Fellow with Soillse at the University of the Highlands Islands, during which time she held a visiting fellowship at the Institution for Advanced Studies in Humanities (IASH) at the University of Edinburgh, where she completed her monograph, *Family Language Policy: Maintaining an Endangered Language in the Home* (Palgrave, 2016). Her research has been published in the *International Journal of the Sociology of Language*, *Current Issues in Language Planning* and the *Journal of Multilingual and Multicultural*

Development. She is currently co-editor of a volume arising from a European COST network, entitled *New Speakers of Minority Languages: Linguistic Ideologies and Practices.* Her research interests include discourse analysis, language alternation, pragmatics, child language and natural language use.

Iain Taylor is a Lecturer at Sabhal Mòr Ostaig, where he teaches courses on language planning and sociolinguistics as well as Gaelic language. He recently contributed to two research projects, with Gillian Munro, on language usage in the Western Isles and into the training needs of Gaelic development workers. He has published a number of articles on Gaelic language skills and the demographics of Gaelic society.

Colin H. Williams is an Honorary Professor and Director of the Language, Policy and Planning Research Unit, Cardiff University and a Senior Research Associate of the VHI Institute and Visiting Fellow, St Edmund's College, Cambridge University. He is a former member of the Welsh Language Board and currently advises the Welsh Government on its Official Language Policy. He has served as an expert advisor to the Soillse project and chairs its international advisory committee. Currently, he is engaged in research which compares the influence of senior civil servants on policy development in a number of jurisdictions, including Scotland, Wales, Ireland, Catalonia, Finland and Canada.

Foreword: Assailed yet Resolute

Under what conditions can an endangered minority language community offer hope and a vision to its members and a programme of action that is acceptable to its fellow majoritarian citizens? This is one of the most challenging of questions in any pluralist democracy, for so much of a minority's ambition is predicated upon the majority's recognition of its right to exist and, if valued, to flourish. From contemporary Catalan, to Nahuati and Yucatec Maya to Maori, the fate of minoritised languages could be taken as a temperature gauge of a society's approach to cultural diversity and the worth of human dignity.

This volume represents a very welcome synthesis of our current understanding of the social context of Gaelic. Based in large part on the research undertaken by the Soillse network it represents the current state of the art with respect to the multiple dimensions of Gaelic, but the issues raised are indicative of wider, global trajectories. How the contributors approach their topics and together provide evidence-based policy recommendations thus has resonance far beyond the shores of Scotland. However, we acknowledge that there are many, often contradictory or ambiguous types of evidence, so much so that decision-makers tend either to be wary of such data or select those which fit their ideological predispositions as to the role of Gaelic in society.

This innovative volume is replete with scholarly analyses, insights, critical judgements and pragmatic observations. The fundamental questions asked refer to meanings and relevance, for the speakers and their neighbours, local authorities and national political representatives. As indicated in the introductory chapter the civil society platform upon which recent language revitalisation efforts have been constructed is relatively fragmented, deeply scarred and politically rather marginal. Questions of low social prestige, the hegemonic power of English and the political rhetoric of successive Scottish administrations still act as barriers to Gaelic being considered as a universal public good in society. Thus, it is critical that newer language affiliations and practices not only provide meaning-seeking experiences but also offer a robust defence for the promotion, protection and regulation of Gaelic.

Several interlinking methodologies and threads are given substantive, empirical life in the constituent chapters. Linguistic ideologies and authority are interpreted in settings as diverse as Edinburgh schools or within the NHS Eileanan Siar Gaelic language plan. There is an emphasis on discourse analysis, detailed ethnographic approaches and real-time observations to supplement self-reported or participant narratives on language usage and variety. Ideological spaces, the lack of adequate language resources and the sufficiency of formal language plans are also analysed using approaches developed within a variety of disciplines.

Attention is drawn in the various chapters to the development of different types of speakers and their social contexts, to the layered complexity of the challenges they face in realising their sociolinguistic skills within social communication. However, the golden thread which runs throughout the volume is the ability of the community to draw on its own resources, initiatives and programmes for action which are negotiated with those in power who set the official agenda and control the fiscal allocations to enable the visions to become social reality.

Of course, one of the more profound difficulties of being such a small minoritised community is that structure and agency are often influenced by strong and readily identifiable personalities. Thus, whether one is discussing the actions of Bòrd na Gàidhlig, the policy decisions of government ministers or the programme priorities implemented by senior civil servants, there is an element of recognition, of accountability and of engagement which does not figure so readily in larger speech communities. Neither are academics, including several in this collection, allowed to remain anonymous; for several public intellectuals simultaneously combine being activists, government advisers and critics of public policy. This is both a strength and weakness. It is a strength because there is often an immediacy born of a long-term acquaintance, if not always instant access to those who are the wielders of influence and power. But it is also a weakness for within the neoliberal climate, most Gaelic-medium organisations are grant-dependent agencies, and an unbridled amount of public criticism and unfavourable reports, often authored in tandem with academic specialist, can in theory result in a downturn in funding or, at the very least, an unresponsive detachment to the issues under consideration. And yet, in so many instances, the official response to specialist policy recommendations has been to fund and action them, as and when political and fiscal conditions allowed. The problem is that such responses happen over the long term and, as so many of the contributors to this volume stress, there is an urgency to the current crisis facing the Gaelic community. Clearly within this community there is no single category of speaker for it represents a range of nuanced identities, varieties of speech and skill sets. Thus, knowing where to place one's priorities is an understandable conundrum. That there are so many options available and described in this volume attests to the currency and richness of the analysis.

There is clearly much that needs further explication. Further work could be undertaken on the strategies for teaching and learning Gaelic, to native speakers, new speakers and migrants. Analysing the relationship between building up the skills capacity and the daily usage of Gaelic within the public sector, voluntary, entertainment and sporting domains would be profitable, and would feed in to the finessing of language plans, let alone any proposed language standards and more robust legislation. An agenda which identified the need for a more convincing language-related discourse, greater social cohesion, behavioural policy tools undergirding interventions, comprehensive and actionable language rights, the specification of language standards of service delivery, a closer engagement with and empowerment by political parties would all build on the pioneering work of the earlier initiatives.

However, the most pressing imperative perhaps is a clearer specification of the economic, regional development and infrastructural needs of the Gaelic-speaking workforce together with the identification and then construction of newer opportunities that a working knowledge of Gaelic alongside English and other selected languages could fulfil.

The harvest may yet be plentiful but the workers are few, to paraphrase Mathew 9:37. Yet what is needed above all to allow Gaelic not only to navigate into the mainstream but to be accepted as a public good, is regular high-quality evaluations of the impact of civil society initiatives and government plans so that the time-series evidence related to the impact of current schemes, plans and actions can be scrutinised, debated and fed into future proposals.

It is argued below that through the study of the practices and ideologies of speakers in a range of contexts, the findings presented here force one to reconsider the very meaning of Gaelic 'revitalisation' and cause one to rethink what would constitute a success in Gaelic revitalisation in Scotland.

So, what would count as success in the short and medium term? At a bare minimum the stabilisation of existing numbers and communities would require considerable energies being expended. For me, stabilisation would count as a necessary but not a sufficient minimum success. A more telling success story would involve increased numbers of speakers, largely through the statutory education and adult education systems; a more profound sense of rootedness and legitimacy of Gaelic in new domains and locales; a greater usage of the language in a wider range of both public and private contexts; a more robust economic sphere within which Gaelic would gain instrumental credit and repay higher levels of fluency and communication skills; and a generous acknowledgement of the role that new speakers could play in language revitalisation efforts. It will be noted that I am emphasising skills acquisition, usage and capacity building. But for this to become binding on the public authorities as social action, then clearly there is a need for a greater specification of the legal rights of speakers, a greater satisfaction of their expectations when faced with the frustration of not receiving the services that are advertised as theirs by statutory obligation, and a deeper sense that Gaelic policy is an integral part of public policy writ large. All this has to be layered upon the protection and development of *A' Ghàidhealtachd* as an integral part of national language planning and policy and socio-economic development. A tall order indeed and a challenging pathway. But it is one to which the contributors to this volume have provided a sensitive road map if we were but willing to use it and follow their directions rather than wait à la Chekhov for the wind in the graveyard!

Colin H. Williams, Cardiff University and
Cambridge University, UK

Acknowledgements

The editors wish to start by sincerely thanking all contributors to the studies upon which this book is based. In this book, Gaelic speakers, learners, activists and practitioners rightfully take centre stage. We would also like to acknowledge the significant contribution of those who have helped us to bring this work to completion. Chief among them are our contributors to this volume. In particular, we would like to single out Nicola Carty, who was initially on the editorial team and contributed to the original proposal, as well as co-authoring the introduction. We are also indebted to our international colleagues with whom we share similar concerns about endangered language communities, and who have stimulated dialogue and debate since the inception of the Soillse network. We owe a huge thank you to colleagues who reviewed individual chapters and responded with such enthusiasm to this project. We are most grateful to the readers who evaluated our proposal for their insightful comments and suggestions. Without the exceptional patience and guidance from Edinburgh University Press, this project would not have been possible and we are grateful to Laura Williamson for encouraging us to pursue it. We also thank Ordnance Survey and the National Records of Scotland for allowing us to reproduce material from the 2011 Census. Finally, the editors gratefully acknowledge the financial support and assistance of the Scottish Funding Council, Bòrd na Gàidhlig and Highlands and Islands Enterprise to the Soillse research network.

List of Abbreviations

BnaG	Bòrd na Gàidhlig
CnaG	Comunn na Gàidhlig
CNES	Comhairle nan Eilean Siar
CPD	continuing professional development
EME	English-medium education
GIDS	Graded Intergenerational Disruption Scale
GLP	Gaelic language plan
GME	Gaelic-medium education
GP	general practitioner (medical doctor)
GOC	Gaelic Orthographic Conventions
HIE	Highlands and Islands Enterprise
IGT	intergenerational transmission
L1	first language
L2	second language
NGO	non-governmental organisation
NHS	the National Health Service
NMS	National Museum of Scotland
NRS	National Records of Scotland
RLS	reversing language shift
SFC	Scottish Funding Council
SLA	second languge acquisition
UNESCO	United Nations Educational, Scientific and Cultural Organization

I

Introduction

Marsaili MacLeod, Cassie Smith-Christmas and Nicola Carty

It seems apt to open this volume with a quote from Nancy C. Dorian, whose work on the Gaelic spoken in East Sutherland has not only profoundly shaped scholarship on Scottish Gaelic sociolinguistics as a whole, but has guided research on language shift and maintenance for decades now. In 1987 Dorian wrote:

> In the fifteen years during which I was constantly visiting the East Sutherland district of the northeast Scottish mainland or living there, actively studying its distinctive and unique flavor, I was asked many times whether my activities or indeed anyone else's could make any difference to the ultimate fate of the dialect. But I was never asked that question by a native of the region. (Dorian 1987: 233)

More than thirty years later, as the authors in this volume can attest, this question still lies at heart of conducting research on the social and linguistic dynamics of the Gaelic (*Gàidhlig*) language. Collectively, we have been asked this same question by various interlocutors, dozens, if not hundreds of times – sometimes with genuine interest and concern, sometimes pejoratively, with clear intent to aggravate. Indeed, a cursory glance at the mainstream and regional Scottish press will reveal that in popular discourse, the answer to this question is a loud and resounding 'no'. Gaelic is referred to as a 'dead language', or a language that only a tiny proportion of the population speak; and children receiving their education through the medium of Gaelic, or attempts of any integration into public signage (recently, for example, the use of Gaelic – *Poileas Alba* – on the Police Scotland logo), cause public outcry.[1] These acts are considered 'vanity projects' and deemed 'a waste of money'. In other words, the fate of the language is sealed, and any attempt to alter this trajectory goes against deep-seated notions of what 'ought' to be (cf. Duchêne and Heller 2007). These types of discourses occur contemporaneously with – and sometimes even in tandem with – overly romanticised framings of the language: 'Scotland's ancient language', evocative of the 'wild' landscape of the language's perceived heartland, the Outer Hebrides. As McLeod (2001: 27) aptly summarises the situation: 'The position of Gaelic in Scottish public life and discourse is contradictory: a dominant softcore, romanticized support coexists with a residual contemptuousness that borders on racism' (see also McEwan-Fujita 2006 and MacKinnon 2011 for further discussions on these discourses).

Gaelic is not alone in its paradoxical framing within the public discourse; indeed, as discussed for instance in Jaffe (2007) and Sallabank (2013), this type of exultation in concert with denigration is reproduced across a number of minority language contexts. It is against this discursive backdrop that Gaelic, and other minority languages, however, undertake the process of revitalising the language, a process that the most eminent of language revitalisation scholars, Joshua Fishman (2002: 270), describes from the collective viewpoint as one which is 'more complicated than most of us had originally thought it would be, and indeed it is'. As the chapters of this volume show, the constant struggle against the denigrating discourses, as well as the balancing act between at points capitalising on and at times distancing from the more 'essentialising' (Jaffe 2007) discourses, underpins the wider milieu of language revitalisation in contemporary Scotland. On the ground, so to speak, the fact that the language is only spoken by 57,375 speakers in Scotland remains a formidable challenge (National Records for Scotland (NRS) 2013a). It is important to point out that in the case of many endangered language situations, where speaker numbers may be in the hundreds or dozens, this may seem like a relatively 'healthy' number, especially when considering the fact that languages can be indeed 'healthy' with relatively few speakers (for instance, Kulick's 1997 well-known example of Taiap pre-Tok Pisin contact) and given Urla's (1993) caution against playing the numbers game in revitalisation efforts. However, in 2011, the findings of Munro et al.'s study conducted on Shawbost, on the Isle of Lewis – a community chosen because of its legacy as a Gaelic stronghold – revealed that intergenerational transmission 'has all but ended' and that 'the language is falling apart and may be dead as a community language in Shawbost within one or perhaps two generations' (p. 3). This finding underscores the precarious position of the language, which aligns with Kulick's study alluded to earlier, where although Taiap was healthy despite its small speaker base, a rupture in intergenerational transmission left the language in a critical situation. Such evidence lends support to Fishman's (2001: 467) characterisation of Stage 6 on his well-known GIDS scale – intergenerational transmission in the home – as the 'fulcrum' of reversing language shift and to Spolsky's 2012 characterisation of family language policy as the 'critical domain'.

Despite the formidable challenges of maintaining a language in which intergenerational transmission has 'all but ended' even in its historical strongholds, Gaelic revitalisation nevertheless continues. The naissance of the current revitalisation coincides with a growing interest in the last thirty years or so in the fate of indigenous languages worldwide (see, for example, Edwards 1984; Grenoble and Whaley 1998; Janse and Tol 2003; Brenzinger 2007; King et al. 2008); its naissance, however, is markedly later than its Celtic cousins and geographic neighbours, Ireland and Wales. The timing of the current revitalisation, as well as its ideological underpinnings, is discussed within the chapters in this volume. At the heart of this volume, however, is the resilience of the *people* who engage in revitalisation efforts – their agency, how they enact their agency, and the various barriers they face in doing so. For, as James Costa (2016) writes in his recent volume on language revitalisation:

> For although of course language is the central rallying point, the actions we are referring to are primarily not about language but about people: people coming together to act in the world, people articulating opinions about how society should be ordered and about who should take part in that order. (Costa 2016: 4)

The chapters in this volume reveal how people who engage in language revitalisation in various ways conceptualise their actions, the ideological underpinnings of such actions, and how these relate other aims as well as broader sociolinguistic and socio-political realities (cf. Glaser's 2006: 181 concept that the 'Gaelic community' may perhaps best be understood as a social movement). As the chapters will also show, many of these revitalisation efforts revolve around 'new' speakers of the language, defined by O' Rourke et al. (2015) as speakers who have acquired the minority language not in the home or community, but in an institutional context such as the school and which Ó Murchadha et al. (2018: 4) have recently re-conceptualised as 'social actors who use and claim ownership of a language that is not, for whatever reason, typically perceived as belonging to them or "people like them"'. Not only have efforts around new speakers guided a number of language revitalisation efforts (for example, integrating the minority language into the school; see Baker 2007), but in cases where there are no native speakers, or where native speakers are past childbearing age, revitalisation efforts may depend almost entirely on new speakers (for example, Manx, see Ó hIfearnáin 2015; or Giernesiei, see Sallabank and Marquis 2018). For Gaelic where, as emphasised earlier, intergenerational transmission remains precarious, new speakers indeed have a part to play in the future of the language, although as various chapters also illustrate (see, for example, McLeod, this volume), this role is often not without its contestation.

This volume shows how, for those people taking part in the revitalisation, the future of the language is not already written, and it is certainly not written in obituary form. That does not mean that these social actors are ignorant of the advanced state of the language shift, nor that they are unwilling to acknowledge the gravity of the situation. It means that they are prepared to keep swimming against the proverbial tide of language shift to take part in something so that their language (however this notion of 'their' might be conceptualised) may continue to be spoken in Scotland. This is their story, of how they navigate the vast complexities of revitalising a minority language in the twenty-first century, and the continual challenges they face in doing so.

The minoritisation of Gaelic speakers in Scotland

We turn our attention now to consider the main socio-historical processes through which speakers of Scottish Gaelic have been marginalised up until the present day. It should be noted that this section is only intended to provide a general background for the chapters which follow, and that much more advanced treatments of Gaelic in Scotland can be found in the various references throughout this section. Linguistically speaking, Scottish Gaelic is most closely related to Irish Gaelic and Manx Gaelic, and more distantly to the other Celtic languages, Breton, Cornish and Welsh. There is evidence of a Scottish Gaelic variety distinct from Irish Gaelic emerging in the twelfth century (Ó Maolalaigh 2008), yet the continuing linguistic similarities between the three Goidelic languages also draw our attention to the concept that in addition to linguistic differences, different languages exist because they have been circumscribed by the borders – both physical and conceptual – of an ever-evolving socio-historical landscape (cf. Ó Baoill 2000; Smith-Christmas and Ó hIfearnáin 2015). What follows is a brief account of how a language that once was spoken over nearly all of present-day Scotland came to be minoritised to the point that a sizeable proportion of the Scottish public has already erected the language's metaphoric tombstone, or at the very least wishes for its imminent erection.

In common with other small languages in Europe, Gaelic has a long history of demographic decline and geographical retreat to the periphery. In the case of Gaelic, this meant a retreat to the mountainous north and west of the country, commonly referred to as the Highlands, which stands in contrast to the fertile and more urbanised area of the country, known as the Lowlands. As detailed in Devine (1994: 1), by 1380 we see this geographic difference conceptualised in socio-cultural terms, with the chronicler John Fordun writing that people of the Lowlands (*Galldachd*) spoke 'Teutonic' (Scots) and the people of the Highlands (*Gàidhealtachd*) spoke 'Scottish' (Gaelic), the former of whom he considered 'domestic and civilised', while the latter of whom he considered 'a savage and untamed nation'. This image of the 'savage' Highlander became deeply embedded in Lowland cultural consciousness. The Highlands therefore, needed to be 'civilised', and education, coupled with religion, provided the key mechanisms by which to do so. The aims of imposing this 'civility' on the people of the Highlands were twofold: a) to introduce Presbyterianism into this still predominantly Catholic area; and b) to induce a shift to English. The preface to the Statutes of Iona, ratified in 1616, for example, state that there is 'there is no means more powerful' to 'abolish and remove' the Gaelic language than the establishment of schools (MacKinnon 1991: 47[2]) and the initial English-only policy of The Society in Scotland for the Propagation of Christian Knowledge, founded in 1701, similarly echoed the entwined nature of religion, education and anti-Gaelic sentiment. In addition to this climate of hostility towards the language, the end of the eighteenth century marked the beginning of significant change in the Highlands, with the transition from the clan system to that of landlord-tenant; forced migration (as tenants could be forced off the land if – as was the case during The Clearances, lasting from 1792–1886 – sheep-farming was deemed more profitable than small tenant holdings); and migration to urban Lowland areas such as Glasgow following due to the desperate socio-economic conditions in the *Gàidhealtachd*. Thus, not only did the language suffer due to depopulation within its heartland area, but English became firmly associated with economic survival and Gaelic with abject poverty (see Withers 1988, 1998).

The low status of Gaelic was further compounded by the Education (Scotland) Act 1872, which made no provision for the language within compulsory education (see O'Hanlon and Paterson 2014). MacKinnon (1974: 55) writes that up until 1930s there were reports of children being punished for speaking Gaelic in school on the Isle of Lewis. By this time, although the language continued to be spoken in various areas of the Highlands, attested to for instance by the Scottish Dialect Survey conducted primarily between 1950–1963, and Dorian's (1981) well-known work on East Sutherland Gaelic, Gaelic was steadily retreating to the country's westernmost islands, the Hebrides. In this area (as well as in rural areas of the mainland Highlands), the local infrastructure meant that most children had to 'board away' for secondary school, which in turn meant either going to the mainland or living in one of the more urbanised areas, such as Stornoway on the island of Lewis, or Portree on the Isle of Skye. These two towns were areas where the language shift was most acute, with the 1961 Report for the Scottish Council on Education (p. 31) characterising them as 'English pales'. Until recently, university education most certainly meant leaving for the mainland, and thus many young Gaelic speakers not only spent much of their lives in more Anglicised areas, but these experiences further contributed to the low value of language. The low value attributed to Gaelic as a result of educational policy is considered one of the primary reasons for the widespread language shift following the Second World War, when various places in the Hebrides saw gaps in intergenerational transmission. Moreover, the language become further confined to the westernmost of the Hebrides, referred to as the Outer Hebrides, and governed by the local authority, Comhairle nan Eilean Siar (Western Isles Council). This island archipelago is now commonly perceived as the remaining traditional 'heartland' area (see Figures 1.1 and 1.2).

However, despite the language's long decline, its resilience too must be emphasised. As MacKinnon (1991: 181) writes,

> The Gaelic communities have surprisingly maintained themselves into the late 20th century despite the most formidable adversities. The modern history of Gaelic society since the Clearances and the establishment of the crofting community, has included two world wars, a profound intervening depression, and a subsequent history of both neglect and exploitation with little regard for community and ecological values.

The most recent census (2011) recorded 57,375 Gaelic people in Scotland with the ability to speak Gaelic, which comprises 1.1 per cent of the Scottish population. Remarkably, given the language's continuing shift, the 2011 Census results showed the rate of decline to be slowing (2.2 per cent decline as opposed to 11.1 per cent between 1991 and 2001) and, for the first time, a 0.1 per cent growth in the percentage of young speakers under the age of twenty. As Dunmore (2014) points out, this slight increase was heralded as indicative of the success of Gaelic-medium education (GME), but Dunmore's own work in this area (this volume; 2014) aligns with other discussions of minority language education as a revitalisation strategy (see for example Spolsky 1991; Hornberger 2008; Woolard 2011) in highlighting the layered complexities of this endeavour. This again returns to Fishman's (2002: 270) point mentioned earlier, of language revitalisation being 'more complicated than most of us had originally thought it would be, and indeed it is'. The following is meant to delineate some of the most pertinent complexities that will be further explored in the following chapters.

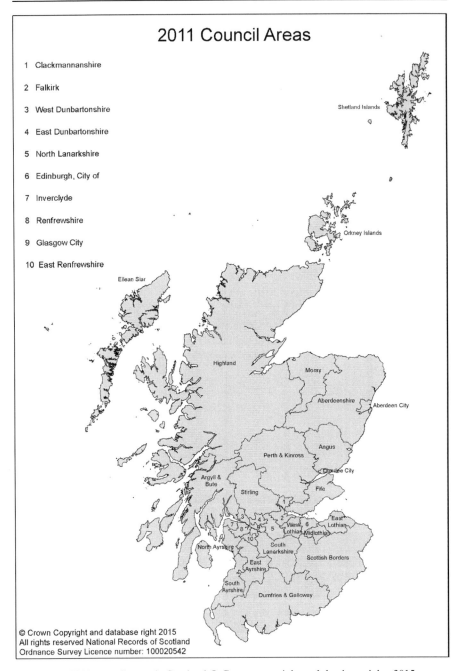

Figure 1.1 2011 council areas in Scotland © Crown copyright and database rights 2015
OS100020542

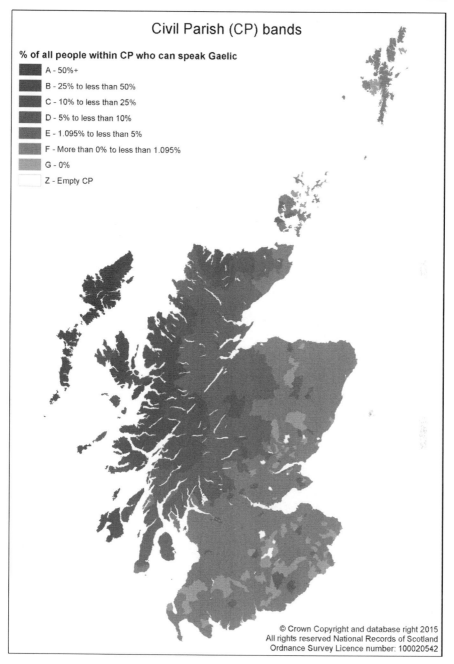

Civil Parish (CP) bands

% of all people within CP who can speak Gaelic

- A - 50%+
- B - 25% to less than 50%
- C - 10% to less than 25%
- D - 5% to less than 10%
- E - 1.095% to less than 5%
- F - More than 0% to less than 1.095%
- G - 0%
- Z - Empty CP

Figure 1.2 Density of Gaelic speakers in Scotland (2011) © Crown copyright and database rights 2015 OS100020542

The modern Gaelic revival

As mentioned previously, the modern Gaelic revival coincides broadly with what many consider to be a growing interest in the fate of minority languages world-wide. Indeed, as McLeod (2006: vii) emphasises in the introduction to the volume *Revitalising Gaelic in Scotland*, some have even gone so far as to term recent Gaelic revitalisation efforts a 'renaissance'. As alluded to in the last section, education has been one of the key terrains in which these revitalisation efforts have played out. In the 1970s, bilingual education (Gaelic and English) was instituted by *Comhairle nan Eilean Siar* and initially involved twenty primary schools under the council's remit. The implementation of immersive Gaelic education is attributed to the forma-tion of 'cròileagan' (playgroups for 3–4-year-olds), which will be discussed in much greater detail in Kirstie MacLeod's chapter (this volume). In 1985, immersive Gaelic education was introduced in primary schools, as parents, frustrated with the lack of Gaelic fluency pupils were attaining in the bilingual programme, witnessed the comparative success of the *cròileagan* (Robertson 2003). The first two GME units were set up in Glasgow and Inverness in 1985, the total number of students of which was twenty-four. The term 'unit' is used here because, with a few exceptions, GME streams are usually part of English-medium schools. Since its initial inception, GME has continued to grow, and in lowland and urban communities in particular GME has introduced the language to hitherto non-Gaelic-speaking families. In fact, most of the 3,145 children in Gaelic primary education (BnaG 2017) are believed to learn Gaelic as a second language (Education Scotland 2015). As well as the slight upward trend in the number of young speakers, the 2011 Census also recorded, for the first time, a higher proportion of Gaelic speakers in Lowland Scotland than in Highland Scotland. For instance, some 9,000 speakers alone live in the Greater Glasgow area (NRS 2013b); even though, historically, this city has been a stronghold of Gaelic-speaking migrants from the Highlands (see Kidd 2007), this number is viewed as mirroring the change in other minority language revitalisation contexts, such as Wales (see Aitchison and Carter 2004; Jones 2012), Ireland (see Ó Riagáin 2000), Galicia (see O'Rourke 2005; O'Rourke and Romallo 2011) and the Basque country (see Ortega et al. 2015), where new speakers comprise a significant proportion of the younger speaker base, particu-larly in urban contexts (see also Nance 2018 for more on young new speakers of Gaelic in Glasgow).

Despite the expansion of GME at the primary level, it remains less available at the secondary level, and, similarly, in terms of adult education. Although there have been significant gains on these fronts – such as, for example, the establishment of the Gaelic-medium college Sabhal Mòr Ostaig UHI, which offers degree courses through the medium of Gaelic, as well as a myriad of other adult-learning opportunities – this gap in provision poses a significant challenge for language planning, especially in terms of intergenerational transmission (MacCaluim 2007; McLeod et al. 2010; Smith-Christmas and Armstrong 2014). Lack of secondary school opportunities jeop-ardise young speakers' use of the language into adulthood; and, similarly, the lack of opportunities available for adults to become fluent, confident speakers does not bode well for maintaining a speaker base of childbearing age (cf. Fishman 1991). As discussed in Carty's (2014) work and M. MacLeod (this volume), current efforts are underway to address issues such as fluency in adult language learning, and these efforts also underscore the importance of taking attitudinal and affective factors into language pedagogy as a means to language revitalisation.

As emphasised earlier, unlike its Celtic neighbours Ireland and Wales, Gaelic has generally been perceived as a regional and not national language of Scotland. This perhaps accounts in part for the fact that Gaelic was not recognised in national statutory terms until 2005 with the Gaelic Language (Scotland) Act 2005. The Act was modelled upon the first Welsh Language Act 1993, and, while it bears similarity to Ireland's 2003 Official Languages Act, is less demanding in several respects (see Walsh and McLeod 2007; Dunbar 2010). It does not, for example, grant Gaelic speakers any language rights; however, it has increased the status and visibility of Gaelic in official life, including its use in the Scottish Parliament. Perhaps most importantly, the Gaelic Language (Scotland) Act 2005 established the statutory body Bòrd na Gàidhlig, which is charged with implementing a National Gaelic Language Plan and with guiding the delivery of Gaelic education by local government. The main powers of the Bòrd are exercised through placing a requirement on certain public bodies to produce plans to give equal status to Gaelic and English, and to incrementally increase bilingual service provision in their organisation (see McLeod 2010 and Dunbar, this volume). Efforts at the national level have also included the media, and both the Gaelic radio service, Radio nan Gàidheal, and television service, BBC Alba, are currently available throughout Scotland, now free of charge. Along with these developments, we also see what could be considered as a shift in attitude, with O'Hanlon et al.'s (2013) research showing a general support for the language by the Scottish public as well as the desire for it to be maintained in the future; however, it is important to note that since this research was conducted, as pointed out at the beginning of this chapter, the denigrating discourses still persist in wider Scottish consciousness.

Taken together, these processes are producing a Gaelic community which is increasingly mobile, urban, networked and, as a result, socio-culturally diverse. What might this mean for the language practices of different kinds of speakers? The contributions in this volume reveal how Gaelic speakers are negotiating novel ways to maintain and enact their bilingual identities in socio-spatially diverse contexts. In doing so, they challenge older understandings of the Gaelic community as a single collective identity. A central concern is to identify the functions crucial to continued use of the language and the social conditions necessary to reproduce a speech community in the likelihood of minority identities being more or less decoupled from place or traditional forms of use (cf. Romaine 2007).

The present collection

Following in the wake of *Revitalising Gaelic in Scotland* (McLeod 2006), *Coimhnearsnachd na Gàidhlig an-Diugh / Gaelic Communities Today* (Rothach and Mac an Tàilleir 2010) and *A' Cleachdadh na Gàidhlig: slatan-tomhais ann an dìon cànain sa choimhearsnachd* (Cox and Armstrong 2011), our volume draws on scholarship from Soillse, the national research network for Gaelic language revitalisation in Scotland, in critically examining recent planning and policy initiatives. This inter-university network, established in 2010, was formed to contribute international-quality research to inform Gaelic revitalisation efforts. Soillse builds on a valuable, albeit fragmented, research base on the sociology of Gaelic, which is summarised by Emily McEwan-Fujita in the *Edinburgh Companion to the Gaelic Language* (Watson and Macleod 2010). Our intention in this volume is to further intellectually challenge the changing nature of the sociology of Gaelic in Scotland through critically interrogating processes and patterns of Gaelic language acquisition, use and management across key spaces of interaction: the community, educational settings, and in organisations. Using this approach we can go at least some way to addressing McEwan-Fujita's calls for further research on 'the actual proficiencies, usage patterns and ideologies of Gaelic speakers in residential community contexts' and 'more of the ethnography of communication in everyday life' (2010: 200). In doing so, the volume aims to contribute fresh theoretical insights into processes of small language revival and decline in Western globalised society.

In the eleven chapters which follow, we move from micro sociolinguistic levels of analysis to the macro, beginning first with analyses of children's language acquisition, use and management in pre-school and school years. In Chapter 2, Timothy C. Armstrong unpacks the fifteen-year-long campaign for a dedicated Gaelic school in Edinburgh city through archival research and stakeholder interviews. Armstrong's analysis reveals how some parents and activists imagined the out-of-classroom spaces in the immersion school would serve as sites for Gaelic normalisation and identify formation. The campaign therefore involved an ideological struggle over language practice, ultimately producing a micro-level language-in-education policy. His chapter challenges us to consider how the 'language in the playground' problem reflects wider tensions over the role of schooling in language revitalisation.

In Chapter 3, Kirstie MacLeod extends the discussion of the interaction between the school and home by adopting an ethnographic research approach to understanding the role of Gaelic parent and toddler groups in promoting and facilitating Gaelic language acquisition and use in families. The chapter investigates how families of differing Gaelic competencies conceptualise the parent and toddler group within the wider milieu of GME and presents a nuanced discussion of the relationship between educational domains, the family sphere and Gaelic language revitalisation more generally. In keeping with her linguistic anthropological approach, MacLeod's account tells of the everyday challenges and rewards of early years' bilingualism in an endangered language from the perspectives of parents and other carers.

In Chapter 4, Sìleas L. NicLeòid builds on this theme by linking language ideologies to psychological processes of language acquisition, addressing Gaelic-medium educated children's understanding and use of Gaelic idiomatic language. Through interviews with pupils, their teachers and their parents, NicLeòid draws out the complex attitudes behind children's recognition and use of idioms, exploring how perspectives on the relevance of Gaelic in the twenty-first century influence children's linguistic practices at school. NicLeòid further argues that attitudes towards Gaelic have an important role to play in language change, highlighting the relationship between ideology, practice and language form.

The volume then shifts its focus from educational settings on to wider meso levels of sociolinguistic interaction in Chapters 5–7, through addressing language practices and ideologies in the community. Chapter 5 begins the exploration of this topic, with Stuart Dunmore's discussion of the extent to which adults schooled through the medium of Gaelic between 1985 and 1995 report using Gaelic today. Results indicate that the majority of participants' day-to-day Gaelic language use is limited, although exceptions are found among speakers socialised in Gaelic at home during childhood, and those who work in Gaelic-oriented professions. Dunmore's findings emphasise the importance of maintaining Gaelic in a range of domains in order to foster pro-Gaelic ideologies and patterns of usage across the lifetime.

The 'exceptional cases' described by Dunmore – that is, those GME-educated adults who maintain use of the language in their adult lives – fall into the category of 'new speakers', a group which is addressed by Wilson McLeod in Chapter 6. McLeod argues that although new speakers do not represent a new phenomenon in the Gaelic community, they have been, until recently, numerically few and their sociolinguistic experiences unexplored. McLeod contends that despite the challenges involved in producing new speakers, the role they can play in Gaelic revitalisation efforts and in the wider Gaelic community is crucial. As such, he argues that it is imperative to understand the identity, ideological positions and linguistic practices of these individuals. In Chapter 7, Marsaili MacLeod addresses some of the questions raised by McLeod through presenting the findings from a study into second language (L2) adult learners of Gaelic who are engaged in a community classroom learning programme. The findings highlight the typical slow rate of progression and the limitations of an extensive programme of learning, with little conversational practice, in facilitating learners to become active speakers of Gaelic.

In Chapter 8, Bell and McConville argue for Gaelic speakers' input into planning endeavours, again highlighting the importance of a community-based approach to language planning. Their argument draws on adult Gaelic users' ideological approaches to Gaelic corpus planning. A clear ideology emerged from their observations, with participants overwhelmingly identifying the 'best' Gaelic as the traditional, idiomatic vernacular of the mid-twentieth century, when the last generation of Gaelic-dominant bilinguals grew up. They conclude that language management can benefit from an understanding of speakers' relationships to formal Gaelic, which echoes NicLeòid's insights on the value of examining attitudes to a specific language form.

If speakers' ideologies and linguistic practices are to influence language revitalisation policy, it is important not only to examine self-reported language practices, but also to consider real-time observations of Gaelic usage. In Chapter 9, Ingeborg Birnie uses participant observation to report on language choices in conversations in a variety of publicly accessible open spaces. Her findings are compared to official Gaelic language management policies in an argument that focuses on bottom-up interventions in formal language planning.

Those responsible for the design and implementation of Gaelic language plans are considered in Chapter 10, by Michelle Macleod, Timothy C. Armstrong, Gillian Munro and Iain Taylor. This chapter marks the move from the meso level of interaction to the macro level, as chapter themes begin to address Gaelic at the level of larger-scale organisations. The authors note that the increase in strategic planning for Gaelic has naturally led to an increase in the number of individuals involved in this activity. However, they raise the question of how the language practices and ideologies of this new and growing taskforce are brought to bear on this work. This chapter illustrates how increasing professionalisation means a new sector of the Gaelic community is evolving, and that their attitudes and practices should be considered in our understanding of the sociolinguistic realities of Gaelic at the macro organisational level.

In Chapter 11, Robert Dunbar argues that the implementation of public sector language plans falls somewhat short of the policy rationale that inspired their statutory requirement. Through his critical examination of existing plans, and the mechanisms used to enforce the measures outlined therein, Dunbar calls into question the potential of Gaelic language plans to contribute to the revitalisation of Gaelic without redress to language rights. This chapter raises larger questions relating to the attitudinal and behavioural implications of official plans for increasing the status and use of Gaelic in Scotland.

In dealing with these domains of the family, school, community and organisations, this volume highlights the important links between the ideologies and practices of different communities, which may have varying degrees of language competence. These insights are possible based on the work done to date by members of the Soillse network. But as language shift towards English continues, the urgency of developing new ways for future generations to transmit, use and identify with Gaelic in a meaningful way increases. In the final chapter, we synthesise the findings and reflect on the key themes that thread through the contributed chapters. We consider the potential consequences of the research findings for Gaelic communities in Scotland, and reflect on why Gaelic in Scotland is endangered still.

Notes

1. For example, 'Police Scotland unveil new logo with its name in Gaelic despite just 1.1% of the population speaking it' (*The Scottish Sun*, 19 September 2017); 'Police Scotland are blasted after spending taxpayers' money rebranding their force helicopter in Scots Gaelic' (*Mail Online*, 31 August 2015), 'Forcing Gaelic on our schools is wrong, says MSP' (*The Shetland Times*, 2 February 2016).
2. MacKinnon presents the quotes from the document in their original spelling; for simplicity, we have chosen to simply show them in their standard English form.

References

Aitchison, John and Harold Carter. 2004. *Spreading the Word: The Welsh Language 2001*. Ceredigion: Y Lolfa Cyf.
Baker, Colin. 2007. Becoming Bilingual through Bilingual Education. In P. Auer and L. Wei (eds), *Handbook of Multilingualism and Multilingual Communication*, 131–154. Berlin: Mouton de Gruyter.
Bòrd na Gàidhlig. 2017. *Dàta Foghlaim 2016–17 [Education Data 2016–17]*. Inverness: Bòrd na Gàidhlig.

Brenzinger, Matthias (ed.). 2007. *Language Diversity Endangered*. Berlin: Mouton de Gruyter.

Costa, James. 2016. *Revitalising Language in Provence: A Critical Approach*. Oxford: Blackwell and Philological Society.

Carty, Nicola. 2014. The Adult Learner in Gaelic Language-in-Education Policy: Language Revitalisation and the CEFR. *European Journal of Language Policy* 6(2), 195–217. Available online at https://doi.org/10.3828/ejlp.2014.11

Cox, Richard A. V. and Timothy Currie Armstrong (eds). 2011. *A' cleachdadh na Gàidhlig: slatan-tomhais ann an dìon cànain sa choimhearsnachd*. Slèite: Clò Ostaig.

Devine, Tom M. 1994. *Clanship to Crofters' War: The Social Transformation of the Scottish Highlands*. Manchester: University of Manchester Press.

Dorian, Nancy C. 1981. *Language Death: The Life Cycle of a Scottish Gaelic Dialect*. Philadelphia: Pennsylvania University Press.

Dorian, Nancy. C. 1987 [2014]. The Value of Language-Maintenance Efforts which are Unlikely to Succeed. *Small Language Fates and Prospects*, 223–233. Leiden: Brill.

Duchêne, Alexandre and Monica Heller (eds). 2007. *Discourses of Endangerment: Ideology and Interest in the Defence of Languages*. London: Continuum.

Dunbar, Robert. 2010. Language Planning. In Moray Watson and Michelle Macleod (eds), *The Edinburgh Companion to the Gaelic Language*, 146–171. Edinburgh: Edinburgh University Press.

Dunmore, Stuart. 2014. Bilingual Life after School? Language Use, Ideologies and Attitudes among Gaelic-medium Educated Adults. Edinburgh: University of Edinburgh PhD thesis.

Education Scotland. 2015. *Advice on Gaelic Education*. Livingstone: Education Scotland.

Edwards, John. 1984. *Linguistic Minorities, Policies, and Pluralism*. New York: Academic Press.

Fishman, Joshua A. 1991. *Reversing Language Shift*. Clevedon: Multilingual Matters.

Fishman, Joshua. A. 2001. *Can Threatened Languages be Saved? Reversing Language Shift, Revisited: A Twenty-First Century Perspective*. Clevedon: Multilingual Matters.

Fishman, Joshua. A. 2002. Endangered Minority Languages: Prospects for Sociolinguistic Research. *International Journal on Multicultural Societies* 4(2), 270–275.

Glaser, Konstanze. 2006. Reimagining the Gaelic Community: Ethnicity, Hybridity, Politics and Communication. In Wilson McLeod (ed.), *Revitalising Gaelic in Scotland: Policy, Planning and Public Discourse*, 169–184. Edinburgh: Dunedin Academic Press.

Grenoble, Lenore A. and Lindsay J. Whaley (eds). 1998. *Endangered Languages: Current Issues and Future Prospects*. Cambridge: Cambridge University Press.

Hornberger, Nancy (ed.). 2008. *Can Schools Save Indigenous Languages? Policy and Practice on Four Continents*. Basingstoke: Palgrave Macmillan.

Jaffe, Alexandra. 2007. Discourses of Endangerment: Contexts and Consequences of Essentializing Discourses. In Alexandre Duchêne and Monica Heller (eds),

Discourses of Endangerment: Ideology and Interest in the Defence of Languages, 57–75. London: Continuum.

Janse, Mark and Sijmen Tol (eds). 2003. *Language Death and Language Maintenance: Theoretical, Practical, and Descriptive Approaches*. Amsterdam: John Benjamins.

Jones, Hywel J. 2012. *A Statistical Overview of the Welsh Language*. Cardiff: Welsh Language Board.

Kidd, Sheila M. (ed.). 2007. *Glasgow: Baile Mor nan Gaidheal City of the Gaels*. Glasgow: Roinn na Ceiltis.

King, Kendall A., Natalie Schilling-Estes, Lyn Fogle, Jia Jackie Lou and Barbara Soukup (eds). 2008. *Sustaining Linguistic Diversity: Endangered and Minority Languages and Language Varieties*. Washington, DC: Georgetown University Press.

Kulick, Don. 1997. *Language Shift and Cultural Reproduction: Socialization, Self, and Syncretism in a Papua New Guinean Village*. Cambridge: Cambridge University Press.

MacCaluim, Alasdair. 2007. *Reversing Language Shift: The Social Identity and Role of Adult Learners of Scottish Gaelic*. Belfast: Cló Ollscoil na Banríona.

McEwan-Fujita, Emily. 2006. 'Gaelic Doomed as Speakers Die Out?' The Public Discourse of Gaelic Language Death in Scotland. In Wilson McLeod (ed.), *Revitalising Gaelic in Scotland: Policy, Planning and Public Discourse*, 279–293. Edinburgh: Dunedin Academic Press.

McEwan-Fujita, Emily. 2010. Sociolinguistic Ethnography of Gaelic Communities. In Moray Watson and Michelle Macleod (eds), *Edinburgh Companion to the Gaelic Language*, 172–217. Edinburgh: Edinburgh University Press.

MacKinnon, Kenneth. 1974. *The Lion's Tongue: The Original and Continuing Language of the Scottish People*. Inverness: Club Leabhar.

MacKinnon, Kenneth. 1991. *Gaelic: A Past and Future Prospect*. Edinburgh: Saltire.

MacKinnon, Kenneth. 2011. *'Never Spoken Here', 'Rammed Down our Throats' – The Rhetoric of Detractors and Denigrators of Gaelic in the Press*. Report to Bòrd na Gàidhlig, Inverness, and MG Alba, Stornoway, 7 March 2011. (Evidence to Press Complaints Commission, and Leveson Enquiry.)

McLeod, Wilson. 2001. Gaelic in the New Scotland: Politics, Rhetoric and Public Discourse. *Journal on Ethnopolitics and Minority Issues in Europe* 2, 1–33.

McLeod, Wilson (ed.). 2006. *Revitalising Gaelic in Scotland: Policy, Planning and Public Discourse*. Edinburgh: Dunedin Academic Press Ltd.

McLeod, Wilson. 2010. Leasachadh na Gàidhlig: paradaim ùr? In Gillian Munro and Iain Mac an Tàilleir (eds), *Coimhearsnachdan Gàidhlig An-diugh / Gaelic Communities Today*, 1–17. Edinburgh: Dunedin Academic Press.

McLeod, Wilson, Irene Pollock and Alasdair MacCaluim. 2010. *Adult Gaelic Learners in Scotland: Opportunities, Motivations and Challenges*. Inverness: Bòrd na Gàidhlig.

Munro, Gillian, Iain Mac an Tàilleir and Timothy Currie Armstrong. 2011. *Cor na Gàidhlig ann an Siabost; Barail agus Comas Cànain ann an Siabost / The State of Gaelic in Shawbost; Language Attitudes and Abilities in Shawbost*. Inverness: Bòrd na Gàidhlig.

Nance, Claire. 2018. Linguistic Innovation among Glasgow Gaelic New Speakers. In Cassie Smith-Christmas, Noel P. Ó Murchadha, Michael Hornsby and Máiréad

Moriarty (eds), *New Speakers of Minority Languages: Linguistic Ideologies and Practices*, 213–226. Basingstoke: Palgrave Macmillan.

National Records of Scotland (NRS). 2013a. *Statistical Bulletin – Release 2A*. Available online at http://www.scotlandscensus.gov.uk/documents/censusresults/relea se2a/Stats Bulletin2A. pdf (last accessed 26 September 2013).

National Records of Scotland (NRS). 2013b. *2011 Census: Table LC21205DZ – Gaelic Language Skills by Age.*

Ó Baoill, Colm. 2000. The Gaelic continuum. *Éigse* 32, 121–134.

O'Hanlon, Fiona and Lindsay Paterson. 2014. Gaelic Education Since 1872. In Robert D. Anderson, Mark Freeman and Lindsay Paterson (eds), *The Edinburgh History of Education in Scotland*, 304–325. Edinburgh: Edinburgh University Press.

O'Hanlon, Fiona, Lindsay Paterson, Rachel Ormiston and Susan Reid. 2013. *Public Attitudes to Gaelic in Scotland*. Soillse Research Digest 3. Available online at http://www.soillse.ac.uk/wp-content/uploads/SRD3.pdf (last accessed 15 June 2015).

Ó hIfearnáin, Tadhg. 2015. Sociolinguistic Vitality of Manx After Extreme Language Shift: Authenticity Without Traditional Native Speakers. *International Journal for the Sociology of Language* 231, 45–62.

Ó Maolalaigh, Roibeard. 2008. The Scottishisation of Gaelic: A Reassessment of the Language and Orthography of the Gaelic Notes in the Book of Deer. In Katherine Forsyth (ed.), *Studies on the Book of Deer*, 179–275. Dublin: Four Courts Press.

Ó Murchadha, Noel P., Michael Hornsby, Cassie Smith-Christmas and Máiréad Moriarty. 2018. New Speakers, Familiar Concepts? In Cassie Smith-Christmas, Noel P. Ó Murchadha, Michael Hornsby and Máiréad Moriarty (eds), *New Speakers of Minority Languages: Linguistic Ideologies and Practices*, 1–17. Basingstoke: Palgrave Macmillan.

Ó Riagáin, Pádraig. 2000. Irish Language Production and Reproduction 1981–1996. In Joshua A. Fishman (ed.), *Can Threatened Languages be Saved?* 195–214. Clevedon: Multilingual Matters.

O'Rourke, Bernadette. 2005. Expressing Identity through Lesser-used Languages: Examples from the Irish and Galician Contexts. *Language and Intercultural Communication (Politics, Plurilingualism and Linguistic Identity)* 5(3–4), 274–283.

O'Rourke, Bernadette and Fernando Ramallo. 2011. The Native-non-native Dichotomy in Minority Language Contexts: Comparisons between Irish and Galician. *Language Problems & Language Planning* 35(2), 139–159.

O'Rourke, Bernadette, Joan Pujolar and Fernando Ramallo. 2015. New Speakers of Minority Languages: The Challenging Opportunity – Foreword. *International Journal of the Sociology of Language* 231, 1–20.

Ortega, Ane, Jaqueline Urla, Estibalitz Amorrortu, Jone Goirigolzarri and Belen Uranga. 2015. Linguistic Identity among New Speakers of Basque. *International Journal of the Sociology of Language* 231, 85–105.

Robertson, Boyd. 2003. Gaelic Education. In Tom Bryce, Walter Humes, Donald Gillies and Aileen Kennedy (eds), *Scottish Education*, 250–261. Edinburgh: Edinburgh University Press.

Romaine, Suzanne. 2007. Preserving Endangered Languages. *Language & Linguistics Compass* 1(1–2), 115–132.

Rothach, Gillian and Iain Mac an Tàilleir (eds). 2010. *Coimhearsnachdan na Gàidhlig an-Diugh/Gaelic Communities Today*. Edinburgh: Dunedin Academic Press.

Sallabank, Julia. 2013. *Attitudes to Endangered Languages: Identities and Policies*. Cambridge: Cambridge University Press.

Sallabank, Julia and Yan Marquis. 2018. 'We Don't Say it Like That': Language Ownership and (De)Legitimising the New Speaker. In Cassie Smith-Christmas, Noel Ó Murchdha, Michael Hornsby and Mairead Moriarty (eds), *New Speakers of Minority Languages: Linguistic Ideologies and Practices*. Basingstoke: Palgrave.

Scottish Council for Research in Education. 1961. *Gaelic-Speaking Children in Highland Schools*. London: University of London Press.

Smith-Christmas, Cassie and Timothy. C. Armstrong. 2014. Complementary RLS Strategies in Education: The Importance of Adult Heritage Learners of Threatened Minority Languages. *Current Issues in Language Planning* 15(3), 312–326.

Smith-Christmas, Cassie and Tadhg Ó hIfearnáin. 2015. Gaelic Scotland and Ireland: Issues of Class and Diglossia in an Evolving Social Landscape. In Dick Smakman and Patrick Heinrich (eds), *Globalising Sociolinguistics*, 256–269. London: Routledge.

Spolsky, Bernard. 1991. Hebrew Language Revitalization within a General Theory of Second Language Learning. In Robert L. Cooper and Bernard Spolksy (eds), *Influence of Language on Culture and Thought: Essays in Honor of Joshua A. Fishman's Sixty-Fifth Birthday*, 136–156. Berlin: Walter de Gruyter.

Spolsky, Bernard. 2012. Family Language Policy – The Critical Domain. *Journal of Multilingual and Multicultural Development* 33(1), 3–11.

Urla, Jackie. 1993. Cultural Politics in an Age of Statistics: Numbers, Nations, and the Making of Basque Identity. *American Ethnologist* 20(4), 818–843.

Walsh, John and Wilson McLeod. 2007. An Overcoat Wrapped around an Invisible Man? Language Legislation and Language Revitalisation in Ireland and Scotland. *Language Policy* 7(1), 21–46. doi:10.1007/s10993-007-9069-0

Watson, Moray and Michelle Macleod (eds). 2010. *Edinburgh Companion to the Gaelic Language*. Edinburgh: Edinburgh University Press.

Withers, Charles W. J. 1988. The Geographical History of Gaelic in Scotland. In Colin H. Williams (ed.), *Language in a Geographic Context*, 136–166. Clevedon: Multilingual Matters Ltd.

Withers, Charles W. 1998. *Urban Highlanders*. Edinburgh: Tuckwell Press.

Woolard, Katherine A. 2011. Is There Linguistic Life after High School? Longitudinal Changes in the Bilingual Repertoire in Metropolitan Barcelona, *Language in Society* 40, 617–648.

2

The Language of the Playground: Activists Building Consensus on the Language Policy and Ethos of a New Gaelic Immersion School

Timothy C. Armstrong

Language ideology in Edinburgh and Gaelic-medium education

As an alternative pedagogical model, additive immersion education is clearly a success; by a range of measures and in a variety of contexts, students in immersion schools have been shown to equal and even surpass the attainment of their mainstream peers (for research on attainment in Scottish Gaelic immersion see: Johnstone et al. 1999; Highland Council 2009; O'Hanlon et al. 2013). However, as a tactic for language revitalisation, the efficacy of immersion education is far less certain; while students may attain reasonable communicative competence in their classroom language, that competence does not always translate into much social use of the language outside of school (Dunmore 2014, 2016 and this volume; O'Hanlon 2012). Parents and educators often hope that out-of-classroom spaces in the immersion school – the cafeteria, the hallways and particularly the playground – might serve as sites where students can be encouraged to use the school language informally together, thereby normalising the school language as a social language for use outside of the classroom. If immersion education is to function as an effective tactic for language revitalisation, children would need to not only acquire full proficiency in the threatened language, but also be motivated to take the language out of the classroom and use it in their daily lives outside of the school, and then, ideally, in the future as adults. This is a difficult aim, but it is not impossible or unprecedented, and language ideology plays a central role in this regard. If immersion schooling is founded on a clear revivalist ideology linking language and identity, an ideology that leads to a strong, independent school ethos and a coherent school language policy, immersion schools can both provide excellent bilingual education to their students and serve as an effective means for language revival in their communities (cf. Nahir 1998; Brenzinger and Heinrich 2013).

Immersion education does not always develop in this way, but it can, and this naturally raises the question, when it does, why? Why do some immersion schools develop a strong ideological focus and others less so? In this chapter, I will suggest that part of the answer may be found by examining the history of the establishment of immersion schools. All organisations are profoundly ideological, and the ideology of any given organisation is to a greater or lesser extent a function of the wider ideological environment in which it was founded (Simons and Ingram 1997, 2004). Between 1997 and 2011, parents and other language activists in Edinburgh engaged in a long and difficult campaign to establish a dedicated Gaelic-immersion primary school in the city, and in the course of this campaign the language policy and ethos of the proposed school were points of debate. Drawing on data collected for a social history of this grass-roots campaign, I will show how out-of-classroom language policy in Gaelic-medium education (GME) was imagined and contested in the public sphere, and, then, how parents and other language activists worked to build a consensus on what sort of language policy *they* would like to see for their new school. In this chapter, I will use these data to discuss how local language ideologies inform debates on micro-level language-in-education policy.

The social history that follows draws on a wide range of data that includes newspaper coverage of the Gaelic school campaign, letters to the editor and blog/newsgroup posts, official reports, City of Edinburgh Council meeting minutes and consultation documents, consultation submissions and commissioned research conducted in the course of the campaign, as well as data from extensive archives of documents collected and preserved by the Gaelic-school activists themselves, including correspondences with officials and politicians, meeting minutes of activist groups, drafts of speeches, newsletters, campaign plans and lobbying documents. In addition, semi-structured narrative interviews were conducted with thirteen key activists involved at different stages of the campaign, and, together, this archive and interview data were analysed with a particular focus on the ideologies articulated in the debates around the development of GME provision in Edinburgh. In this analysis, the proposed Gaelic school is understood as an organisation that is founded and that functions in its own historically-dependent ideological context. The linguistic and political ideologies which obtain in this context influence the form and function of the Gaelic school as an organisation, and, in turn, once established, the school itself serves as a key site where political and linguistic ideologies are circulated and reproduced in the next generation of Gaelic speakers.

The campaign to establish a dedicated Gaelic school in Edinburgh is notable for being particularly drawn-out and difficult. Parents and other activists began agitating for a Gaelic school in 1998 and the new school was not opened until September of 2013, about fifteen years later. The overall drive for a Gaelic school can be divided into two distinct campaigns: the first, unsuccessful, campaign from 1998 to 2000; and the second, successful, campaign from 2009 to 2011, separated by almost a decade of quieter but persistent lobbying. The parents and other activists organised their campaigns in the face of a powerful and pervasive ideology in Edinburgh, rooted in the Scottish Enlightenment (cf. Walsh 2006: 136–139), that understands Scottish Gaelic as a vestigial Highland language that has no place in Scotland's modern and cosmopolitan capital city. As an example of a particularly concise articulation of this ideology, here is Gina Davidson, the Scottish Press Association's 2013 Journalist of the Year, arguing in the *Edinburgh Evening News* against the Gaelic school:

> Gaelic may well be a lovely, lyrical, ancient language and well worth keeping alive, but surely that should be in places where it is traditionally spoken, not in a modern,

cosmopolitan city, where the only Gaelic word known to the most is 'slainte' [sic].
(Davidson 2011)

In this ideological context, the debates around the development of GME in Edinburgh
were strikingly contentious, and it is perhaps not surprising that it took more than
a decade to convince the City of Edinburgh Council to approve a dedicated Gaelic
school. In the following analysis, I will show how these larger ideologies about the
appropriateness of Gaelic development in Edinburgh coloured the debates about language policy in the proposed school, among activists, politicians and in the public
sphere in general.

Problems in the playground and out-of-school language use

GME in Scotland is atypical in comparison to minority immersion education in
many other countries in that GME in Scotland has been established predominantly as streams (or units) in mainstream English-medium schools, rather than
as stand-alone, dedicated Gaelic-medium schools (cf. McLeod 2003; Rodgers and
McLeod 2007). There are fifty-nine schools in Scotland which offer Gaelic-medium
primary education (Bòrd na Gàidhlig 2016), but only five of these are dedicated,
stand-alone Gaelic-medium schools, one of which is the new Gaelic school in
Edinburgh.[1] Prior to the establishment of this school, Edinburgh was served by a
single Gaelic-medium unit at Tollcross Primary School. This unit was established in
1988 with one teacher and seven children,[2] and then grew steadily over the years to
the point that, in 1997, the unit had three teachers and fifty-eight primary students,[3]
and was nearing approximately a quarter of the total school roll. Motivated in part by
concerns about language policy and language use at Tollcross, parents in Edinburgh
began campaigning for the establishment of a dedicated school in the city. Here
is how one parent explained her concerns in a letter to the editor of *The Scotsman*
newspaper:

> When we first visited the unit, I expected to enter a Gaelic zone similar to what I had
> seen in a French school in the middle of Germany. Such a unit or school would have
> *only* the minority language spoken, from headmaster, janitor and secretary to every child
> on the playground. It would mean a complete immersion. It would give the minority
> language a more respectable status. However, the unit at Tollcross gives me the feeling
> of it being 'tacked on' to a mainstream school. All of the central emotionally very
> important activities of the school are in English: weekly assembly, the Christmas play
> (with weeks of preparation), the Christmas fair, outings to theatre, concerts, etc. This
> gives everyone involved the feeling of Gaelic being inferior, a second language.
> (Rhein 2000)

This letter demonstrates a common feature of the discourse surrounding school language policy in the debates about the proposed school in Edinburgh. In this letter,
and in many other cases, language use in the playground is not simply named indica-
tively, but also metonymically, to stand for the language policy and linguistic ethos of

the whole school (see also Aldekoa and Gardner 2002: 341). In this letter, the parent names the headmaster, the janitor and the secretary, in addition to children in the playground, as people who should speak Gaelic in an immersion school, but in other instances in the data I collected, only the playground itself is invoked. In discourse about school language policy in these debates, language use in the playground appears to be understood as a bell-wether for the vitality of Gaelic in the school in general and its normalisation as a social language between the children; in other words, what language they might use if unsupervised or what language they might use 'naturally' together.

This parent implies that English was the language spoken in the playground to some degree at Tollcross, and this is supported by reports from the children themselves. As part of the ongoing consultations about the proposed dedicated school, the City of Edinburgh Council conducted research in 2004 into parents', teachers' and students' perceptions of GME in Edinburgh (City of Edinburgh Council 2005). Three focus groups were conducted with GME students: one group from primary six and seven at Tollcross; one group in secondary one and two at James Gillespie's High School; and a final group in secondary three through five also at James Gillespie's. James Gillespie's High School is the local high school in the Tollcross catchment area with a Gaelic programme for former Tollcross students. All three groups indicated that Gaelic use at school was at times problematic:

> P6/7: Do you enjoy speaking Gaelic?
> 'Yes, but in the playground you sometimes have to speak English.'
> S3–5: Do you enjoy speaking Gaelic?
> 'If you speak it together, you get criticised.'
> P6/7: What has been good and what has been bad [about GME]?
> 'The others make fun of you and call you the "Garlic group."'
> 'You exclude some people if you use it in the playground.'
> S1–2: What has been good and what has been bad [about GME]?
> 'Others might feel excluded if you use Gaelic in the playground.'
> 'In primary, the "Garlic's"(!): in secondary it "cuts you off a bit" from others.' (City of Edinburgh Council 2005: 13–15)

In the same survey, parents of GME students were asked: 'Are you aware of your child using Gaelic outside of the school day?' and 89 per cent answered that they were not (City of Edinburgh Council 2005: 8). This survey included parents of students from nursery to high school, so it is difficult to interpret, but, nonetheless, it suggests that, at the time, students at Tollcross were not making much use of their Gaelic outside of class. If the peer reproval reported in the above study was causing GME students at Tollcross Primary School to form negative affective associations (cf. Smith-Christmas 2017) with informal Gaelic use on the playground and in other sites in the school, clearly this could militate against the students' further development as confident, active Gaelic speakers outside of the school, and one can understand why some parents were concerned.

How is ethos, culture and language policy at immersion schools understood in Scotland?

Concerns about language policy and language use in schools with Gaelic units were not limited to parents at Tollcross. Language policy and problems with language use in the playground were named as reasons that parents in Glasgow began organising to establish a dedicated school in that city (MacNeacail 1999; Comann nam Pàrant 2000a: 26), and also featured in the highly contentious debates about converting Sleat Primary School on the Isle of Skye to an all–GME school in 2006 (Highland Council 2006: 2; see also MacLeod 2008: 145–147). At the time of the Edinburgh school campaign, there was no specific national guidance available on language policy for schools that offer GME; rather, individual councils were charged with developing their own guidelines. In 2004, the Scottish Executive issued guidance to local councils stating that council GME policy should contain a commitment to a 'bi-lingual ethos' in schools that offer GME, but the guidance was very general and did not define a bilingual ethos, did not specify how a bilingual ethos might be realised in concrete language policy in a school, or detail how a bilingual ethos might translate into actual Gaelic and English use in a school (Scottish Executive 2004; see also O'Hanlon 2010: 113–115 for a relevant discussion of the 'Language of the School' in taxonomies of immersion education).

As different communities around Scotland consulted on the establishment of dedicated Gaelic schools, various politicians, civil servants, educators and journalists entered the public debate on the question, often discussing their understanding of language policy in Gaelic schools and in schools with Gaelic units. Some commentators took strong issue with the fundamental notion of separate dedicated schools where only Gaelic would be spoken, calling the idea elitist, separatist, divisive, and even akin to apartheid. As an example, in an article and follow-up letter that appeared in the *Times Educational Supplement Scotland*, a secondary teacher, Hugh Donnelly, used just such language to describe the proposal to close the secondary Gaelic unit at his school and open a new 3–18 dedicated Gaelic school in Glasgow. Here, in the following extract from his follow-up letter, he is refuting several correspondents who wrote letters in response to his initial article:

According to one correspondent, what we have here is the creation of a brand new socially inclusive, comprehensive secondary which is a welcome addition to educational choice for all Glasgow pupils regardless of class, creed, or ethnic diversity. Yet another makes the claim for a separate school and the promotion of a Gaelic ethos (whatever that might be) where the medium of instruction will be exclusively Gaelic. Indeed, Gaelic cultural uniqueness is argued as a justification for a separate and exclusive campus for Gaelic speakers. Your correspondent alludes to the limitations of a big school where the opportunities for Gaelic pupils are diluted by the presence of others. Indeed, it is argued that Gaelic pupils just end up talking to their friends in English. (In Glasgow? Surely there would be elements of Scottish urban dialect creeping in also. Knock me down with a feather). (Donnelly 2004)

There is much which could be said about the political and linguistic ideologies that appear in this extract, in Donnelly's article, and the letters that followed it, but here

I will comment briefly on just one point. Donnelly does pick up on a difficult contradiction that parents and other activists faced when framing their arguments for a dedicated school. On the one hand, activists argued that GME is simply the normal curriculum but taught through the medium of Gaelic, or 'mainstream education delivered through Gaelic' as it was sometimes framed. Activists sought to reassure parents, politicians and the public that GME would be no more expensive than English-medium education (EME) but, also, that GME did not represent a radical or divisive departure from mainstream Scottish education. But at the same time, activists were also arguing that dedicated Gaelic schools with a unique Gaelic culture or ethos and an all-Gaelic language policy were necessary to provide GME students with the best chance at developing their Gaelic/English bilingualism, to normalise Gaelic as a social language amongst the students, and to realise GME's full potential as a tactic in the Gaelic revival. As Donnelly identifies here, in this respect, activists *were* arguing that GME should be more than simply 'mainstream education delivered through Gaelic'.

The first Edinburgh Gaelic school campaign: establishing consensus

Against this background debate in the national press, parents in Edinburgh began seriously agitating for a dedicated Gaelic school in the city in 1998. From the very beginning of the first campaign to the end of the final successful campaign in 2011, GME parents in Edinburgh worked diligently through their advocacy group, Comann nam Pàrant, to build a strong consensus around the goal of establishing a dedicated Gaelic school. As part of this consensus-building process, Comann nam Pàrant held a series of meetings in early 1999, and the language policy of the proposed school was one important point of debate at these meetings. The most significant of these meetings was an open 'information day' for parents held on 20 March at the University of Edinburgh, and after this meeting Comann nam Pàrant published detailed proceedings. As part of the day, the parents broke up into smaller groups to discuss the future of GME in Edinburgh, and we can read in the published proceedings that at least one group explicitly discussed language use in the playground and language policy at the proposed school:

> [A] fear that Gaelic will be the language of the school. Opportunities for this? Gaelic needs to move on from the classroom. Not extremism, just common sense. How is that achieved? Gaelic in the playground? Experience says not possible in English-speaking playground. Irish schools have varying success in this: Irish teachers must contribute ideas and incentives, rewards, etc; language of playground must be taught: this is done successfully in Ireland; resources needed, e.g. tapes, children's culture [. . .] 'Gaelic ghetto' a concern for some; but this can be worse if done in units, cf. labels such as 'the Gaelics' [. . .] a non-Gaelic-speaking parent anxious about pressure being placed on his children through language difficulties: how to achieve Gaelic in playground without pressure. (Comann nam Pàrant 2000a: 36)

After the meeting, parents continued to discuss language policy at the proposed school and questioned if expecting children to speak Gaelic in the playground might constitute an unreasonable infringement on their liberty (Comann nam Pàrant 1999a; MacNeacail 1999). In a follow-up meeting of Comann nam Pàrant held on 27 April, discussions on the proposed school continued, and parents took up the issue of language policy again. In response to concerns that an all-Gaelic rule might lead to students being punished for speaking English, the meeting reached a consensus that there was no support for compulsion, coercion or any draconian measures to enforce language policy in the playground. It appears from the meeting minutes that consensus on this point was an important step towards the meeting reaching a general consensus that, 'We, the parent body, agree in principal that we want a Gaelic school for Edinburgh' (Comann nam Pàrant 1999b).

In the following year, the City of Edinburgh Council conducted a consultation on the proposal to move the Gaelic unit at Tollcross to a new dedicated school. The consultation included a survey of all the parents at Tollcross, both GME and EME, and even though a clear majority of the GME parents supported the move (89 per cent), at a meeting on 17 February 2000 the Council Education Committee voted down the proposal. Comann nam Pàrant had asked three GME students at Tollcross to give presentations at the meeting, and the students reportedly spoke eloquently of problems with out-of-classroom language use at Tollcross and of their desire to be educated in an all-Gaelic environment (Campbell 2000; Comann nam Pàrant 2000b). However, others at the meeting speaking against the proposal cited language use in the playground at Tollcross and the opportunity for GME and EME students to mix together as reasons *not* to establish a dedicated school. A teaching representative reportedly called the proposal separatism (Comann nam Pàrant 2000b), and one councillor, Bob Cairns, was quoted as describing the proposal as a form of apartheid and that he found the idea of a school with children speaking only Gaelic frightening (MacLeòid 2000; Silvis 2000). In the end, the Education Committee voted 24 to 4 not to sanction a new dedicated Gaelic school. In explaining the decision in a letter to a parent, the convenor of the committee, Cllr Paul Williamson, made explicit reference to whole-school language policy:

> Whilst the pupils might be surrounded by the Gaelic language to a greater extent [in a dedicated Gaelic school], it has been nobody's intention to prevent these pupils from speaking English in their free time. As bilingual pupils, the current arrangements [of a Gaelic unit in an English-language school] allow them to choose Gaelic or English as a form of communication outside classroom hours. (Williamson 2000)

In this excerpt, Cllr Williamson has framed the question of school language policy using the neoliberal language of free choice (cf. May 2003: 96–99; Clayton 2008; Armstrong 2014: 580), but of course very little of a students' experience in compulsory state schooling in the UK could be considered truly free from constraint. Students' attire and deportment, language, movements through the school over the course of the school timetable, behaviour in the school and learning activities are all circumscribed by a comprehensive system of rules and norms over which the students have almost no voice. Cllr Williamson is not arguing here for a school without compulsion; rather, he is arguing against compelling primary students to speak the Gaelic language specifically. The decision of the Education Committee, and Cllr Williamson's rationalisation of that decision, betray a normative bias in support of the use of the English language in Edinburgh, and it appears that this language ideology was behind much of the tenacious opposition to establishing a Gaelic school in Edinburgh, a school that would have its own language policy that would privilege (and possibly enforce) Gaelic use. In its decision, the Education Committee recommended that the proposal for a dedicated Gaelic school be reconsidered in two years, but, in reality, it was a decade before a proposal for a Gaelic school in Edinburgh was seriously considered again.

The second campaign: full immersion as the rallying point

The second campaign was at least as tortuous and protracted as the first, but almost ten years later it was organised and executed in a very different context in several respects, and these differences both informed the activists' approach to how they framed their campaign and also contributed to their success where the first campaign failed. Significantly, in the years leading up to the second campaign, as dedicated Gaelic schools were established in Glasgow and Inverness, and then as these two schools grew and succeeded, the idea of a dedicated Gaelic school in Edinburgh appeared far less radical in 2009–2011 than it did in 1998–2000. As a consequence, parents had greater latitude to build the second campaign explicitly around the theme of the advantages of full immersion and a strong Gaelic ethos. Here is how Comann nam Pàrant described these advantages in their official response to the final consultation on the Gaelic-school proposal:

> With Gaelic being the language of the whole school, there are more instances, and more diverse opportunities (playground, dining-room, assembly, trips, etc) to use Gaelic [. . .] It is important that pupils see Gaelic as more than just a 'classroom language'. As with any minority language, the perceived status and value attached to Gaelic is an important factor influencing retention and use by young people [. . .] The more that the minority language features in the school experience, the stronger will be the pupils' competence and confidence in the language. The stronger the pupils competence and confidence in the language; the more likely they will be to use it in later life in work, home and in leisure. (Comann nam Pàrant 2011: 7–8)

Around the time of the beginning of the second campaign, students reported that the language in the playground at Tollcross primary was still English (City of Edinburgh Council 2009: 45) and parents feared that this diglossia – Gaelic in the classroom; English in the rest of the school – was leading students to see Gaelic as a language only connected to school work (Comann nam Pàrant 2009: 4). In the extract above, we see the parents making an argument that by extending Gaelic use to the whole school students would not only develop better competency in the language but would also be more likely to use Gaelic as adults, a key step towards creating a new generation of active Gaelic speakers and contributing to the revival of the language.

Again, in the course of the second campaign, some opponents did use emotive language like 'segregation' to describe the proposal for a dedicated Gaelic school, and the

Gaelic-school activists were opposed by powerful local politicians and media organisations in the city, but, in the end, by dint of carefully-planned and persistent activism, Comann nam Pàrant prevailed, and on 27 October 2011 the City of Edinburgh
Council approved the establishment of a dedicated Gaelic school in the city, ultimately
accepting in broad terms Comann nam Pàrant's arguments about full immersion:

> The establishment of a dedicated school [. . .] reaffirms the Council's commitment to the
> preservation and development of the Gaelic language; a dedicated school offers the potential
> for a fuller immersion experience making fluency and bilingualism more likely educational
> outcomes[.] (City of Edinburgh Council 2011: 2)

While the Council's document in response to the consultation on the Gaelic school
does not provide any detail about the language policy of the newly-approved school, it
does name 'increased exposure to the Gaelic language outside the context of the classroom' as a key advantage of a dedicated Gaelic school over a Gaelic unit in an English-
language school (City of Edinburgh Council 2011: 16), strongly suggesting that the
City of Edinburgh council accepted that whole-school language policy would be an
important factor in the potential success of the new school, a significant shift in ideology
from the position of the council in 2000. Extensive repairs were required to make the
mothballed Bonnington Primary building in Leith ready to house the new school, Bun-
sgoil Taobh na Pàirce, delaying its opening by a year, but in that time Comann nam
Pàrant continued to rally parental support for the new school and advance its vision of
GME in Edinburgh. Here is how they described that vision in November 2012:

> CnP is working towards a stated goal of taking **all** of our GME families with us when we
> move to Bun-sgoil Taobh na Pàirce. It is also our vision that the new school will have a **Gaelic
> cultural ethos** and be a **flagship for Gaelic education** in Scotland, promoting the growth
> of Gaelic throughout the country. (Comann nam Pàrant 2012: 2; emphasis in the original)

With the approval of the new school, the question of language policy in GME in
Edinburgh passed from being a debate held in the public sphere, to being a quotid-
ian issue for parents and staff as they prepared to transition from GME provision in a
unit at Tollcross Primary to all-school GME provision at Bun-sgoil Taobh na Pàirce.
How language policy developed in the new school, while an interesting question, is
beyond the scope of this study and its social-history methods. Nonetheless, if parents
and other activists remain as closely involved in the day-to-day operation of the new
school as they were in the operation of the Gaelic unit at Tollcross Primary, it is very
likely that activist ideologies about language value and use in the school will strongly
influence the continuing development of language policy and practice at Bun-sgoil
Taobh na Pàirce.

What does a language policy for a Gaelic school look like?

I have presented only a tiny fraction of the data collected on the ideological side of the
struggle over a dedicated Gaelic school in Edinburgh, but I hope I have successfully

(if briefly) illustrated two things: first, how language policy in the proposed school was imagined and contested by activists, politicians and the public, and how the question of out-of-classroom language use was central in the debates on the development of GME in Scotland; and, second, how linguistic ideology delimits the scope for establishing minority language immersion education, that the arguments around the founding of immersion education in Scotland are ideologically charged, and that it is likely that these ideological contests influence the ethos and language policy in units and in dedicated schools once established.

Recently there has been research conducted, and also public debate, on the definition of GME, in terms of the curriculum and also in terms of the mix of Gaelic and English instruction at different levels (cf. O'Hanlon et al. n.d.; O'Hanlon 2010; Nicholson 2014). This debate has culminated in the publication of the document, 'Advice on Gaelic Education', by the Scottish Government education agency, Education Scotland (2015), which goes some way to clarifying standards of pedagogical good practice in GME. The research presented here demonstrates that a similar consensus-building debate is required on the ideology, ethos and language policy of Gaelic-medium schooling in Scotland. We still do not have clear vision among activists, policy-makers or educationalists of exactly what a 'Gaelic school' means in Scotland in terms of language policy, ethos or ideology. How exactly should the two languages (Gaelic and English) be used throughout a Gaelic school, and how will Gaelic use be encouraged outside of class? What do we expect from the administration of a Gaelic school in terms of leadership and guidance when it comes to establishing the ideology, ethos and language policy of a Gaelic school? Do we expect a relatively laissez-faire policy with regards to language use outside of class, that the school children themselves will 'choose' which language they prefer to use together, or do we expect an all-school policy for language use developed as an instance of a particular ideology about the purpose of the school and the purpose of GME in particular?

Indeed, what is the purpose of GME in Scotland? Discussions of school language policy around GME inevitably lead to deeper questions about the fundamental rationale for GME. Is GME solely established for the sake of the better education of the children involved, so these children can enjoy the cognitive and educational benefits of bilingualism, or are activists also motivated by GME's perceived role as a tactic in the Gaelic revival, as a way to create the next generation of young Gaels in Scotland? And are these two purposes in conflict – immersion education for the advantages of bilingualism and GME as a tactic in the Gaelic revival – or can these two aims be reconciled? Do we expect that a Gaelic school will teach the national curriculum, but through the medium of Gaelic, for example, 'mainstream education delivered through Gaelic', or teach something else, a curriculum that is particularly 'Gàidhealach' in some way perhaps, a curriculum that fosters a clear link between the Gaelic language and students' identity as Scots, or perhaps as Gaels? If a strong language ideology and language policy are advanced in a Gaelic school, will this put off those parents who are more interested in GME as immersion education for bilingual advantage, those without much interest in the Gaelic revival *per se*? And if so, is that necessarily a bad thing? Can GME providers realistically hope to satisfy all potential parents and all possible stakeholders?

These questions of language policy in minority language education are not unique to Scotland. Other educators in other countries have also struggled with the problem of 'language in the playground' at minority-language immersion schools. In her study of the establishment of an Irish-medium school as part of the urban Irish community development, the Shaw's Road Gaeltacht, in Belfast, Ireland, Gabrielle Maguire observed that Irish use had to be deliberately encouraged in the school, and that 'in the school playground; there, constant supervision is required to halt the children's tendency to turn to English' (1991: 123). Thomas and Roberts also show that Welsh-medium-educated school children in Wales tend to use English outside of class, and that while all the schools they studied evidenced a strong Welsh-language ethos, the children's own perceptions of language policy in the playground were inconsistent. Not surprisingly, the tendency of children to use English socially outside of class was particularly strong among those children whose home language was English (Thomas and Roberts 2011; see also Price and Tamburelli 2016).

Experience has shown that effective minority-language education requires detailed and well-funded whole-school language policy and planning (Aldekoa and Gardner 2002), and while Scotland's recent guidance document does contain a brief section on Gaelic use outside of the classroom and on the promotion of a Gaelic ethos in schools that offer GME (Education Scotland 2015: 32–33), and while in several places throughout the text general mention is made of school language policy, of hiring Gaelic-speaking support staff, and of promoting a Gaelic school ethos, nowhere in the document do the authors clearly state what a Gaelic policy for a Gaelic school might actually look like in practice nor engage with the difficult ideological questions raised in debates about language policy in Gaelic schools. Practically, how do you make 'Gaelic the language of the School' (Education Scotland 2015: 32) as proposed in the guidance? What does that policy look like in detail and what sort of ideological work would be required to implement it? This research shows that school language policy in support of Gaelic is politically contentious in Scotland, and yet there is still no national guidance available that addresses these issues openly.

But perhaps it is unrealistic to expect leadership from government agencies on this issue. Perhaps official organisations like Education Scotland simply are not in a position to take the lead on controversial ideological questions like those raised in this study. Rather, it is possible that on-the-ground language activists are in a better position to advance this debate. We have seen that the parents and other activists in Edinburgh did not simply understand the proposed Gaelic school as a policy black box, but, rather, that they had clear ambitions for the ethos of the proposed school. The language policy of the proposed school was contested throughout the campaign, at times in some detail, and indeed the question of language policy was salient and controversial enough that the debate contributed to the long delay in establishing the Gaelic school. As GME expands and develops in the future, it is inevitable that this controversy will continue, and this consensus-building debate cannot be avoided if GME is to succeed in its educational and language-revival aims.

Acknowledgements

Portions of this chapter were first presented at the 46th Annual Meeting of the British Association for Applied Linguistics, Heriot-Watt University, Edinburgh, Scotland on 6 September 2013, and at the BAAL/Cambridge University Press Applied Linguistics Seminar: Languages in the UK: Bridging the Gap between the Classroom and the Community in Language Learning, at Lews Castle College UHI, Stornoway, Scotland, 29 and 30 May 2014, and I would like to thank the delegates for their comments. I am indebted to Fiona O'Hanlon who provided helpful advice while preparing an early draft of this chapter. I would like to thank Liz NicIllEathain and the anonymous activists who read and commented on the text. I would also like to thank the parents and other activists who gave interviews and who allowed access to their archives. I could not have conducted this research into the Edinburgh Gaelic school campaign without their generous support.

Notes

1. While most Gaelic provision in Scotland fits neatly into this simple binary taxonomy, there are a small number of schools/units that are more difficult to classify. In the Highlands and Islands there are schools like Bun-sgoil Shlèite (Sleat Primary School) that are designated as 'Gaelic schools' but with an English-medium unit, and in Glasgow there is also Bunsgoil Ghàidhlig Ghleann Dail (Glendale Gaelic Primary School) which is a dedicated Gaelic school but which sits immediately adjacent to Glendale Primary School, an English-medium school.
2. Accounts differ on the number of children in the unit when it opened, with some sources claiming five and others seven.
3. Accounts also differ on the number of children in the unit in 1998, with some sources claiming fifty-eight and others sixty.

References

Aldekoa, Jasone and Nicholas Gardner. 2002. Turning Knowledge of Basque into Use: Normalisation Plans for Schools. *International Journal of Bilingual Education and Bilingualism* 5(6), 339–354.

Armstrong, Timothy Currie. 2014. Naturalism and Ideological Work: How is Family Language Policy Renegotiated as Both Parents and Children Learn a Threatened Minority Language? *International Journal of Bilingual Education and Bilingualism* 17(5), 570–585.

Bòrd na Gàidhlig. 2016. *Dàta Foghlaim Ghàidhlig/Gaelic Education Data: 2015–16*. Available online at http://www.gaidhlig.org.uk/bord/wp-content/uploads/sites/2/Dàta-Foghlaim-AM-FOLLAIS-2015-16-egn-2-PUBLIC-Education-Data.pdf (last accessed 3 February 2017).

Brenzinger, Matthias and Patrick Heinrich. 2013. The Return of Hawaiian: Language Networks of the Revival Movement. *Current Issues in Language Planning* 14(2), 300–316.

Campbell, Mary T. 2000. Letter. *The Scotsman.* 1 March 2000.

City of Edinburgh Council. 2005. *Gaelic Education Review 2004/05.* 26 March 2005. Edinburgh: City of Edinburgh Council.

City of Edinburgh Council. 2009. *Gaelic Education Needs Feasibility Study.* 7 December 2009. Edinburgh: City of Edinburgh Council.

City of Edinburgh Council. 2011. *Outcomes Arising from Consultation on Proposals for the Future Development of Nursery and Primary Gaelic Medium Education.* 27 October 2011. Edinburgh: City of Edinburgh Council.

Clayton, Stephen. 2008. The Problem of 'Choice' and the Construction of the Demand for English in Cambodia. *Language Policy* 7(2), 143–164.

Comann nam Pàrant. 1999a. *Meeting Minutes, 30-3-1999.*

Comann nam Pàrant. 1999b. *Meeting Minutes, 27-4-1999.*

Comann nam Pàrant. 2000a. *Sgoil Ghàidhlig airson Baile Dhùn Éideann: Latha Fiosrachaidh/A Gaelic-medium School for Edinburgh: Information Day.*

Comann nam Pàrant. 2000b. *Education Committee Meeting – Thursday 17th February 2000; Recollection of Proceedings.* An anonymous unpublished report [n.d.].

Comann nam Pàrant. 2009. *Meeting Minutes, 9-2-2009.*

Comann nam Pàrant. 2011. *Response to the City of Edinburgh Council Proposals to Develop Gaelic Medium Education in Edinburgh.* 21 March 2011.

Comann nam Pàrant. 2012. *Report on Results of Parent Survey November 2012.*

Davidson, Gina. 2011. Gaelic School is Just More Vanity. *The Edinburgh Evening News.* 20 December 2011.

Donnelly, Hugh. 2004. Letter. *TES Scotland.* 17 December 2004.

Dunmore, Stuart S. 2014. Bilingual Life after School? Language Use, Ideologies and Attitudes among Gaelic-medium Educated Adults. Edinburgh: University of Edinburgh PhD thesis.

Dunmore, Stuart S. 2016. Immersion Education Outcomes and the Gaelic Community: Identities and Language Ideologies among Gaelic-medium Educated adults in Scotland. *Journal of Multilingual and Multicultural Development.* Available online at http://dx.doi.org/10.1080/01434632.2016.1249875 (last accessed 30 November 2016).

Education Scotland. 2015. *Advice on Gaelic Education.* Available online at https://education.gov.scot/improvement/gael3-advice-on-gaelic-education (last accessed 21 May 2015).

Highland Council. 2006. *Consultation on a Proposal to Designate Sleat Primary School as a Dedicated Gaelic School.* Inverness: Highland Council.

Highland Council. 2009. *SQA Attainment in Gaelic.* Inverness: Highland Council.

Johnstone, Richard, Wynne Harlen, Morag MacNeill, Bob Stradling and Graham Thorpe. 1999. *The Attainments of Pupils Receiving Gaelic-Medium Primary Education in Scotland.* Stirling: Scottish CILT.

MacLeod, Marsaili. 2008. Revitalising Rural Europe's Indigenous Languages: 'Technologisation' and the Gaelic Language. In Grete Rusten and Sarah Skerratt (eds), *Information and Communication Technologies in Rural Society: Being Rural in a Digital Age*, 125–151. Oxon, UK: Routledge.

McLeod, Wilson. 2003. Gaelic Medium Education in the International Context.

In Mairead Nicolson and Mata MacIver (eds), *Gaelic Medium Education*, 15–34. Edinburgh: Dunedin Academic Press.

MacLeòid, Murchadh. 2000. Cainnt mhaslach mu sgoil Ghàidhlig. *The Scotsman*. 23 February 2000.

MacNeacail, Aonghas. 1999. Sgoil Ghàidhlig sa phrìomh-bhaile? *The Scotsman*. 12 May 1999.

Maguire, Gabrielle. 1991. *Our Own Language, An Irish Initiative*. Clevedon: Multilingual Matters.

May, Stephen. 2003. Rearticulating the Case for Minority Language Rights. *Current Issues in Language Planning* 4(2), 95–125.

Nahir, Moshe. 1998. Micro Language Planning and the Revival of Hebrew: A Schematic Framework. *Language in Society* 27, 335–357.

Nicholson, Linda. 2014. *Consultation on the Gaelic Medium Education Bill: Analysis of Written Responses*. Available online at www.scotland.gov.uk/socialresearch

O'Hanlon, Fiona. 2010. Gaelic-medium Primary Education in Scotland: Towards a New Taxonomy? In Gillian Munro and Iain Mac an Tàilleir (eds), *Coimhearsnachd na Gàidhlig an-diugh/Gaelic Communities Today*, 99–116. Edinburgh: Dunedin Academic Press.

O'Hanlon, Fiona. 2012. Celtic-medium Education and Language Maintenance in Scotland and Wales: Language Use, Ability and Attitudes at the Primary to Secondary School Stage. In Nancy R. McGuire and Colm Ó Baoill (eds), *Rannsachadh na Gàidhlig 6*, 323–354. Obar Dheathain: An Clò Gàidhealach.

O'Hanlon, Fiona, Lindsay Paterson and Wilson McLeod. 2013. The Attainment of Pupils in Gaelic-medium Primary Education in Scotland. *International Journal of Bilingual Education and Bilingualism* 16(6), 707–729.

O'Hanlon, Fiona, Lindsay Paterson and Wilson McLeod. n.d. *Soillse Research Digest 1: Language Models in Gaelic-medium Pre-school, Primary and Secondary Education*. Soillse.

Price, Abigail Ruth and Marco Tamburelli. 2016. Minority Language Abandonment in Welsh-medium Educated L2 Male Adolescents: Classroom, not Chatroom. *Language, Culture and Curriculum* 29(2), 189–206.

Rhein, Helga. 2000. Letter. *The Scotsman*. 3 August 2000.

Rogers, Vaughan and Wilson McLeod. 2007. Autochthonous Minority Languages in Public-sector Primary Education: Bilingual Policies and Politics in Brittany and Scotland. *Linguistics and Education* 17(4), 347–373.

Scottish Executive. 2004. *Education Guidance Issued Under Section 13 of the Standards in Scotland's Schools etc Act 2000 on Gaelic Education*. Office of the Minister of Education, Peter Peacock, MSP, 17 September 2004.

Silvis, Helen. 2000. Medium Rare: Will Gaelic-only Schools be Quaint and Isolated? *The Scotsman*. 15 March 2000.

Simons, Tal and Paul Ingram. 1997. Organization and Ideology: Kibbutzim and Hired Labor, 1951–1965. *Administrative Science Quarterly* 42, 784–813.

Simons, Tal and Paul Ingram. 2004. An Ecology of Ideology: Theory and Evidence from Four Populations. *Industrial and Corporate Change* 13(1), 33–59.

Smith-Christmas, Cassie. 2017. 'Is it Really for Talking?': The Implications of

Associating a Minority Language with the School. *Language, Culture and Curriculum* 30(1), 32–47.

Thomas, Enlli Mô and Dylan Bryn Roberts. 2011. Exploring Bilinguals' Social Use of Language Inside and Out of the Minority Language Classroom. *Language and Education* 25(2), 89–108.

Walsh, John. 2006. Language and Socio-economic Development: Towards a Theoretical Framework. *Language Problems & Language Planning* 30(2), 127–148.

Williamson, Paul. 2000. Letter to Martin G. MacIntyre. 18 February 2000.

Mismatches between National and Local Gaelic Development: Cròileagan Dùn Èideann and the Promotion of Gaelic-medium Education

Kirstie MacLeod

In this chapter, I will describe how a colourful new information pack produced by the national statutory language board, Bòrd na Gàidhlig, and the reaction to it of the play leaders at a Gaelic parent-and-child group helped me to understand parents' first stages of involvement with Gaelic. Research into Gaelic-medium education choice has focused on why parents choose Gaelic-medium education (Roberts 1991; Stockdale et al. 2003; O'Hanlon et al. 2010; Goalabré 2011; O'Hanlon 2012; Rice 2012; McLeod and O'Rourke 2015; O'Hanlon and Paterson 2016). Most of this research asked parents with children already in Gaelic-medium primary education about their reasons for enrolling their child in the provision some, often many, years previously. Exceptions to this include Stephen et al. (2010), whose research into early years provision included exploring Gaelic-medium education choice amongst parents of pre-school children, and also O'Hanlon and Paterson (2016: 2), which utilised a national social attitudes survey to investigate what factors influenced respondents to tick that 'they would be likely to choose Gaelic-medium primary education for their own child'. There is a paucity of research into parents who are in the process of considering Gaelic-medium education or are yet to consider formal education but are involved in Gaelic provision at the early years. Rather than focusing on education choice, in this chapter I will examine how parents are supported by play leaders and fellow parents at Gaelic parent-and-child groups at this initial stage of involvement in Gaelic-medium education and how the role of these groups is wider than promoting and encouraging Gaelic-medium education enrolment at primary level.

This chapter is based on six-months of ethnographic fieldwork within Cròileagan Dùn Èideann. I regularly attended Cròileagan sessions across all locations, including participant observation at fifty-seven sessions, and I conducted semi-structured interviews with play leaders, parents – from twenty-six families in total – and Gaelic-medium education staff. Researchers in Language Planning and Policy are increasingly engaging with ethnography as a research method to understand the 'interpretation and implementation' of language policy at a local level (Hornberger and Johnson 2007: 511). Rather than examining the interpretation of a specific policy at a local level, in this chapter I will explore how concerns regarding a new information pack illuminated differences in priorities and understandings between local- and national-level organisations.

Parent-and-child groups

Parent-and-child or parent-and-toddler groups provide weekly sessions for pre-school children and their caregivers and are run in community centres, village halls and church halls across Scotland. The exact content of the groups and the organisations involved in the provision vary. Gaelic parent-and-child groups and playgroups were established in the early 1980s and predate Gaelic-medium education. These groups played a crucial role in creating sufficient demand for Gaelic-medium primary education (O'Hanlon and Paterson 2015: 313). Three Gaelic-speaking mothers living in Edinburgh established a Gaelic parent-and-toddler group in the city in in 1981 (Gaelic Education in Edinburgh 2016). In 2013/2014, when I conducted my fieldwork, Cròileagan Dùn Èideann ran six sessions each week during school term time; over 100 families attended their sessions weekly. Sessions ran in Tollcross Community Centre, Leith Community Centre and at Bun-sgoil Taobh na Pàirce (Edinburgh's Gaelic School).[1] Each location has a volunteer parent committee; however, paid play leaders deliver and plan the sessions and are supported by the Gaelic development officer at the City of Edinburgh Council, the local authority. Children aged 0–5 years attend sessions with a parent or caregiver;[2] children aged 3–5 years old are less likely to attend because most attend some kind of nursery provision from age of three.

The Cròileagan parent-and-child groups and other early years provision are a key entry point into Gaelic-medium education. Stephen et al. (2010) conducted a review of Gaelic early years provision and stressed the importance of 'high quality GM early years and childcare provision' in Gaelic development:

> The great majority of children who enrol in GM primary education come up through GM playgroups and nurseries. Well structured, well co-ordinated, well publicised and high quality GM early years and childcare provision, based on careful research and analysis, is therefore an important priority within Gaelic development. (Stephen et al. 2010: 1)

The linguistic and educational importance of high-quality Gaelic early years provision for children is clearly detailed here by Stephen et al. (2010). Gaelic-medium early years provision is also where most parents experience Gaelic-medium education for the first time, and for some it may be their first encounter with the Gaelic language. This stage requires careful support for both parents and children in order to establish a strong basis for Gaelic-medium education at primary level. Information packs is one form of support available to parents.

The new pack

Play leaders at the Cròileagan brought my attention to the differences in understanding of the support necessary for parents attending these groups when a new information pack arrived. The new pack replaces a previous pack given to parents that had been provided for the group by Comann nam Pàrant – a national organisation for Gaelic-medium education parents. The new pack 'Fios is Freagairt' ('Information and Answers') replaced this Comann nam Pàrant pack and was developed in 2013 by the statutory national language planning board, Bòrd na Gàidhlig. The new pack is available in a range of locations including in schools and nurseries where Gaelic-medium education is provided and in the Gaelic bookshop in Glasgow. It has been distributed for free to parents with children of different ages in Gaelic-medium education and is not specifically for distribution in Gaelic parent-and-child groups. The new pack was delivered to Gaelic parent-and-child groups for distribution to parents. The Edinburgh group started distributing these new packs to parents on their first visit to the group along with an Edinburgh specific information pack, as they had done with the previous pack.

Not only was the new pack physically different – it was brightly coloured, bigger and rather clumsy, as, for example, the CDs provided in the pack continually fell out – but the new pack also differed significantly in terms of content and focus. The change in content and focus prompted concern among play leaders, who worried that the new packs were too focused on the promotion of Gaelic-medium primary education rather than functioning as an all-round introduction to Gaelic for parents – including information on Gaelic-medium education and other parents' experiences of it. They believed that parent-and-child groups such as the Cròileagan provide distinct support for parents and children and do not exist merely to promote immersion education in formal education. Therefore, the new pack may not be suitable, especially initially, for parents of young children. The play leaders understand that parents attend the groups for a variety of reasons, many who have not yet begun to carefully consider their children's schooling; receiving the pack on their first visit, play leaders fear, could ultimately put off parents from returning. These concerns raised encouraged me to consider more fully the role of Gaelic parent-and-child groups and led me to understand how the national-level support, and its narrow focus on primary enrolment figures, contrasted with their own view of the role of such groups.

Mismatch

At a national level a far more explicit connection is made between primary Gaelic-medium enrolment figures and support for early years groups than was the case in these groups. The groups themselves focus on the current needs of parents and caregivers, on creating a place that provides a welcoming and supportive environment, a broad and gentle introduction to Gaelic, and opportunities to learn about Gaelic-medium education if sought. This discrepancy can be viewed as an example of a mismatch between national-level language planning goals and objectives and the understandings and practices at a local level. Ó hIfearnáin (2010) has identified such a mismatch between national-level language goals in Ireland and the language ideologies and practices of native Irish speakers in Gaeltacht areas:

> The problem is that the aims and linguistic desires of the national collective do not necessarily coincide with those of the residual Irish-speaking population, in the Gaeltacht

and elsewhere. Subtle mismatches in the aims and objectives of language management initiatives which favour the national language ideology over that of Irish-speaking core have led to
situations where policies in favour of promoting Irish as a community language may actually
have contributed to its decline. (Ó hIfearnáin 2010: 38)

Such mismatches can arise where the national-level ideology or planning goals do not
fit with a particular group of speakers. Ó hIfearnáin (2010: 41) believes that such mismatches are prevalent where 'a particular language ideology [that] has national goals,
which may not be appropriate to the smaller residual speech community'. As I will
show in what follows, such mismatches may also be evident in predominantly language
learner environments such as the Gaelic parent-and-child groups in Edinburgh and
in resources developed to support language planning goals. Ó hIfearnáin (2010: 41)
stresses the importance of understanding local 'linguistics beliefs and practices' if 'successful language management' is going to be achieved through national goals:

> The key element of this approach is that it shows that in order to undertake successful lan-
> guage management from the institutional point of view, such as an official national language
> plan, it is first important to understand the linguistic beliefs and practices of the speech com-
> munity so as to be able to steer them towards productive measures.

In what follows, I will outline the national language planning context and how it
appears to connect support for early years groups, such as the Cròileagan, with the
national language plan's overarching goal of increasing the numbers in primary on
enrolment.

The national language planning context

Bòrd na Gàidhlig, the statutory national language planning board, has two distinct
areas of involvement in Gaelic parent-and-child groups such as the Cròileagan
in Edinburgh. Established in 2006, following the passing of the Gaelic Language
(Scotland) Act 2005, Bòrd na Gàidhlig must write and implement a National
Gaelic Language Plan every five years (Gaelic Language (Scotland) Act 2005: 2(1)).
Since 2011, Bòrd na Gàidhlig has also given 'direct support to early years groups
across the country' (Bòrd na Gàidhlig 2014: 10, 2012a). This 'direct support' includes
financial support given to groups directly or through partnership projects with local
authorities and other organisations such as the Scottish Books Trust, for resource
development and training for play leaders (Bòrd na Gàidhlig 2014: 12–13). The
amount and manner of support given by Bòrd na Gàidhlig varies across locations.
Support for the Cròileagan in Edinburgh takes the form of resource provision, such
as the information packs, and training for play leaders at the annual An t-Alltan Beag
conference.

In their latest National Gaelic Language Plan 2012–17, Bòrd na Gàidhlig consider Gaelic
development in eight development areas including 'Home & Early Years' and 'Education:
Schools & Teachers'. One of three outcomes stated in 'Education: Schools & Teachers'
is 'an increase in the number of entrants to primary one Gaelic-medium education

from 400 to 800 by 2017' (Bòrd na Gàidhlig 2012b: 22). This target has become the headline goal of the 2012–2017 National Plan for Gaelic and Bòrd na Gàidhlig release primary one [P1] enrolment figures annually to the media (Bòrd na Gàidhlig 2014; Munro 2014). The outcome for 'Home & Early Years' is to increase 'the acquisition and use of Gaelic by young people in the home and increased numbers of children entering Gaelic-medium early years education' (Bòrd na Gàidhlig 2012b: 18).

In Bòrd na Gàidhlig's annual report for 2013–2014, the relative success of their 'direct support' for early years groups is assessed in terms of increases in enrolment at P1 level before the importance of the outcome of increasing P1 enrolment is reiterated. There is an association made between supporting early years groups such as the Cròileagan with increasing P1 enrolment rather than the goals outlined for the home and early years:

> We continue to give direct support to early years groups across the country and saw signifi-
> cant growth in the numbers of children entering Gaelic-medium education at P1. This is a
> key element in the National Gaelic Language Plan 2012/17, as it is fundamental to the aim of
> stabilizing and growing the numbers of Gaelic speakers. (Bòrd na Gàidhlig 2014: 12)

The aim of increasing enrolment at primary level emerges as a recurrent theme in association with support given to Gaelic early year groups, rather than supporting the national goals pertaining to the 'Home & Early Years'. Bòrd na Gàidhlig outline the development of the new 'Fios is Freagairt' information pack in the same annual report. The Bòrd states that promotional activities including the new pack are to 'increase the number of children currently registered for Gaelic-medium education' and are for 'parents interested in Gaelic education':

> The Bòrd supported 5 different areas across the country through promotional activities
> and advertising campaigns in order to help increase the number of children currently reg-
> istered for Gaelic-medium education. This work was carried out in partnership with Local
> Authorities. In order to support the local promotional activities and the work of the Parental
> Advisory Scheme, Bòrd na Gàidhlig published a new resource for parents interested in
> Gaelic education. The bi-lingual information pack, 'Fios is Freagairt', provides people with
> an audio and visual resource and contains a clear and informative guide to Gaelic-medium
> Education. In the package, there is information on the benefits of bilingualism and Gaelic-
> medium education, FAQs, information on organisations who can support parents, and it
> highlights the opportunities there are in Gaelic teaching. (Bòrd na Gàidhlig 2014: 12–13)

Although increasing P1 enrolment is an explicit goal for Bòrd na Gàidhlig it is not a key priority for the Cròileagan. The Cròileagan orientates itself to the promotion and facilitation of Gaelic language acquisition and use in families with young children and supports parents considering Gaelic-medium education within its generally sup-portive environment for parents of young children and wider support for Gaelic. In so doing it supports the national language planning goals of increasing acquisition and numbers in Gaelic-medium early years education, and ultimately primary education, but not through explicit promotional activities.

Play leaders understand the unique position of the groups; for most parents this is their first encounter with Gaelic-medium education and first opportunity to meet other parents with children attending such provision. Play leaders are mindful that attendance does not reflect a decision about formal education and the enrolment of a child into Gaelic-medium education at nursery or primary level. They appreciate that parents take time to experience and learn from others' experiences of Gaelic-medium education and that decisions regarding formal education are made over time and are based on an ongoing process of experiencing, researching and considering whether Gaelic-medium education is the best option for their child and their family. In what follows, I will outline the role of the Cròileagan as understood by play leaders and parents, and the various reasons that parents attend the groups.

Why do parents attend the Cròileagan?

Cròileagan Dùn Èideann welcomes all families. Cròileagan groups are not exclusively for Gaelic speakers or those considering Gaelic-medium education at nursery or primary level. A range of adults attends groups such as the Cròileagan: parents, grandparents, other relations, childminders, nannies, au pairs. Even if all caregivers wanted their child to attend because of a strong interest in Gaelic or Gaelic-medium education, then it would not always be the case that the caregiver with this interest was the adult in attendance with their child. Many parents, especially those with very young children (0–2 years), do not attend the Cròileagan as a result of a desire to learn Gaelic or with a specific interest in enrolling their child in Gaelic-medium education. Rather, parents often reported attending Cròileagan sessions because they are 'well-run and well-organised' local parent-and-child groups where they are made to feel welcome and supported.

Play leaders at the Cròileagan focus on creating a well-structured, welcoming environment that is rich with opportunities to sing songs, play and do craft activities and that supports both adults and children in learning and using Gaelic. Parents are attracted to the groups and continue to attend because of this well-structured and welcoming environment and it is hoped that their interest in Gaelic will often increase over time. Given parents' lack of focus on formal Gaelic-medium education and formal education more generally, play leaders' unease about the new packs is understandable.

Choice over time

Play leaders are mindful both of the multitude of reasons parents attend the Cròileagan initially and the likely low level of consideration given to primary education by parents with very young children. Play leaders understand that parents can become interested in formal Gaelic-medium education through their positive experiences at the Cròileagan and ultimately go on to enrol their child in Gaelic-medium education, as this play leader outlined:

> There is another group [of parents] that come without an intention of doing GME that find
> that they actually really like the group and the way it runs and then they thought of GME

and then do end up sending their children [to Bun-sgoil] Taobh na Pàirce and parents do tell me. I know that there are other families, you know, with children much higher up the school that say Cròileagan is the reason that the children are here.

Play leaders, distributing the new packs to parents on their first visit, fear that their focus on primary education and promoting Gaelic-medium education may intimidate parents and dissuade them from returning. Parents may become more interested in Gaelic-medium education over their time at the Cròileagan if they continue to attend, but initially should be welcomed into the sessions and given a small amount of information that is broad and unintimidating. The Cròileagan's approach is gentle and supportive and is based on an understanding that parents' attendance reflects a wide range of reasons and that parents of children of different ages have different needs and considerations.

The appeal of the Cròileagan

Parents reported a range of different reasons for attending the Cròileagan with their children – some attend for its social and education purposes, some for Gaelic language purposes. They nevertheless agree about the Cròileagan's appeal: it provides social opportunities for children and parents in a well-organised and welcoming environment. One mother explained that she started attending the Cròileagan with her four-month-old daughter because she was looking for a welcoming parent-and-child group to enable herself and her daughter to meet others. The group needed to be at a time and in a place that was convenient for her, and the Cròileagan group happened to fit her criteria, which did not include Gaelic language education. She was not put off by Gaelic as she had some knowledge of Irish, but she made clear the primacy of social considerations: if she had not been made welcome on her first visit and enjoyed the group, then she would not have returned. Another father, who was interested in the Gaelic language and Gaelic-medium education, explained that, over and above the Gaelic content of the sessions, he enjoyed the high-quality educational environment and the social opportunity it affords for both himself and his child:

> I think that it is a very good social occasion for the kids and for the adults. I think that it is incredibly well run, well organised. The fact that it has elements of free play, elements of craft, elements of song, all the kids sit down together and have a snack, everything, all those things make it the best adult and child experience that I think that [my child] has had, the two of us have had, from going to all sorts of things all over Edinburgh.

Play leaders as well as parents conveyed the importance of the well-run and welcoming nature of the groups in attracting parents. One play leader identified the structure of the sessions as a key attractive feature to parents:

> They might come because it is quite a nice group, so it's quite structured, it is pretty friendly, the children aren't just left to run around on their own as they are at some playgroups, there

is always a craft activity, the parents tend to sit with their child and engage with them at circle time so there are lots of reasons why it is just a nice group.

The Cròileagan serves an important social purpose for parents with young children. Parents' and play leaders' awareness of the attractive features of Cròileagan reflects an understanding of the needs and considerations of parents and other adults looking after very young children. Parents seek a supportive structured environment for their young child that also welcomes them and is a place where they can enjoy the company of other adults.

Stephen et al. (2010: 35) noted in their review of Gaelic-medium early years provision that parents interested in Gaelic held a concern that other parents attending groups for non-language related reasons detracted from the Gaelic environment of the group. In my time attending sessions, all adults took part in the Gaelic activities including those without an explicit or initial interest in Gaelic. Many parents shared their experiences of having come along to this nice and welcoming group and over time their interest in Gaelic and Gaelic-medium education had increased. The variation in interest levels of adults in Gaelic was not raised as an issue to me during the research. All adults took part in the Gaelic elements of the sessions, circle time and craft activities and there was an understanding amongst parents and play leaders that a parent not attending primarily to access Gaelic might increase their interest in the language over time.

'Learning Gaelic as a family'

Cròileagan Dùn Èideann may not explicitly or strongly promote Gaelic-medium education but it does clearly promote Gaelic language acquisition and use and encourage 'learning Gaelic as a family'. The Gaelic language content is an integral part of the structure and organisation of the sessions and parents are required to use Gaelic in sessions. Across all locations, Cròileagan Dùn Èideann sessions follow an almost identical structure, one filled with opportunities to learn and use basic Gaelic vocabulary, songs and rhymes. Play leaders speak Gaelic to all children and attempt to use Gaelic with other Gaelic-speaking or Gaelic-learning parents despite some play leaders not being fluent speakers themselves. Play leaders, parents and older children sing Gaelic songs at circle time at the beginning and end of the sessions, with one of the songs reflecting the topic of the week. The play leader distributes a phrase of the week, often a command to be used with children at home, and then practises pronunciation with the parents. Following circle time, the week's craft activity builds on the recently introduced theme of the week. Play leaders engage in Gaelic with children and parents as they complete the task while learning and revising basic Gaelic vocabulary relevant to the week's topic. Parents and play leaders circulate at snack time offering 'uisge no bainne?' (water or milk) to children and 'tì no cofaidh?' (tea or coffee) to adults, before returning to the circle time and more Gaelic songs. Play leaders end sessions by informing parents of news relating to the groups themselves but also of information about Gaelic classes and events taking place in the city.

In addition to the Gaelic content of the sessions themselves, the Cròileagan promotes Gaelic language learning and use outside of the session. Gaelic language-learning materials are available for parents to take home from the Cròileagan's lending libraries that are displayed at each session. Parents can, and are encouraged to, sign out Gaelic children's books,[3] Gaelic children's DVDs and story sacks[4] from the Cròileagan's lending libraries. Because parents are present throughout sessions, the Cròileagan affords opportunities to support and encourage the simultaneous language learning of parents and young children, an opportunity that is not possible at any other stage of Gaelic-medium education. Cròileagan Dùn Èideann continues to engage in the acquisition and development of resources to support families in using and learning Gaelic as a family. Thus, the Cròileagan contributes to the national language planning goal of increasing 'the acquisition and use of Gaelic by young people in the home' by supporting and gently encouraging parents and young children with no Gaelic to learn and use Gaelic within and outwith the sessions (Bòrd na Gàidhlig 2012b: 18).

The Cròileagan's orientation towards supporting and facilitating Gaelic language acquisition leads to another difficulty with the new pack. The 'Cluich Còmhla' CD which accompanied the previously distributed pack contained more than twenty songs and many matched the songs sung at the Cròileagan in their circle time at the beginning and end of sessions. A number of parents commented that they played this CD at home and in the car. The new pack also contains a CD; however, it has only five songs, and most of them are not sung in the Cròileagan. The information pack's CD, coupled with the reduced focus on Gaelic in the home contained within the pack, does not appear to align with the notion of 'learning Gaelic as a family', the orientation of the Cròileagan.

Support for parents considering Gaelic-medium education

Some parents do, indeed, attend the Cròileagan in order to learn about Gaelic-medium education and the Cròileagan supports such parents. One mother explained that she wanted to meet other parents before making a decision about Gaelic-medium education for her child who was to be enrolled for P1 in the coming months. Attending the Cròileagan afforded her this opportunity and she particularly appreciated other parents' willingness to reflect on their experiences, both positive and negative. Parents and play leaders with older children often outlined how they had overcome difficulties that had arisen and pointed out positives that parents may not have identified during discussions about Gaelic-medium education. For parents considering Gaelic-medium education, meeting other parents who openly admit to having had similar anxieties proves a valuable aspect of their research into Gaelic-medium education. Parents' and play leaders' experiences were felt to be authentic and grounded in their own experiences; parents who sought others' views and experiences expressed gratitude at such opportunities, which they felt to be independent of the school or any explicit promotion agenda.

The promotion of Gaelic-medium education at the groups takes the form of support for parents already considering Gaelic-medium education. One play leader conveyed her own understanding of the role of the Cròileagan as being a 'dual role,' serving as both an introduction to Gaelic-medium education and to the language:

I think personally that the biggest role is actually to be that first easy step into accessing Gaelic-medium education. The second part of, whether it as important, they are both pretty important, but the second thing is for the children and the parents to both hear and learn some Gaelic but yeah it is definitely dual role for me [. . .] So yeah, so that the, so definitely two things, a bit of Gaelic learning and a bit of promotion.

This play leader clarified her approach to promoting Gaelic-medium education within the Cròileagan. This involves being available to parents with questions about Gaelic-medium education and also informing them of the positive experiences that she has had:

The promotion, as it was, not that I am going out and saying 'you must come to Gaelic-medium', but definitely being somebody that they can ask about or that I can say 'do you know how good it is' the things that they might not know, things, about the things that I value about GME which is things to do with the community, the Gaelic community, or the culture that the children are exposed to, or the children getting to go and do the Mòds, those kind of things that parents wouldn't know about even if they were interested in bilingual education.

The gentle approach to the promotion of Gaelic-medium education taken by play leaders reflects the Cròileagan's position as an introduction to Gaelic language learning and Gaelic-medium education. The Cròileagan is a place of information and experience sharing on a range of matters including Gaelic-medium education and it remains open to adults looking after young children, whether they are considering formal education choice or not.

The new information pack is appreciated by parents who attend the Cròileagan in an effort to research and experience Gaelic-medium education while considering formal education. One mother who had enrolled her three-year-old child for Gaelic-medium education at nursery level praised the information and support that she had received from the Cròileagan, including the new information pack, stating that 'the literature that I have been given has been really helpful'. The Cròileagan recognises that information on Gaelic-medium education is important to parents considering formal education but not all parents in attendance are currently doing so. The Cròileagan differs from nursery and other formal education in that it provides opportunities for engaging the whole family in language learning, and the support and resources available to parents and children at the Cròileagan evidences their appreciation of these opportunities.

Gaelic-medium enrolment in Edinburgh

The Cròileagan's approach does indeed support the national language planning goals of increasing enrolment in Gaelic-medium primary education and also supports parents to begin learning and using Gaelic with their young children in the home. Edinburgh's approach is also successful in terms of supporting parents in considering formal Gaelic-medium education. Enrolment in Gaelic-medium education in

Edinburgh has grown significantly in recent years, particularly since Bun-sgoil Taobh na Pàirce, the first dedicated Gaelic school in the city, opened in 2013. During my research, over sixty pupils were registered to start in P1 in 2014, meaning that the P1 intake was just below its capacity of sixty-six. During my fieldwork the nursery had ninety-six registered pupils, which was a record, and was at capacity.[5] As a result, Edinburgh contributes significantly to enrolment figures for Gaelic-medium education nationally.

Those involved in Gaelic-medium education at nursery and primary level acknowledge the crucial role of the Cròileagan as the initial stage of Gaelic-medium education, and note that many families come to Gaelic-medium education as a result of their attendance at the Cròileagan. The head teacher of the Gaelic School acknowledged the pivotal role of the Cròileagan in introducing parents to Gaelic and Gaelic-medium education and the value of parents meeting each other during their considerations. The Cròileagan provides the foundation for Gaelic-medium education in Edinburgh, not only supporting parents considering Gaelic-medium education but also attracting parents to Gaelic and Gaelic-medium education through their well-structured and welcoming parent-and-child groups. Thus, the Cròileagan contributes to the national language planning goal of increasing entrants into P1 by introducing parents and young children to Gaelic and Gaelic-medium education, and supporting them in their research and decision-making. This contribution is achieved without emphasising and overtly promoting Gaelic-medium primary education.

Conclusion

Cròileagan Dùn Èideann contributes to national language planning goals set forward by Bòrd na Gàidhlig in relation to both Gaelic-medium education and home use of Gaelic. The Cròileagan groups achieve this by way of their welcoming, inclusive, Gaelic language-orientated approach rather than active and overt promotion of Gaelic-medium education. The examination of the Cròileagan's role illustrates its highly nuanced approach to supporting parents with young children in Edinburgh. The discrepancy between the national focus on primary enrolment and the Cròileagan's approach clearly illustrates how local endeavours are grounded in an understanding of the needs and requirements of people within their area. National-level support should actively seek to understand how local endeavours currently contribute to national language planning goals and appreciate that providing appropriate support for parents requires an understanding of their current considerations and interests.

Notes

1. Sessions were also held in Corstorphine Community Centre until it was severely damaged by fire in October 2013.
2. I will refer to all adults attending the Cròileagan as parents, given that parents were the most common adults to attend. Other adults in attendance included: grandparents, other relatives, childminders, nannies and au pairs.
3. A CD of a fluent Gaelic speaker reading the story is included with each book.

4. Storysacks were developed by one of Cròileagan Dùn Èideann's play leaders. They are based around a topic such as colours, numbers or shapes and include a related book with CD, and an activity to be done at home.
5. Forty children can attend the Gaelic-medium nursery in Bun-sgoil Taobh na Pàirce at one time. There are two sessions per day and children are entitled to five sessions per week. During my research, a small number of children were attending a number of sessions in the Gaelic-medium nursery and the remainder in the English-medium nursery elsewhere. As a consequence, the number of children registered exceeded the daily capacity of eighty.

References

Bòrd na Gàidhlig. 2012a. *National Gaelic Language Plan 2012–2017: Growth & Improvement*. Available online at http://www.gaidhlig.org.uk/bord/wp-content/uploads/sites/2/National-Gaelic-Langauge-Plan-2012-2017.pdf (last accessed 7 May 2015).

Bòrd na Gàidhlig. 2012b. *Aithisg Bhliadhnail 2011/2012; Annual Report 2011/2012*. Available at http://www.gaidhlig.org.uk/bord/wp-content/uploads/sites/2/Annual-Report-2011-12.pdf (last accessed 7 May 2015).

Bòrd na Gàidhlig. 2014. *Aithisg Bhliadhnail 2013/2014; Annual Report 2013/2014*. Available at http://www.gaidhlig.scot/wp-content/uploads/2017/01/Annual-Report-2013-14.pdf (last accessed 31 August 2017).

Gaelic Education in Edinburgh. 2016. *Edinburgh's GME Story*. Available online at http://gaelic-education.org/edinburgh-council/ (last accessed 10 October 2016).

Gaelic Language (Scotland) Act 2005. Available online at http://www.legislation.gov.uk/asp/2005/7/contents (last accessed 31 August 2017).

Goalabré, Fabienne. 2011. *Parental Choice of Minority Language Education in Language Shift Situations in Brittany and Scotland*. Aberdeen: University of Aberdeen unpublished doctoral thesis.

Hornberger, Nancy H. and David Cassels Johnson. 2007. Slicing the Onion Ethnographically: Layers and Spaces in Multilingual Language Education Policy and Practice. *TESOL Quarterly*, 509–532.

McLeod, Wilson and Bernadette O'Rourke. 2015. *Irish Parents and Gaelic-Medium Education in Edinburgh and Glasgow*. Edinburgh: Soillse.

Munro, Alistair. 2014. Growth of Gaelic Education Hailed a Success. *The Scotsman* [online]. 8 July. Available online at http://www.scotsman.com/gaelic/growth-of-gaelic-education-hailed-a-success-1-3470404 (last accessed 31 August 2017).

O'Hanlon, Fiona M. 2012. *Lost in Transition? Celtic Language Revitalization in Scotland and Wales: The Primary to Secondary School Stage*. Edinburgh: University of Edinburgh unpublished doctoral thesis.

O'Hanlon, Fiona and Lindsay Paterson. 2015. Gaelic Education Since 1972. In Robert Anderson, Mark Freeman and Lindsay Paterson (eds), *The Edinburgh History of Education in Scotland*, 304–325. Edinburgh: Edinburgh University Press.

O'Hanlon, Fiona and Lindsay Paterson. 2016. Factors Influencing the Likelihood of Choice of Gaelic-medium Primary Education in Scotland: Results from a National Public Survey. *Language, Culture and Curriculum*, 1–28.

O'Hanlon, Fiona, Wilson McLeod and Lindsay Paterson. 2010. *Gaelic-Medium Education in Scotland: Choice and Attainment at the Primary and Early Secondary School Stages*. Report for project 'The Output of Gaelic Education'. Inverness: Bòrd na Gàidhlig.

Ó hIfearnáin, Tadhg. 2010. Institutionalising Language Policy: Mismatches in Community and National Goals. In Gillian Munro and Iain Mac an Tàilleir (eds), *Coimhearsnachdan na Gàidhlig an-diugh/Gaelic Communities Today*, 35–49. Edinburgh: Dunedin Academic Press.

Rice, Fiona. 2012. *Sgrùdadh air adhbharan phàrantan an cuid cloinne a chur tro Fhoghlam tro Mheadhan na Gàidhlig ann an Uibhist agus Barraigh 2011*. Sabhal Mòr Ostaig: unpublished honours dissertation.

Roberts, Alasdair. 1991. Parental Attitudes towards Gaelic Medium Education in the Western Isles, *Journal of Multilingual and Multicultural Development* 12(4), 253–269.

Stephen, Christine, Joanna McPake, Wilson McLeod, Irene Pollock and Tessa Carroll. 2010. *Review of Gaelic-medium Early Education and Childcare*. Edinburgh: The Scottish Government. Available online at http://www.gov.scot/Resource/Doc/315694/0100403.pdf (last accessed 31 August 2017).

Stockdale, Aileen, Bryan MacGregor and Gillian Munro. 2003. *Migration, Gaelic-medium Education and Language use*. Sleat, Isle of Skye: Ionad Nàiseanta na h-Imrich, Sabhal Mòr Ostaig.

4

Gaelic amongst Schoolchildren: Ideas on Language Change and Linguistic Choices in Gaelic

Sìleas L. NicLeòid

Today's children's Gaelic is different in a number of ways from the Gaelic that their grandparents' generation would speak (cf. Gillies 1980; MacAulay 1982; NicLeòid 2016). Sometimes Gaelic-medium[1] pupils receive harsh reactions from older, native speakers, such as: 'Chan eil fhios 'am dè tha thu ag ràdh an sin! Dè seòrsa Gàidhlig a th' agad an sin?'('I don't know what you're saying there! What kind of Gaelic is that?').[2] Comments of that kind usually refer to different aspects of change which native speakers recognise in the children's speech in comparison to their own. The most obvious change manifests itself in the choice of vocabulary. Sometimes this means that the younger generation uses Gaelic terms where the older would traditionally use English (for example, for names of the months), but also newly coined terminology which is established in schools and other educational institutions, for specific subjects (mathematics, science and so on) – a necessary prerequisite for minority language immersion education in order to teach subjects which had never been taught through that particular language before (cf. Slaughter 1997; Baker 2011) – but unknown to speakers who were not educated through the medium of Gaelic (cf. McIntyre 2009; Baker 2011). Further changes concern grammatical structures in the language (cf. NicLeòid 2016).

To an extent, linguistic differences may be expected as a part of normal language change between generations, in any language (cf. Dorian 1981, 1994; Johnstone 2002; Thomason 2007). However, the process of language change is different for minority languages, due to the strong, continuous influence of the majority language(s) (Clyne 1992; Sankoff 2001; Baker 2011). Apart from that, language attitudes of the minority language speakers themselves can influence linguistic domains and speaking patterns as well (Baker 1992; Bradley 2013 [2002]). This means that, in general, minority languages deal with more complex linguistic and meta-linguistic factors in the process of language change (Martin-Jones 1988; Aitchison 2001). These will be discussed later, within the context of the research data.

To examine this process of language change, this qualitative chapter focuses on analysing (i) schoolchildren's understanding of Gaelic idioms (such as similes (along the lines of e.g. 'to be as strong as an ox') and sayings (along the lines of e.g. 'to take to one's heels')),[3] and (ii) their attitudes towards them, as a possible example of an important part of language change between generations in a minority language, but also as an example of the influence of micro-language attitudes on speaking patterns and habits.

Idioms are an important part of language in general, both from a linguistic and cultural point of view. They are invaluable for a deeper understanding of how very differently languages are constructed, and often make use of completely different images and references in order to express the same content (Burke 1998; Vulchanova et al. 2011; Pushpanathan 2016). In addition, idioms give the speakers different pragmatic options within a language, since the pragmatic meaning conveyed through idioms may be very different from simple, non-idiomatic expressions in the same context (cf. Glucksberg 2001; Mäntylä 2004; Vega Moreno 2007).

As Mäntylä (2004: 79), citing Ellis, summarises, when discussing productive language skills, 'an important index of nativelike competence is that the learner uses idioms fluently' (Ellis 1997: 130). The levels to which young speakers, especially second-language (L2) speakers, use idioms in a language can therefore serve as an indicator of their proficiency in the language, both active and passive. The nature of their use of idioms may also indicate their understanding of underlying differences in languages and that it is not automatically correct to translate idioms from one language into another.

The indicative nature of idioms in the context of both language acquisition and language attitudes in connection with minority languages was the main reason for including them in my research. The analysis of pupils' knowledge, use and attitudes towards idioms in Gaelic has added invaluable information to our overall picture of the children's language abilities, their language attitudes and linguistic identities.

The empirical study

My analysis is based on linguistic data from interviews with eighty Gaelic-medium pupils between P4 and S2 (in 2011), at nine different schools situated in four areas across Scotland, including traditional and non-traditional Gaelic-speaking areas.[4] These were different from each other not only with regards to the linguistic environment, but also in terms of lifestyle, infrastructure and choices of out-of-school activities. This way, the research was able to generate results that were not typical for one certain school or area only, but valid on a much broader level.

In every area, one primary school and one high school were chosen.[5] The research focused on pupils from the last three to four years in primary school and the first two years in high school based on the assumption that children from these age groups were able to express their own ideas coherently.[6] Moreover, these school years represent important stages in their lives in which they experience new learning situations and make their own choices.[7] Apart from the children, sixteen Gaelic-medium education (GME) teachers (two in each school) and thirty-two parents (four in each school) were interviewed, in order to add an additional and independent perspective on the children's linguistic abilities and choices.

All interviews were semi-structured (Kvale 1996); based on a script, but leaving room to follow up on important points brought up spontaneously by the interviewees.

The transcribed data was analysed using thematic content analysis according to Grbich (2007) and Spencer et al. (2003), based on the epistemological positions of postmodernism and interpretivism (cf. Snape and Spencer 2003; Grbich 2007). This methodology allowed the researcher to analyse the data according to the main topics and categories arising from the interviews, through 'segmentation, categorisation and relinking of aspects prior to the final interpretation' (Grbich 2007: 16). The data went through this process several times, taking into account the different contexts and how they may influence the final interpretation (Kvale 1996). For the type of qualitative research my doctoral research was based on, this methodology was the most efficient one since it allows the researcher to handle complex data from different sources and in different contexts within one analysis.

In this chapter, I will present results from these interviews and discuss several outcomes, focusing on, first, the children's general knowledge of Gaelic idioms (active and passive, and how they acquired it) and, second, on their attitudes towards idioms and their place in modern Gaelic.

Since idioms are an essential and particularly individual part of every language, their use (or the lack thereof) not only reflects the speakers' knowledge, but may also reveal information about the speakers' attitudes towards the language (cf. Ellis 1997; Gumperz 2009) and, in connection with minority languages, its status. If, for example, speakers mainly use idioms directly translated from the majority language (calques) in the minority language, could it be that they rarely hear traditional idioms and therefore do not know the difference, or do they assume that because English, for example, is a majority language, its structures and idioms will automatically work for any minority language as well, thus not acknowledging the minority language's individual and unique features?[8]

Part of the analysis in this research focused on how the pupils feel about idioms in Gaelic in general; their attitudes did reveal valuable information about their everyday linguistic choices, including their own point of view on what constitutes 'modern Gaelic'.

Findings: the use of idioms by primary school pupils

Primary school pupils' perspectives

At first, the pupils were given different examples of idioms and were asked whether or not they recognised them and if they knew any further, similar examples. They were not asked to actively present a list of all the idioms they knew; rather, the question aimed at finding out if the children were used to hearing idiomatic expressions in Gaelic and if they were aware of the use of idioms in their linguistic surroundings. The pupils were not given a definition of 'idiom', but, following a practical rather than a theoretical approach, were provided with different examples of idioms (similes and sayings) as soon as the term was introduced. As a next step, they were asked whether they would use these kinds of expressions at all themselves, in speaking or in writing. In order to ensure that the question was not too abstract, it was framed in a context the children knew well, that is, school work.[9] Based on the quality of the children's answers, it appears that this system of questions worked very well, without putting too much pressure on the children, for example, by making them feel they had to fulfil tasks similar to school assessments. Whenever an interviewee seemed unsure about an example or a question, they were given further, more detailed explanations or questions until it was clear that they fully understood what was being asked of them.

Out of forty primary school pupils interviewed, eight said that they did not know Gaelic idioms very well at all and were not aware of them being used in their surroundings. Most of the interviewees (twenty-six) expressed that they knew Gaelic idioms to some extent. Amongst those pupils, levels of understanding varied from struggling to understand idioms and only knowing two or three, to feeling confident that they understood most idioms in general, but sometimes needed a bit of time to work out their meanings.

In addition, some pupils confirmed they were comfortable with idiomatic expressions in terms of understanding them, and that they were happy to use some of them sometimes at school, in creative writing projects or other written school work. However, they would not use them at all in spoken language, because they felt that idioms would demand too much effort in comparison to simple, straightforward language:[10]

> Interviewer: Ma smaoinicheas tu air abairtean is gnàthasan-cainnt anns a' Ghàidhlig, mar 'Tha mi cho sgìth ris a' chù' no 'cho sona ri bròg', rudan mar sin, a bheil thu eòlach air sin? . . . A bheil thu eòlach air [. . .] dòighean mar seo a bhith ga ràdh?
> Pupil: Tha, ach tha e doirbh airson mise a' cur a-staigh gach seantans no rudeigin mar sin, so tha mi dìreach mar, ag ràdh an rudan *basic*.[11] (Pu-19-PS)[12]

> (If you think about sayings and idioms in Gaelic, like 'Tha mi cho sgìth ris a' chù' ('I'm as tired as a dog') or 'cho sona ri bròg', ('as happy as a shoe') things like that, do you know those? . . . Do you know [. . .] ways like this to say it?
> Yes, but it is hard for me to put this into every sentence or something like that, so I just, like, say the basic things.')

Three pupils from a traditional Gaelic-speaking area said that idioms were completely natural to them and that they would understand and use them, but, according to their own statements on where they received their input on Gaelic idioms, it was very likely that those pupils, who all came from Gaelic-speaking families, had acquired this understanding and speaking pattern at home. This analysis was confirmed by their teachers. Not many pupils stated that they made use of idioms in speech (two from traditional Gaelic-speaking areas), but around a quarter of the children claimed to use idiomatic expressions sometimes for writing tasks at school, such as stories.

A closer look will now be taken at their attitudes and ideas towards idioms in Gaelic. Many of the pupils understood Gaelic idioms as a discrete part of the language, which could be separated out completely from basic Gaelic, with no close connection between the two at all. Many pupils expressed that they preferred 'Gàidhlig bhunaiteach' ('basic Gaelic') or 'Gàidhlig àbhaisteach' ('normal Gaelic'), because, from their point of view, anything else was too complicated, old-fashioned and no longer connected to modern Gaelic as they understood it (cf. Harrison 2007; Ó Giollagáin 2011). One pupil went a step further, stating that basic and simple Gaelic was 'Gàidhlig cheart' ('proper/right Gaelic'), implying that any other kind of Gaelic, such as Gaelic including idiomatic expressions, was 'wrong':

> Interviewer: Thuirt thu gum bi thu a' bruidhinn Gàidhlig aig amannan ri do sheanair, am bi thu a' cluinntinn abairtean an uair sin?
> Pupil: Uaireannan. Bhidh . . . uaireannan, cha bhi tòrr. Airson, tha e mar, tha iadsan a' bruidhinn an Gàidhlig mar nach eil sinn a' bruidhinn a-nis [. . .] Chan eil iadsan a' cleachdadh a' chànain mar sin. Tha iad dìreach ag ràdh dìreach Gàidhlig cheart, chan eil iad a' cleachdadh 'tha mi cho sgìth ris a' chù' is rudan. (Pu-5-PS)

> (Interviewer: You said that you sometimes speak Gaelic to your grandfather, do you hear sayings then?
> Pupil: Sometimes. Yes . . . sometimes, not often. Because, it is like, they speak Gaelic in a way we don't speak now [. . .] They don't use the language like this. They just say just proper Gaelic, they don't use 'tha mi cho sgìth ris a' chù' ['I'm as tired as a dog'] and things.)

It is interesting that some pupils seem to look at idiomatic expressions in Gaelic as representing something which can be interpreted like a lower register of the language (separate from 'Gàidhlig cheart'), rather than a feature of a higher-register, more elaborated code, and that it is not appropriate even in older generations' speech. This is different from believing that idioms and sayings are old-fashioned, and therefore no longer compatible or adequate in modern Gaelic; this attitude is far more generic. It concerns both modern Gaelic and Gaelic as spoken by older generations, ignoring a possible effect of language change over time and generations. If these pupils accept idioms as appropriate to modern Gaelic at all, it is only in the context of their school work, as a feature of an academic register, but not outside of the classroom:

> Uill . . . nuair a tha mi a' cluinntinn e, tha mi mar a' tuigsinn dè tha iad a' ciallachadh, ach chan eil daoine *really* a' cleachdadh iad tòrr a-nise, aig an sgoil. Tha, *yeah*, tha iadsan dìreach a' canail 'Tha e sgìth' no 'Chaidh e air falbh' [an àite 'cho sgìth ris a' chù' agus 'Thug e a chasan leis']. (Pu-3-PS)

> ('Well . . .when I hear it, I do, like, understand what they mean, but people don't *really* use them a lot now, at school. They say, *yeah*, they just say 'Tha e sgìth' ['He is tired'] or 'Chaidh e air falbh' ['He left'] [i.e. instead of their idiomatic equivalents 'Tha e cho sgìth ris a' chù' ['He is as tired as the dog'] or 'Thug e a chasan leis' ['He took his legs with him'].')

These examples demonstrate a linguistic simplification which has been noted in the Gaelic of young people in Scotland at different levels (cf. Dorian 1981, 1994; Bateman 2010; Bell et al. 2014). While Dorian's research focuses on grammatical simplification which happens as a part of language decline, my own research has shown that some simplification also happens at the level of idioms (higher-level structures), suggesting that children are not acquiring a clear command of the use of Gaelic idioms. This point was corroborated by Bell et al. (2014) in their research on the language community's priorities and ideas concerning 'good Gaelic' within the context of corpus planning (see Chapter 8 this volume). The majority of participants/interviewees in that project showed a clear preference for a traditional target variety of Gaelic, or retro-vernacular, 'in contrast to the evolving, English-influenced usages of the younger generation' and expressed their worries about the 'loss of basic lexical distinctions and traditional idioms' (Bell et al. 2014: 8–9). According to the Gaelic language community itself, this overall simplification and adaptation of Gaelic to English structures and idioms makes it difficult for the younger speakers to be integrated into the language community.

If idiomatic expressions are not a habitual feature of language use in the children's daily lives in the first place, they will not know them well enough to use them spontaneously, without having to make a conscious effort. Their awareness of this extra effort, however, as well as their feeling that idioms have no part in modern Gaelic, leads them to make a distinction between 'normal' Gaelic (the unelaborated language) and 'old-fashioned, complicated' Gaelic, that is, idiomatic Gaelic. Consequently, it is likely that most of them will decide to speak only what they understand as 'normal' and 'modern' Gaelic.

Teacher and parent perspectives

Many statements from teachers supported the conclusion that the majority of GME pupils do not know Gaelic idioms well at all and speak the language in a relatively simple and unelaborated form, without making much use at all of its idiomatic resources:

> Chanainnsa nach eil sin aca . . . uaireannan tha sinn air bruidhinn mu dheidhinn seo anns an sgoil, ach *no*. San fharsaingeachd, chan eil gnàthasan-cainnt is sin aca. (T-7-PS)

> (I would say that they don't have it . . . sometimes we'll talk about this at school, but no. In general, they don't have idioms and the like.)

As noted above, some teachers explained that it was difficult for children who had no exposure to Gaelic at home or in their community to learn the language idiomatically and as naturally spoken by its native speakers. Due to that lack of both input and opportunities to use Gaelic idioms informally, these children's Gaelic would very often be simpler and lack idioms. At the same time, idiomatic language is not a subject covered much in the schools, and therefore it is no surprise that GME pupils do not get enough input in this area from the school itself, either, in order to acquire a broad understanding and knowledge of Gaelic idioms.

Parental opinion supports the conclusion that the school as an institution is not currently a site where children make significant progress in learning Gaelic idioms. Rather, those few pupils who use Gaelic idioms as a habitual and unselfconscious part of their speech, are understood to have acquired that competence as a function of language use in the home or in their community. Many parents felt that the Gaelic their children learned in school was quite formal, and some of them suggested that this register of simple, formal speech as used at school – often the only Gaelic register their children could speak, since most of the pupils do not learn and speak the language in a linguistically natural and informal environment – was the reason that many children felt that Gaelic idioms were no longer relevant in modern Gaelic. Some parents complained that the schools did not make a sufficient effort to present and familiarise the children with different registers and types of Gaelic speech, claiming that the teachers themselves would not use idiomatic expressions in front of the children:

> Chan eil rud sam bith mar sin aca [a' chlann] idir idir idir [. . .] Chan eil na tidsearan a' cleachdadh abairtean [Gàidhlig] is chan eil mise, agus mar sin, [gàire], chan eil eisimpleirean aca. (Pa-2-PS)

> (They [the children] don't have anything like that at all, at all, at all [. . .] The teachers don't use [Gaelic] sayings and neither do I,[13] which means [laughter] that they don't have any examples.)

There was no clear agreement among the parents as to what schools were supposed to do about this situation. Some pointed out that there was no proper way to teach a topic such as idioms in the first place, while others said that it would be of great importance for the children to learn more about them at school. Several parents just accepted the situation that the pupils had a certain understanding of idioms, even if that was limited, and that the Gaelic language as spoken by the younger generation had changed in general, towards a simpler, more formal mode of speech.

Findings: the use of idioms by high school pupils

High school pupils' perspectives

The forty high school pupils were interviewed in the same manner as the primary schoolchildren. More than half of the children (twenty-four) said that they knew idioms in Gaelic, or, at least, that they were aware of them even if they did not understand them all. Among those pupils, there were seven who admitted that they only 'knew them a little' ('beagan eòlach orra') or 'understood some' ('a' tuigsinn feadhainn'). Taking a closer look at the full answers, it becomes clear that some of the pupils were unsure about idioms in general language use, looking at them as a specific topic at school rather than a normal part of the language. Furthermore, six pupils felt that they barely knew any idioms at all and that they were a very difficult part of the language that they were not willing to take on. At high school level, none of the children claimed that Gaelic idioms were completely natural to them or that they had a very good knowledge of them.[14]

When asked if they would use idioms in Gaelic themselves, over a quarter of the pupils (thirteen) stated that they would not use them at all, either in writing or in speaking. According to their answers, they did not consider idiomatic language as contemporary. They felt that they would sound extremely old-fashioned in front of their friends and peers if they used idiomatic expressions of that kind themselves, as one pupil told me:

> Tha mi eòlach orra [abairtean is gnàthasan-cainnt], ach chan eil mi really ga chleachdadh . . . Yeah . . . It's not cool. (Pu-50-HS)

> (I know them (i.e. sayings, idioms), but I don't really use them . . . Yeah . . . It's not cool.)

However, twelve pupils claimed that they would sometimes use idioms in written work at school, for example when they had to write a creative story. Some of them were very aware of the impact idiomatic language could have on their marks: they understood that 'good Gaelic' was expected to contain idiomatic expressions. They perceived idioms to be part of their work at school only, rather than a natural element of the language that would be used in an everyday context. There were only three interviewees out of forty who claimed that they used Gaelic idioms in speech:

> Pupil: Uaireannan, dìreach . . . airson rud beag gàire, ach cha bhi mar. Bhidh mi ag ràdh 'Mo chreach is a thàinig'. (Pu-56-HS)

> (Sometimes, just . . . for a bit of a laugh, but I won't, like. I will say 'Mo chreach is a thàinig' ('My ruin that came').)

> Interviewer: Am bi thu fhèin gan cleachdadh? (Do you use them yourself?)
> Pupil: Nuair a tha mi mar, *being sarcastic* no rudeigin, leis na caraidean agam, 's dòcha gun can mi e, ach . . . cha bhi *really*, cha bhi nuair a tha mi . . . *normally*, cha bhi mi. (Pu-60-HS)

> (When I'm, like, *being sarcastic* or something, with my friends, maybe I'll say it, but . . . not *really*, not when I . . . *normally*, I won't.)

These interviewees did admit that they would use idiomatic Gaelic at times; however, the quotes above make it very clear that they would only use Gaelic idioms in speaking as a joke among friends or when they were being ironic, rather than in normal conversation.

At a more abstract level, interesting attitudes and ideas on idiomatic expressions in Gaelic also came to the surface in the interviews. Two interviewees were not sure what idioms or sayings were in the first place, even after being given several examples. To one of them, idioms were closely connected to the language of the islands (that is, the Outer Hebrides, the current demographic heartland of Scottish Gaelic (cf. National Records of Scotland 2011; Mac an Tàilleir 2013)), as if they belonged to certain dialects and specific geographical areas only and did not have a place in Gaelic in general. Another pupil expressed a particularly unusual attitude towards idioms in Gaelic: in her opinion, Gaelic did not, in fact, have its own idioms, but would avail of calques from English or idioms created ad hoc (cf. Rothach 2006).

Similar to the primary school pupils, many interviewees from high school level regarded Gaelic idioms as a separate part of the language that could be used at times (for school work purposes or when joking with friends), but were not necessary anymore in what the pupils understood as modern Gaelic.

Teacher and parent perspectives

The dominant view held by the eight high school teachers interviewed was that pupils did not typically use idiomatic expressions and that that the formal register used in school did little to support its acquisition. One teacher stated that the majority of her pupils did not know many idioms in Gaelic and confirmed that the small group of children who did have a better knowledge of idiomatic language had acquired those skills at home, not at school. Three other teachers agreed that the majority of the children did not actively know many idioms, although they understood more idioms (passively) than they were able to use themselves in conversation or in writing.

Two further teachers emphasised the point that currently most pupils in GME were not native speakers and would not speak any Gaelic until they started at *Sgoil Àraich* (Gaelic-medium nursery) or even at primary school. Due to this acquisition situation, they did not pick up idiomatic expressions in Gaelic – the way native speakers would acquire it at home, in their family environment – at all. According to these teachers, idioms were not the kind of subject which children could acquire and master completely through the school alone. Idioms were closely connected to informal speech as used and heard in the home domain. This meant that pupils with no Gaelic in the family missed out on this very important kind of input, since all they learned and heard most of the time was the more formal register of the language as taught and used at school.

> Interviewer: Dè mu dheidhinn gnàthasan-cainnt is abairtean is rudan mar sin?
> Teacher: Chan eil sin cho làidir, airson nach eil a' Ghàidhlig aca aig an taigh, aig tòrr aca [. . .] Nì iad an-àirde rudan aca fhèin . . . glè thric tha e stèidhichte fèir air eadar-theangachadh bhon Bheurla [. . .] chan eil iad a' dol a dh'ionnsachadh Gàidhlig dìreach mar a tha i againn ann an leabhar [. . .], airson tha saoghal againn gu math eadar-dhealaichte an-diugh. (T-11-HS)

> (How about idioms and sayings and things like that?
> It is not so strong, because they don't have Gaelic at home, many don't [. . .] They will make them up themselves . . . very often just based on translations from English [. . .] they are not going to learn Gaelic just the way it is in a book [. . .] because our world is quite different today.')

As gathered from the pupils' interviews and confirmed by this teacher, it seems typical for the children to simply make up idioms in Gaelic, very often based on English idioms. Interestingly, these pupils do not seem to feel that this is problematic, despite it being the case that direct translation of idioms will almost never lead to traditionally correct and intelligible results (cf. Rothach 2006; NicLeòid 2015). This attitude reveals a lack of basic understanding of how differently languages work, as well as an intuition of what is correct in one language as opposed to another (even without understanding why) (cf. Baker 2011). Instead, pupils seemed to deal with both languages as if they were based on exactly the same grammatical and idiomatic principles.

Furthermore, this teacher raised another important point, contending that one should not expect today's children to learn the same kind of Gaelic as would be found in books. Instead, she alluded to the idea that it would be natural to expect changes in the language within the younger generations, according to what they felt was suitable. This is a very interesting idea which, again, was reflected in the children's attitudes as well. As Johnstone (2002) pointed out both in regards to Welsh and to Scottish Gaelic, immersion education seems to bring forward new ways of speaking the language, especially in predominantly English-speaking areas with not much input in the minority language out of school. He explains that some people see this as a problem, claiming that it is a:

> sign of linguistic degradation and argue that steps have to be taken to ensure that proper Gaelic or Welsh is taught, learnt and used. Others prefer to consider the 'errors' that the new speakers produce to be a sign of sociolinguistic vitality as they create their own linguistic identity. (Johnstone 2002: 40)

The most realistic assessment of the situation may be somewhere in the middle of these two extremes. Languages generally do change through successive generations of speakers and in tandem with their linguistic identities, speaking patterns and attitudes towards the language (Thomason 2007). There is, however, the danger of accepting any changes in a minority language as spoken by the younger generation as being identical to the natural process of development that happens between generations in all languages, even majority languages.

With minority languages, it is very often the case that these changes include more than what would be expected as a result of natural linguistic adaptation over time (cf. Dorian 1994, 1981). It is hard to determine which parts or elements of a minority language change naturally, the same as they would in a majority language, and which changes take place through the influence of the majority language and through mistakes made by new speakers due to lack of practice and opportunities to use the language, gaps in its acquisition, lack of input, and due to attitudes towards the language and its usage. In the case of Scottish Gaelic, different research projects have shown that most GME pupils do not use the language amongst themselves at all (cf. Oliver 2006; Stiùbhart 2011; O'Hanlon 2013; NicLeòid 2015), and because of this lack of function as a means for peer communication it becomes even more unlikely that the pupils' 'errors' in Gaelic can be classified as new language developments expressing the speakers' linguistic identity and so on. For something like this to happen, in fact, it would be necessary for the language to be used frequently in and out of school among peers. However, this is no longer the case for Gaelic, implying that new linguistic developments as noticed among pupils will mostly have to be considered a result of mistakes and lack of input.

Furthermore, if the children are in no way worried about simply making up idioms in Gaelic nor about the possibility that the result would most likely be unidiomatic and even occasionally unintelligible (NicLeòid 2016), their linguistic choices reveal further information about their attitude towards and esteem for the language as well (cf. Oliver 2005): there is a possibility that they do perceive Gaelic to be a slightly imperfect or incomplete language which has become flexible by getting weaker through its status as a minority language and for which therefore 'right' and 'wrong' no longer have the same meaning as for English or other majority languages. With attitudes of this kind, young speakers may not see any reason to make the required effort to learn the language as a detailed and elaborated code.[15]

The strong influence of English was mentioned several times by teachers. One teacher especially emphasised how difficult it is nowadays for children to learn idiomatic Gaelic, since it can be expected − even for children who come from Gaelic-speaking families – that the input they receive in English is always greater than the input they receive in Gaelic, through their environments, peers and the media.

When the parents were asked how well they thought their children knew Gaelic idioms and sayings, five claimed that their children did not know many at all, although they hoped that their children might understand more than they actively used. A number of parents did not expect the children to learn many idioms at school. Many of them saw a very clear input-output connection: if their children received idiomatic input at home, there would be a good chance that they would be fluent in idioms themselves and able to use them actively. And without input of that kind at home, they would only know few idioms which they would not be likely to incorporate into their own speech.

At the same time, there were a few parents among the interviewees who did believe that the school, as an institution, may have an influence on the pupils' skills concerning idioms, if the children continuously heard enough rich, fluent and profound Gaelic in class. For these parents, the input-output connection was not limited to the linguistic home situation, but true to the school environment, too, claiming that, generally, the children 'are going to pick up idioms and things . . . according to the kind of Gaelic they hear' (Pa-24-HS: 'tha iad a' dol a thogail gnàthasan-cainnt is rudan . . . a rèir na tha iad a' cluinntinn de Ghàidhlig').

Similar to one of the points raised by the teachers, one parent elaborated on the influence of English on the children's abilities in Gaelic in general, and especially concerning idioms. She explained that children would often put grammatical structures and idioms together in English first, in their minds, then translate them into Gaelic. Thus, they would come out with expressions which were not idiomatic at all in Gaelic.

Some parents observed that a few children do not use idioms themselves, in their own speech, although they habitually hear idioms at home and understand them without difficulty. This point reinforces the conclusions drawn from the children's interviews, that patterns of usage of idioms are established on more than the speaker's language skills alone. It appears that some children choose not to use idioms, even if they would be perfectly able to, due to the image idioms and sayings have among young speakers, as being old-fashioned and with no place in modern Gaelic.

Conclusions

It has been shown that among the interviewees in this study, only a very small number of school pupils had a profound knowledge of Gaelic idioms and were willing to use these in their own speech, and that these children all came from Gaelic-speaking families.

Most primary school pupils did not feel idioms to be natural or even linguistically appropriate, but more than half of the primary school pupils claimed that they still knew them to a limited extent. According to interviewees in all three groups (pupils, parents and teachers), primary schoolchildren do not receive much explicit instruction on idioms (for reasons to do with lack of time and teachers' insecurity as to the most appropriate methodology to teach idioms), nor do they have much passive exposure to them at school, and therefore it has become very difficult for pupils without Gaelic-speaking families and communities to acquire them. Pupils explained that their use of idioms was solely for written work at school, which is likely to be explained by their belief that idioms were old-fashioned ways of speaking which were no longer relevant today.

These beliefs were amplified amongst secondary school pupils, who despite having a greater knowledge of idioms, seem to understand idioms as a separate school subject instead of an everyday part of the language. This attitude may be connected to the fact that the school is the main source of linguistic input for Gaelic (and limited to very few subjects and situations) for the majority of GME pupils, and may explain why they generally do not use idioms in their own speech. This is supported by teachers' and parents' opinions, who confirmed that the children did not know many idioms in the first place and stated that mostly they simply used calques of English idioms, without understanding how different languages are constituted very differently, especially concerning idiomatic expressions.

Although the level of usage of idioms in Gaelic and attitudes towards them are similar for both school levels (primary and secondary), a few interesting differences should be noted as well. A higher proportion of high school pupils stated that they would not use idioms at all, in comparison to a much smaller proportion of primary school pupils. This seems to indicate that the pupils' attitudes and speaking patterns have become more established as they get older and that they develop more of their own personal paradigms for speaking Gaelic. At primary school level, children seem less set in their speaking patterns, and are more open to taking in whatever input they receive. Peer pressure may generally be lower at that stage than in high school, and, therefore, children may be more willing to try out what they have learned, rather than thinking first and foremost about how they might be judged by their peers for doing so (cf. Eckert 2003; NicLeòid 2015). At the same time, it became clear that attitudes and ideas on the use of idioms had already started developing at the primary school level. At both school levels, pupils generally preferred to speak 'simple' Gaelic instead of idiomatic Gaelic, since the latter was seen as old-fashioned and, in their opinion, no longer belonged in daily 'normal' Gaelic.

While the data from all groups of interviewees suggested that the language, as both primary and high school pupils spoke it, had undergone a process of simplification, the children had a different view on their own linguistic habits and ways of speaking than did teachers or parents. Several pupils felt that the Gaelic they spoke was modern Gaelic, whereas idioms belonged to a different category which at one time was an inseparable part of the language but, in their opinion, was no longer appropriate in modern Gaelic. While present in the interviews with primary schoolchildren, this attitude was stronger and more common among the high school pupils.

It was interesting to see that many children understood their own language skills in Gaelic as representing the new, modern form of the language. They did not question their own level of ability in Gaelic or consider that they might have more to learn – especially through using the language more – or that they were possibly making mistakes now and again, and that these grammatical, idiomatic and vocabulary deviations were some of the reasons that their way of speaking Gaelic was so different from older generations. Apart from some pupils who did indeed believe that their skills in Gaelic could be improved (mostly in relation to vocabulary and grammar), there was a strong feeling among pupils that they were the new generation of Gaelic speakers, and, therefore, the Gaelic they spoke must be modern Gaelic, ignoring their possible lack of specific skills in different linguistic areas.

Notes

1. Gaelic-medium education (GME): many primary schools in Scotland offer to educate children to a very high percentage through the medium of Gaelic (from nursery level onwards) in order to acquire the language through immersion rather than as a subject. Depending on the council area, English is usually introduced as a subject around P4.
2. Data from research project on GME (NicLeòid 2015).
3. *Idiom/idiomatic expression* defined as: 'A group of words established by usage as having a meaning not deducible from those of the individual words' (Oxford Dictionaries 2017), 'A form of expression natural to a language, person, or group of people' (ibid.), cf. also Burke 1998. By *idiomatic language* the author refers to specific speech patterns and collocations present in conservative Gaelic speech.
4. In order to protect the interviewees' identities, the schools themselves cannot be named.
5. Due to low numbers of pupils, two primary schools had to be included in one particular area.
6. They were also at an appropriate age in terms of understanding and producing idioms in their first language (cf. Levorato and Cacciari 1992; Vulchanova et al. 2011).
7. There is also a considerable difference in the linguistic environment of primary schools, where GME pupils are mainly taught through the medium of Gaelic, whereas those high schools which include Gaelic in the curriculum at all only offer Gaelic as a subject plus, depending on the school, between one and three further subjects through the medium of Gaelic in the first two years, often even less in the higher years (cf. O'Hanlon et al. 2012). This change in the children's linguistic environment at school and its possible implications was part of the reason the author chose to focus the research on the last years at primary school and the first years at high school.
8. Cf. Cronin 1995 on issues concerning translation and minority languages.
9. E.g. literary exercises, such as writing stories; a task which would expect them to make use of higher-level language skills in Gaelic.
10. None of the pupils produced Gaelic idioms spontaneously in the interviews.
11. Possible mistakes made by the pupils in Gaelic will not be considered in the translation unless they affect the meaning of the statement.
12. Abbreviations in transcriptions:
    Pu – pupil
    Pa – parent
    T – teacher

PS – primary school
HS – high school
. . . – *pause*
.. – 'em, mm' etc.
[. . .] – 'part left out'
[word] – 'added word(s)'
Italics – 'English word in Gaelic sentence'

13. This parent was a learner, and aware both of the importance of idioms and of the fact that not only the teachers but parents themselves could do more to ensure that the children successfully acquired them.

14. Apart from other reasons, partly this might be a reflection of the reduced exposure to Gaelic in general at high school level as opposed to primary school level.

15. Pàdraig Ó Duibhir (2009) identified similar attitudes in his research on schoolchildren's skills in Irish. The pupils were genuinely interested in the language and would have liked to be completely fluent. Although they were aware that their skills were not fully developed and that they made mistakes, they accepted this stage as the highest level of Irish that they would ever reach, with all its grammatical, idiomatic and vocabulary related shortcomings, and were not willing to actively make an effort to realise their potential for improvement (Ó Duibhir 2009: 115).

Bibliography

Aitchison, Jean. 2001 [1991]. *Language Change: Progress or Decay?* 3rd edition. Cambridge: Cambridge University Press.

Baker, Colin. 1992. *Attitudes and Language.* Clevedon: Multilingual Matters.

Baker, Colin. 2011 [2001]. *Foundations of Bilingual Education and Bilingualism.* 5th edition. Clevedon: Multilingual Matters.

Baker, Colin and Sylvia Prys Jones. 1998. *Encyclopedia of Bilingualism and Bilingual Education.* Clevedon: Multilingual Matters.

Bateman, Meg. 2010. 'Gàidhlig Ùr'. In Gillian Munro and Iain Mac an Tàilleir (eds), *Coimhearsnachd na Gàidhlig an-Diugh/Gaelic Communities Today*, 87–98. Edinburgh: Dunedin Academic Press.

Bell, Susan, Mark McConville, Wilson McLeod and Roibeard Ó Maolalaigh. 2014. *Dlùth is Inneach: Linguistic and Institutional Foundations for Gaelic Corpus Planning.* Project Report, Bòrd na Gàidhlig.

Bradley, David. 2013 [2002]. Language Attitudes: The Key Factor in Language Maintenance. In David Bradley and Maya Bradley (eds), *Language Endangerment and Language Maintenance: An Active Approach*, 1–10. London: Routledge.

Burke, David. 1998. Without Slang and Idioms, Students are in the Dark! *ESL Magazine* 1(5), 20–23.

Clyne, Michael. 1992. Linguistic and Sociolinguistic Aspects of Language Contact, Maintenance and Loss: Towards a Multifacet Theory. In Willem Fase, Koen Jaspaert and Sjaak Kroon (eds), *Maintenance and Loss of Minority Languages*, 17–36. Amsterdam: John Benjamins.

Cronin, Michael. 1995. Altered States: Translation and Minority Languages. *TTR: traduction, terminologie, rédaction* 8(1), 85–103.

Cummins, Jim. 2000. *Language, Power and Pedagogy: Bilingual Children in the Crossfire*. Clevedon: Multilingual Matters.

DASG (Digital Archives of Scottish Gaelic). 2017. *Corpas na Gàidhlig*. Available online at http://www.dasg.ac.uk/corpus/ (last accessed 23 January 2017).

Dorian, Nancy C. 1981. *Language Death: The Life Cycle of a Scottish Gaelic Dialect*. Philadelphia: University of Pennsylvania Press.

Dorian, Nancy C. 1994. Comment: Choices and Values in Language Shift and its Study. *International Journal of the Sociology of Language* 110, 113–124.

Eckert, Penelope. 2003. Language and Adolescent Peer Groups. *Journal of Language and Social Psychology* 22(1), 112–118.

Edwards, John. 2009. *Language and Identity*. Cambridge: Cambridge University Press.

Ellis, Nick C. 1997. Vocabulary acquisition: Word Structure, Collocation, Word-class, and Meaning. In Norbert Schmitt and Michael McCarthy (eds), *Vocabulary: Description, Acquisition and Pedagogy*, 122–139. Cambridge: Cambridge University Press.

Gallagher, Michael. 2009. Ethics. In E. Kay M. Tisdall, John M. Davis and Michael Gallagher (eds), *Researching with Children and Young People: Research, Design, Methods and Analysis*, 11–26. London: SAGE.

Gillies, William. 1980. English Influences on Contemporary Scottish Gaelic. *Scottish Literary Journal: A Review of Studies in Scottish Language and Literature*, Supplement 12 (Language), 1–12.

Glucksberg, Sam. 2001. *Understanding Figurative Language: From Metaphor to Idioms*. Oxford: Oxford University Press.

Grbich, Carol. 2007. *Qualitative Data Analysis*. Los Angeles: SAGE Publications.

Gumperz, John J. 2009. The Speech Community. In Alessandro Duranti (ed.), *Linguistic Anthropology: A Reader*, 66–73. Chichester: Wiley-Blackwell.

Harrison, K. David. 2007. *When Languages Die: The Extinction of the World's Languages and the Erosion of Human Knowledge*. Oxford: Oxford University Press.

Johnstone, Richard. 2002. *Immersion in a Second or Additional Language at School: A Review of the International Research*. Stirling: Scottish CILT.

Kvale, Steinar. 1996. *InterViews: An Introduction to Qualitative Research Interviewing*. Thousand Oaks, CA: SAGE.

Levorato, M. C. and Cristina Cacciari. 1992. Children's Comprehension and Production of Idioms: The Role of Context and Familiarity. *Journal of Child Language* 19(2), 415–433.

Lewis, Jane and Jane Ritchie. 2003. Generalising from Qualitative Research. In Jane Ritchie and Jane Lewis (eds), *Qualitative Research Practice: A Guide for Social Science Students and Researchers*, 263–286. London: SAGE.

Mac an Tàilleir, Iain. 2013. Cunntas-sluaigh na h-Alba: Clàran mun Ghàidhlig. Paper presented at Research Meeting, Sabhal Mòr Ostaig, Isle of Skye.

MacAulay, D. 1982. Borrow, Calque and Switch: The Law of the English Frontier. In John A. Anderson (ed.), *Language Form and Linguistic Variation*, 203–237. Amsterdam: John Benjamins.

McIntyre, William James Michael. 2009. *The Revival of Scottish Gaelic through Education*. Amherst, NY: Cambria Press.

Mäntylä, Katja. 2004. Idioms and Language Users: The Effect of the Characteristics of Idioms on their Recognition and Interpretation by Native and Non-native Speakers of English. In Minna Riitta-Luukka, Pekka Olsbo and Marja-Leena Tynkkynen (eds), *Jyväskylä Studies in Humanities* 13. University of Jyväskylä.

Martin-Jones, Marilyn. 1988. Language, Power and Linguistic Minorities: The Need for an Alternative Approach to Bilingualism, Language Maintenance and Shift. *The Sociological Review 36* (S1), 106–125.

Müller, Martina. 2006. Language Use, Language Attitudes and Gaelic Writing among Secondary Pupils in the Isle of Skye. In Wilson McLeod (ed.), *Revitalising Gaelic in Scotland: Policy, Planning and Public Discourse*, 119–38. Edinburgh: Dunedin Academic Press.

National Records of Scotland (2011), *Scottish Census Results* 2011. Available at http://www.scotlandscensus.gov.uk/census-results (last accessed 6 January 2017).

NicLeòid, Sìleas L. 2015. *A' Ghàidhlig agus Beachdan nan Sgoilearan: Cothroman leasachaidh ann am Foghlam tro Mheadhan na Gàidhlig*. Slèite: Clò Ostaig.

NicLeòid, Sìleas L. 2016. Cuimseachadh air Cruth ann am Foghlam tro Mheadhan na Gàidhlig (FMG): A' leasachadh chomasan cànain le ceartachadh iomchaidh. In Wilson McLeod, Anja Gunderloch and Rob Dunbar (eds), *Rannsachadh na Gàidhlig 8: Cànan & Cultar/Language & Culture*, 299–314. Edinburgh: Dunedin Academic Press.

Ó Duibhir, Pádraig. 2009. A Comparison of Irish Immersion Students' Attitudes and Motivation to Irish in the Republic of Ireland and Northern Ireland. *Proceedings of the BAAL Annual Conference*, Newcastle University, 113–116.

Ó Duibhir, Pádraig. 2010. 'It's only a Language': The Attitudes and Motivation of Irish-medium Students to the Irish Language. In Wesley Hutchinson and Clíona Ní Ríordáin (eds), *Language Issues: Ireland, France, Spain*, 121–140. Bruxelles: Peter Lang.

Ó Giollagáin, Conchúr. 2011. The Eclipse of the First Language Minority Speaker: Deficiencies in Ethnolinguistic Acquisition and its Evasive Discourse. In Hywel Glyn Lewis and Nicholas Ostler (eds), *Reversing Language Shift: How to Re-awaken a Language Tradition*, 11–22. Carmarthen: Proceedings of the Fourteenth FEL Conference.

O'Hanlon, Fiona. 2013. Celtic-medium Education and Language Maintenance in Scotland and Wales: Language Use, Ability and Attitudes at the Primary to Secondary School Stage. In Nancy McGuire and Colm Ó Baoill (eds), *Proceedings of Rannsachadh na Gàidhlig 6*, 323–354. Aberdeen: An Clò Gàidhealach.

O'Hanlon, Fiona, Lindsay Paterson and Wilson McLeod. 2012. *Language Models in Gaelic Medium Pre-School, Primary and Secondary Education*. Inverness: Soillse.

Oliver, James. 2005. Scottish Gaelic Identities: Contexts and Contingencies. *Scottish Affairs* 51, 1–24.

Oliver, James. 2006. Where is Gaelic? Revitalisation, Language, Culture and Identity. In Wilson McLeod (ed.), *Revitalising Gaelic in Scotland: Policy, Planning and Public Discourse*, 155–168. Edinburgh: Dunedin Academic Press.

O'Rourke, Bernadette. 2011. Whose Language is it? Struggles for Language Ownership in an Irish Language Classroom. *Journal of Language, Identity, and Education* 10, 327–345.

Oxford Dictionaries. 2017. *British and World English*. Oxford: Oxford University Press. Available online at https://en.oxforddictionaries.com/definition/idiom (last accessed 19 January 2017).

Pushpanathan, Thiruvengadam. 2016. Using Games as a Tool in Teaching Idioms. In T. Manichander (ed.), *Emerging Trends in Digital Era through Educational Technology*, 295–298. Solapur: Laxmi Book Publications.

Romaine, Suzanne. 2006. Planning for the Survival of Linguistic Diversity. *Language Policy* 5(2), 441–473.

Rothach, Gillian. 2006. Gàidhlig aig an òir. In Wilson McLeod (ed.), *Revitalising Gaelic in Scotland: Policy, Planning and Public Discourse*, 221–37. Edinburgh: Dunedin Academic Press.

Sankoff, Gillian. 2001. Linguistic Outcomes of Language Contact. In Peter Trudgill, J. K. Chambers and Natalie Schilling-Estes (eds), *Handbook of Sociolinguistics*, 638–668. Oxford: Basil Blackwell.

Slaughter, Helen B. 1997. Indigenous Language Immersion in Hawai'i. In Robert Keith Johnson and Merrill Swain (eds), *Immersion Education: International Perspectives*, 105–130. Cambridge: Cambridge University Press.

Snape, Dawn and Liz Spencer. 2003. The Foundations of Qualitative Research. In Jane Ritchie and Jane Lewis (eds), *Qualitative Research Practice: A Guide for Social Science Students and Researchers*, 1–23. London: SAGE.

Spencer, Liz, Jane Ritchie and William O'Connor. 2003. Analysis: Practices, Principles and Processes. In Jane Ritchie and Jane Lewis (eds), *Qualitative Research Practice: A Guide for Social Science Students and Researchers*, 199–218. London: SAGE.

Stiùbhart, Mòrag. 2011. Cainnt nan Deugairean. In Richard A. V. Cox and Timothy Currie Armstrong (eds), *A' cleachdadh na Gàidhlig: slatan-tomhais ann an dìon cànain sa choimhearsnachd*, 275–282. Slèite: Clò Ostaig.

Thomas, Enlli Môn and Dylan Bryn Roberts. 2011. Exploring Bilinguals' Social Use of Language Inside and Out of the Minority Language Classroom. *Language and Education* 25(2), 89–108.

Thomason, Sarah G. 2007. Language Contact and Deliberate Change. *Journal of Language Contact* – THEMA 1, 41–62.

Vega Moreno, Rosa E. 2007. *Creativity and Convention: The Pragmatics of Everyday Figurative Speech*. Amsterdam: John Benjamins.

Vulchanova, Mila, Valentin Vulchanov and Margarita Stankova. 2011. Idiom Comprehension in the First Language: A Developmental Study. *Vigo International Journal of Applied Linguistics* 8, 207–234.

5

When School is Over and Done With: Linguistic Practices and Socio-demographic Profiles of Gaelic-medium Educated Adults

Stuart Dunmore

Introduction

This chapter presents data from doctoral research conducted by the author, which examined language use and ideologies among a purposive sample of 130 adults who started in Gaelic-medium education (henceforth 'GME') during the first years of its availability in Scotland (Dunmore 2015). As part of this research an online survey of language use and attitudes among this group elicited 112 responses between 2011 and 2013. Twenty-eight of these participants were also interviewed, as were eighteen further individuals. Qualitative and quantitative analyses demonstrated that the majority of participants' social use of Gaelic is limited today, although notable exceptions were found among some speakers who were substantially socialised in the language at home during childhood.[1] Only a small minority of participants may be described as 'new speakers' of Gaelic, that is to say having been raised without Gaelic at home and acquiring the language in GME, but continuing to make frequent use of it in the present day (see McLeod et al. 2014; Dunmore 2018). This chapter focuses specifically on the degree to which questionnaire participants reported using the Gaelic language in the work, home and community environments, before moving on to examine the sociological and educational correlates of these professed language practices statistically. As I hope to demonstrate, the question of former-GME students' socialisation in Gaelic at home during childhood appears from the quantitative analysis to have an important bearing on rates of Gaelic language use with various interlocutors in adulthood. Similarly, continuation with GME after completion of primary school seems from the statistical analysis to play a crucial role, correlating consistently with higher rates of Gaelic use.

Gaelic in Scotland in the early twenty-first century

The 2011 Census in the UK showed a 2.2 per cent decline in the number of people claiming an ability to speak Gaelic in Scotland compared to the 2001 Census.[2] In spite of this, the census also showed growth, for the first time, in the number of Gaelic speakers under the age of twenty. Although the proportion of individuals in this group able to speak Gaelic increased by just 0.1 per cent compared to the figure in 2001, the actual increase in numbers of speakers under twenty-five grew by 8.6 per cent from 2001 (National Records of Scotland (NRS) 2015: 9). This growth compared to a 4.6 per cent decline in numbers of speakers aged twenty-five and over, and a great deal was made of its importance in demonstrating the success of GME in Scotland. The then chief executive of Bòrd na Gàidhlig – the statutory agency charged with the promotion of Gaelic – stated of the figures that:

> [T]he number of Gaelic speakers in Scotland has almost stabilised since the census of 2001. This is mainly due to the rise in Gaelic-medium education [. . . and] shows that within the next ten years the lon- term decline of the language could be reversed. (Bòrd na Gàidhlig 2014)

The significance attached to the development of GME for language policy objectives is similarly emphasised in the following extract, from a consultation paper published by the Scottish Government on a prospective Gaelic education bill. The principles of this document, and the consultation it invited, were subsequently integrated within the Education (Scotland) Act 2016:[3]

> The Scottish Government's aim is to create a secure future for Gaelic in Scotland. This will only be achieved by an increase in the numbers of those learning, speaking and using the language. Gaelic medium [sic] education can make an important contribution to this, both in terms of young people's language learning but also in terms of the effects this can have on language use in home, community and work. (Scottish Government 2014: 3)

Thus, the importance attached by policy-makers to GME as a means by which not only to increase rates of Gaelic language acquisition in school, but also to socialise children into patterns of language use that will later impact on language practices in the domains of home and work, is clearly apparent in such contemporary statements of policy (cf. Bòrd na Gàidhlig (2012) *National Gaelic Language Plan 2012–2017*). There is an identifiable aspiration in current language policy in Scotland that GME will substantially increase numbers of new speakers of Gaelic, by equipping students to use the language to a considerable degree throughout their adolescent and adult lives. Yet very little empirical evidence has previously been available on whether GME indeed does impact on (past or present) students' linguistic practices in this way; while it is the hope and intention of many policy-makers that the system will equip children to lead a bilingual life after school, it has not hitherto been shown clearly that this is (or is not) in fact the case.

Neither, in fact, has comparable research hitherto been conducted in the international context on the long-term outcomes of bilingual and immersion education in revitalisation initiatives. As a response to this apparent lacuna in the literature, the principal research objectives of my doctoral investigation sought to address the role that Gaelic may play in the day-to-day lives of former Gaelic-medium students who started in GME during the first decade of its availability; how and when do they use the language? Additionally, the qualitative and quantitative analyses examined the sociological and ideological correlates of participants' professed language practices in order to shed further light on the interrelationship of these factors.

Language revitalisation and immersion education: theoretical approaches

Lambert and Tucker (1972: 225) first coined the expression 'immersion education', describing an innovative French-medium programme for Anglophone children in 1960s Quebec as 'immersion in a "language bath"', that would lead to bilingualism by the end of primary school. This model, through which children would receive full immersion in the target language until second grade, when first language (L1) instruction was introduced and then gradually increased, was subsequently replicated in diverse contexts internationally as a means of revitalising minority languages. García (2009: 128) has glossed this particular variety as 'immersion revitalisation' education, and GME was established in 1985 on the basis of this model (largely via the experience of Welsh-medium education).

While, as noted above, GME occupies a prominent position in contemporary language policy in Scotland, various leading scholars have theorised that the potential impact of immersion education on language revitalisation initiatives may be undermined by a complex assortment of socio-psychological factors. The late Joshua Fishman, for instance, stated famously that minority languages at which RLS ('reversing language shift') efforts are directed require spaces for their informal use in the domains of home and community *'before* school begins, outside of school, during the years of schooling and afterwards, when formal schooling is over and done with' (Fishman 2001b: 471). Suzanne Romaine (2000: 54) has stated that it is '[the] inability of minorities to maintain the home as an intact domain for the use of their language' that has often proved a fundamental (and deciding) factor in instances of language shift.

Similarly, Nettle and Romaine (2000: 189) highlight that securing intergenerational transmission in the home is often regarded as the most crucial goal of language maintenance, rather than persuading policy-makers and governments to act on behalf of the threatened language in domains such as that of public education. These observations parallel Fishman's emphasis on the difficult task of securing the minoritised variety as the language of the home – and the failure to do so contributing in large part to the failure of language revitalisation initiatives generally (Fishman, 1991: 406; see also Heller 2006, 2010; Romaine 2006; Jaffe 2007a, 2007b; Edwards 2009, 2010a).

On the basis of various meta-analyses of the effectiveness of French immersion education in Canada (cf. Harley 1994; MacFarlane and Wesche 1995; Johnstone 2001), Edwards (2010a: 261) notes that in spite of their greater command in the target language, immersion pupils generally appear not to seek out opportunities to use their second language to a greater extent than, for instance, students studying it as a subject. As Baker (2011: 265) phrases the issue, there is always a risk, in immersion education programmes, that '[p]otential does not necessarily lead to production' of the target language outside of the classroom (cf. Ó Riagáin and Ó Gliasáin 1979; Fishman 1991, 2001a; Heller 1995; Hickey 2001; Potowski 2004).

While the limitations of education in revitalising minority languages (without adequate support in the home) have therefore been widely theorised, empirical research on long-term outcomes of minority language-medium education is notable by its scarcity internationally. Micro-level case studies of former immersion education students in Wales (Hodges 2009), Ireland (Murtagh 2008) and Catalonia (Woolard 2011) have certainly offered some revealing conclusions in this regard, though they are somewhat limited in terms of their generalisability.[4] Use of Welsh and Irish by past immersion students in those contexts was found to be limited in Murtagh (2003) and Hodges' (2009) respective studies. Catalan language use by former immersion students in Woolard's (2011) research was notably greater, likely reflecting that language's divergent setting and stronger demographic base (cf. Pujolar and Gonzalez 2013). Although it is the hope of many teachers, parents and policy-makers that bilingual immersion education will equip children to live bilingual lives – using their two languages in adulthood – the long-term success of this outcome has not previously been adequately assessed.

Method

In response to this apparent shortcoming in the research literature, an online questionnaire to survey former Gaelic-medium students' reported language abilities, use and attitudes was uploaded in September 2011. Gaelic and English versions of the questionnaire were designed, and bilingual invitations to the corresponding web links were subsequently dispatched to potential respondents via email, Facebook or Twitter, with participants offered the choice of completing the questionnaire in whichever language (Gaelic or English) they felt more comfortable with. A catalogue of 210 individuals was eventually collated, and invitations to participate in the research were systematically distributed among contacts, up to a maximum of three times.[5]

A total of 112 questionnaire responses was eventually elicited, representing a response rate of 53.3 per cent to the 210 invitations I distributed personally. This response rate would be smaller (34.3 per cent) if the additional 117 invitations sent by a colleague are factored into this total, though there may well have been some overlap between the two groups. The online questionnaire contained thirty questions, spread over three overarching sections on social background, language use, ability and attitudes. The questionnaire design drew broadly on the Euromosaic (MacKinnon 1994) and Welsh language use surveys (Welsh Language Board 2008), and was also partly informed by Dorian's (1981) questionnaire on language attitudes as part of her research on East Sutherland Gaelic.

In the first section of the online form, questions were asked about the date of birth, sex, occupation, current location and home town of participants, as well as their continuation with GME beyond primary school, and with the study of Gaelic generally. Additional questions in this section were asked on participants' further and higher education attendance, the proportions of languages that were used in their childhood homes and surrounding communities, and change in relation to Gaelic language practices and skills since leaving school. In addition to the social variables of age, sex and occupational class, therefore, data were elicited in the first portion of the questionnaire on the social geography and linguistic socialisation of informants during childhood, including their continuation with GME after primary school. The second section of the questionnaire asked participants to report their abilities in English as well as Gaelic, and to indicate the relative proportions of Gaelic and English that they currently use at work or university, at home, in interaction and during leisure time. Respondents were also asked to quantify the overall frequency of their Gaelic language use at present, to identify which members of their immediate family were *able* to speak Gaelic, and to indicate the relative proportions of Gaelic and English that they currently use in conversation with them. The analysis presented in this article will focus on important findings from participants' responses to these first two sections of the questionnaire.

Results

The following analytic sections of this chapter firstly address the social backgrounds of respondents, particularly in respect of home language socialisation during childhood and continuation with GME and Gaelic study subsequent to leaving primary school. I then move on to consider their reported language practices in various key domains and with different interlocutors, before discussing the statistical correlations that were identified between the sociological and linguistic variables.

Social backgrounds of participants

Seventy-three of the 112 questionnaire respondents were female (65.2 per cent) and thirty-nine were male (34.8 per cent), likely reflecting self-report bias and the self-selected nature of questionnaire responses. Forty-nine of the questionnaires were returned via the Gaelic version of the survey (43.8 per cent), while sixty-three were completed in English (56.2 per cent). As indicated previously, twenty-eight of the 112 questionnaire respondents were also interviewed, representing 25 per cent of the total. In terms of age-group, individuals in the 24–32 age bracket were initially targeted in email invitations so as to ensure coverage of respondents who started in GME between 1985 and 1992, the first eight years of the system's availability in Scotland, although ultimately the average (mean) age of respondents was 25.1 after all completed questionnaires were returned via the online survey tool.

A measurement of socio-economic class was made using a scale based on the National Statistics Socio-economic Classification (NS-SeC) and adjusted for the relatively younger cohort under investigation.[6] Respondents were therefore asked to report their current occupation as an indicator of social class; responses to this are displayed in Table 5.1.

By way of comparison with the data displayed in Table 5.1, the 2011 Census demonstrated that 5 per cent of Scottish adults were unemployed, while only 4 per cent were in education or training (NRS 2013b). As such the data in Table 5.1 are clearly out of proportion to those found nationally. Of course, age is key factor in this respect, and it is likely that many of the 30.4 per cent of respondents currently in education or training will progress to occupations in the first three occupational

Table 5.1 Socio-economic/occupational class

Occupational class[a]	N	%
1. Traditional professional	24	21.4
2. Modern professional	39	34.8
3. Routine manual/service	13	11.6
4. In education/training	34	30.4
5. NEET[b]	2	1.8
Total	112	100

[a] Occupations were classified using the NS-SEC typology (Office for National Statistics 2017).
[b] Not in employment, education or training.

Table 5.2 Reported socialisation in Gaelic

Languages used	What languages were used in the home in which you were raised? N (%)	What languages were used in the wider community? N (%)
Only English	29 (25.9)	40 (35.7)
More English than Gaelic	42 (37.5)	45 (40.2)
Equal amounts of English and Gaelic	12 (10.7)	11 (9.8)
More Gaelic than English	24 (21.4)	16 (14.3)
Other languages	5 (4.5)	0 (0)
Total	112 (100)	112 (100)

categories after graduating. As can be seen in Table 5.1, the traditional and modern professional class categories currently account for 56.2 per cent of all questionnaire respondents. By comparison, the 2011 Census reported 49.1 per cent of Scotland's population to belong to the equivalent socio-economic categories (NRS 2013b). As discussed in greater detail below, the key sociological factors that emerged from the statistical analysis were Gaelic language socialisation in childhood, continuation with GME into secondary school, and with Gaelic study subsequently. Table 5.2 displays informants' reported language socialisation during childhood. Crucially for the analysis presented here, over two-thirds (67.9 per cent) of respondents reported growing up in homes that were predominantly English-speaking during childhood, while over three-quarters (75.9 per cent) were raised in predominantly English-speaking communities.

As may be seen from Table 5.2, thirty-six respondents reported growing up in homes where Gaelic was used to at least an equal degree as English (32.1 per cent), while forty-two reported greater use of English than Gaelic (37.5 per cent) and twenty-nine reported English only (25.9 per cent). More Gaelic use was reported of respondents' homes than communities; this is likely to be at least partly attributable to the responses of informants raised in the Lowlands. It is conceivable that the largest category here – that of 'more English than Gaelic' – is also the broadest in terms of past linguistic practice, ranging from, for example, parents' occasional use

Table 5.3 Continuation with GME at secondary school

GM subjects at secondary	N	%
None	2	1.8
Gaelic only	47	42.0
+1 other subject	27	24.1
+2 other subjects	17	15.2
+3 other subjects	9	8.0
> 3 other subjects	10	8.9
Total	112	100

of the odd Gaelic word or phrase while helping children with homework, to more substantial use of the language in conversation. It is unfortunately impossible to know from these data, but it seems likely, in light of the qualitative analysis conducted, that questionnaire participants may have included more limited Gaelic language usage within this category. The 'more English than Gaelic' category was again the largest reported for language use in the wider community that respondents were raised in, with forty-fiv (40.2 per cent) reporting 'more English than Gaelic' and forty 'only English' (35.7 per cent).

Tables 5.3 and 5.4 display informants' reported continuation with Gaelic study after completing GME at primary school. As can be seen from Table 5.3, continuation with Gaelic-medium instruction in subjects other than Gaelic is greatly reduced at secondary level compared to primary, reflective of limited secondary GME provision during the period in question. Less than a third of respondents (32.1 per cent) studied two or more subjects through Gaelic at secondary school, while a further quarter (24.1 per cent) studied just one other subject in addition to Gaelic. The largest individual group of respondents, however, studied just Gaelic as a subject in secondary school (42.0 per cent):

Levels of continuation with Gaelic as a subject are therefore relatively high, with only two informants reporting that they ceased Gaelic study altogether at the end of primary school (cf. category 9, Table 5.4). Fifty-five further respondents (49.1 per cent)

Table 5.4 Extent of continuation with Gaelic study

Level of study	N	%
1. Postgraduate degree	2	1.8
2. Undergraduate degree	36	32.1
3. Some university (HE)	10	8.9
4. Some college (FE)	7	6.3
5. Advanced Higher	5	4.5
6. Higher Grade	29	25.9
7. Standard Grade	14	12.5
8. Some High School	7	6.3
9. Primary School	2	1.8
Total	112	100.1

reported continuing Gaelic study until some point in high school (categories 5–8), while the same number again continued to study Gaelic at college or university level (categories 1–4). Of the latter group, thirty-eight went on to gain an undergraduate qualification in Gaelic, amounting to just over a third (33.9 per cent) of all questionnaire respondents (categories 1–2). This proportion is likely to be far higher than that among all former Gaelic-medium students, although data on this issue are not currently available. The Scottish Funding Council's (2007: 13) report on Gaelic education suggested that the number of students studying Gaelic to degree level within five Higher Education (HE) institutions was small but rising. If 33.9 per cent of all GME-leavers in the period 1985–95 had gone onto HE Gaelic study, the figure would amount to a considerable number of Gaelic graduates in these years; this appears extremely unrealistic from data presented in the SFC report (2007: 13–14). The self-selected nature of the informant cohort should therefore again be born in mind.

Language use

In response to each question on the language use survey (section 2 of the questionnaire) participants were asked to indicate which language they would normally use in a variety of domains and speech situations (see Hymes 1974), using a 5-point scale ranging from 'Only English' to 'Only Gaelic', with a further option of 'Not applicable'. Figure 5.1 shows respondents' reported use of Gaelic and English at work or university.

As can be seen from Figure 5.1, forty-six respondents (41.1 per cent) indicated that they normally used 'only English' at work or university (thirteen of whom (28.3 per cent) reported being in higher education currently) while a further 16 (14.3 per cent) reported using 'mostly' English. While a clear majority therefore reported using 'only' or 'mostly' English at work or university, 41.9 per cent claimed to use at least 'equal' Gaelic and English. Ten participants claimed to make equal use of English and Gaelic (8.9 per cent; three of whom are at university), with thirty claiming to use 'mostly Gaelic' (26.8 per cent; five of whom are at university) and a further seven claiming 'only Gaelic' (6.3 per cent; two of whom are at university).

This would appear again to be unrepresentative of GME-leavers generally, given the small size of the Gaelic labour market relative to English-medium employment in Scotland (see Campbell et al. 2008; MacLeod 2008). While the extent of this disparity

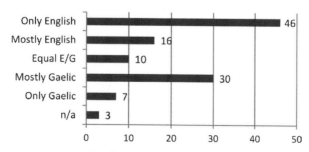

Figure 5.1 Language use at work/university (n)

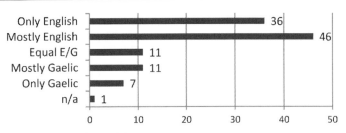

Figure 5.2 Language use at home (n)

is proportionally smaller when the responses of participants currently in education are disaggregated from the data, self-selection bias is clearly at play in the data. It subsequently appears likely that individuals currently engaged in Gaelic employment or education were more likely to participate in the research than those without a professional connection to Gaelic. Yet, crucially, when we compare reported language use in the more formal domain of work to that within the home (Figure 5.2), we see substantially lower levels of Gaelic use in that setting:

Eighty-two participants claimed to use 'only' or 'mostly' English in the home, amounting to 73.2 per cent of the total. By contrast, just 25.9 per cent claimed to use at least 'equal' Gaelic at home, with eleven informants indicating equal English and Gaelic use (9.8 per cent), eleven reporting 'mostly Gaelic' (9.8 per cent) and seven reporting 'only Gaelic' (6.3 per cent). Significantly, therefore, informal use of Gaelic within the home setting appears at first glance to be relatively weak. This finding is perhaps unsurprising in light of literature discussed in respect of immersion pupils' socialisation in minority languages above (see Ó Riagáin and Ó Gliasáin 1979; Fishman 1991, 2001a; Heller 1995; Hickey 2001; Potowski 2004). To clarify the issue of home use of Gaelic further, respondents were then asked 'What are your current living arrangements?' (Figure 5.3).

While Gaelic language use with housemates who cannot speak Gaelic may not, in some cases, be a matter of choice for a speaker, they may be thought to have more influence over their selection of a partner and the languages they speak to them (although of course many other factors may be more influential in an individual's choice of partner). Respondents' answers in this specific connection are displayed in Figure 5.4. As may be seen, English predominates to an even greater extent in relation to language use with a partner.

Figure 5.3 Current living arrangements (n)

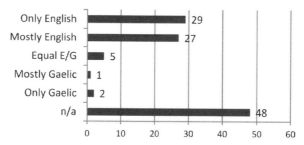

Figure 5.4 Language use with partner/spouse (n)

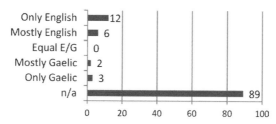

Figure 5.5 Language use with son/daughter (n)

While only sixty-four respondents (57.1 per cent) reported that they were currently in a relationship (Figure 5.4) just eight of these reported 'equal'-to-'only' Gaelic use with their partner or spouse, amounting to just 12.5 per cent of those in a relationship. When we consider respondents' language use with offspring (Figure 5.5), the pattern of relative disuse becomes even more apparent:

While just twenty-three of the 112 participants (20.5 per cent) responded that they have a son or daughter currently, only five of that number (21.7 per cent) reported speaking at least 'equal' Gaelic to their children, with eighteen speaking 'mostly' or 'only' English to them (78.3 per cent). The fact that only eleven of the twenty-three respondents with children (47.8 per cent) reported using *any* Gaelic with them (six of whom report 'mostly English') is particularly notable, especially when the wider policy objectives associated with GME in Scotland are considered. Furthermore, four respondents who reported speaking Gaelic to their children did not claim to do so with their partners. While a large majority of questionnaire participants (79.5 per cent) reported not having children at present, intergenerational transmission (IGT) of Gaelic among the 20.5 per cent of respondents who did so appears from the above data to be weak. Further in-depth research would be needed to ascertain rates of IGT among GME-leavers generally. Again, however, the preliminary finding of low levels of Gaelic use with partners and children is perhaps unsurprising when we consider existing theoretical and empirical contributions to the literature (see Ó Riagáin and Ó Gliasáin 1979; Fishman 1991, 2001a; Heller 1995; Hickey 2001; Murtagh 2003; Potowski 2004; Hodges 2009). If the types of language use into which immersion pupils are socialised at school pertain chiefly to education, it should come as little surprise if they are unable (or unwilling) to speak the target language to loved ones in future, or to transmit it to their own children at home.

Correlational statistics

In light of the self-selected, purposive sample analysed, establishing causality in the relations of sociological and linguistic variables to one another was not an objective of the research, and the ordinal ranks used to code responses to questions on social background, language use and attitudes render the dataset unsuitable for analysis using parametric statistical tests. Instead, Spearman's rank order correlation co-efficient ('Spearman's *rho*') was used to examine relationships between the ranked social and linguistic variables. This test calculates a value (ρ, or 'rho') to represent the correlation between two ranked sets of ordinal data. Again, as the purposive sample analysed was not random, the results of this test are not discussed in relation to statistical significance. Rather, particularly noteworthy correlations are displayed in bold typeface within tables and discussed in light of what they may indicate. The first such table displays rho correlations between sociological factors of age, sex, class, Gaelic language socialisation and continuation in GME, and the linguistic variables Gaelic use and ability:

As can be seen in Table 5.5, the sociological variables of age, sex and class tended not to correlate with reported Gaelic language use to any considerable degree. Conversely, consistent but weak correlations were found between Gaelic language use and having parents who can speak Gaelic; Gaelic ability on the part of mothers correlates somewhat with general frequency of Gaelic use (=.378), work use (=.225) and home use (=.355), while that of fathers correlates with overall frequency of use (=.298), work use (=.296) and home use (=.376). Relatively weak correlations are similarly shown between high levels of socialisation (coded for here as high reported use in the childhood home) and both frequency of Gaelic use (=.344) and high home use (=.452), though the corresponding correlation is weaker for high Gaelic use at work or university (=.107). High levels of Gaelic socialisation are therefore shown to correlate to some degree with higher levels of present-day use of the language in the home, as well as with general higher frequency of Gaelic use. Significantly, however, continuation with GME and Gaelic study after school correlates considerably more strongly with general frequency of Gaelic use (=.690), use of the language at work (=.630) and, to a lesser extent, in the home (=.438). This demonstrates the crucial importance of GME provision beyond primary school as a bolster to socialisation in the home and community.

While socialisation therefore appears not to correlate strongly with linguistic practices observed in Table 5.5, its effect is more apparent when we consider reported

Table 5.5 Reported Gaelic use, socialisation and ability Spearman's rho correlations

Gaelic use	Age	Sex	Class	Home Gaelic socialisation	Mother ability	Father ability	GME cont.
Overall Gaelic use	.076	.008	.209	.344	.378	.298	**.690**
Work use	.038	.016	.224	.107	.225	.296	**.630**
Home use	.035	.014	.078	.452	.355	.376	.438

Table 5.6 Family Gaelic use – linguistic and social variables Spearman's rho correlations

Gaelic use with family member	Age	Sex	Class	Home Gaelic socialisation	GME cont.
Mother	.161	.035	.161	**.511**	.362
Father	.099	.015	.302	**.502**	.154
Partner/spouse	.108	.117	.010	.161	.416
Son/daughter	.145	.323	.196	**.669**	**.645**
Grandmother/-father	.161	.035	.052	**.514**	.465
Brother/sister	.110	.121	.010	.238	.203
Other family	.053	.055	.007	.319	**.521**

Gaelic language use with particular interlocutors. Table 5.6 displays rho correlations for family language use (after 'n/a' responses have been disaggregated from the dataset), correlated with social and linguistic variables.

Again, age, sex and occupational class tend not to correlate with family language use in Table 5.6, with the strongest effect found between occupational class and Gaelic use with a father (=.302). By contrast, high levels of Gaelic socialisation correlate relatively strongly with high reported Gaelic use with mothers (=.511), fathers (=.502), grandparents (=.514) and, crucially, with children (=.669). These correlations highlight the importance of language socialisation in childhood to participants' continued use of Gaelic, and potential ability to pass the language on.

Importantly, however, strong correlations are also observed between present Gaelic use with a child and continuation with GME (=.645), reflecting the importance of these variables to higher rates of IGT of the language. A relatively strong correlation (=.521) is also found between GME continuation and Gaelic use with 'other' family members (such as aunts, uncles and cousins). The correlation of Gaelic use with a partner or spouse is somewhat weaker (=.415), though still notably stronger than with any variable of age, sex or class.

Conclusions

Overall levels of family Gaelic use among the 112 participants (presented in Figures 5.2 to 5.5) are low in comparison with English, particularly with key interlocutors crucial to processes of IGT, such as partners and children. Home use of Gaelic was also generally weak throughout the questionnaire dataset (as well as the interview corpus; see Dunmore 2015) and the more formal domains associated with work predominated in participants' reported Gaelic language use from day to day. In many respects, findings presented in this chapter in respect of limited Gaelic use by former GME students may come as little surprise to the various theorists and researchers who have examined the role of immersion education in minority language revitalisation. Indeed, a large body of literature attests to the limitations of the classroom in influencing children's language socialisation and linguistic practices (cf. Ó Riagáin and Ó Gliasáin 1979; Edwards 1984a, 1984b, 2010a, 2010b; Fishman 1991, 2001a;

Heller 1995, 2006, 2010; Hickey 2001; Jaffe 2007a, 2007b; Potowski 2004; Romaine 2006; Woolard 2011). From this perspective, limited use of the target language by a majority of participants would be the very outcome such scholars would predict. Yet for policy-makers who view the development of GME as the principal mechanism for creating new speakers, the findings of the overall investigation will likely be a source of considerable frustration. Nevertheless, the key correlates of greater Gaelic language use this study has revealed should be beneficial for the development of evidence-based language policy in Scotland.

Significantly, reported experiences of Gaelic socialisation at home during child-hood correlate with higher levels of Gaelic use with key interlocutors later in life, as substantiated in the statistical analysis, which found frequent correlations attesting to the interrelationship of the two variables. Additionally, the statistical analysis demonstrated that continuation with GME in secondary school, and with study of the language after school, was linked to higher levels of present-day Gaelic use generally, and in the domain of work/university study specifically. Higher Gaelic language socialisation and continuation with Gaelic study therefore appear to accom-pany greater use of the language, as might be expected. In terms of the implications of this finding for current language policy in Scotland, it is clear that the goal of strengthening Gaelic language socialisation in the home and community needs to be prioritised alongside developing GME as a policy objective. In connection with the latter goal, correlational statistics presented in this chapter demonstrate that GME provision at the secondary level should be increased in order to ensure that progress made at primary level in relation to Gaelic language learning is not subsequently lost due to a lack of continuity in provision at high school (see also O'Hanlon et al. 2010; O'Hanlon 2012).

It is clear that the influence of each of these factors on former GME students' Gaelic use later in life, and the relationship of each to the other, are in need of further research. In particular, fine-grained ethnographic and longitudinal research would yield invaluable data on the relationship of these variables to Gaelic language use in school years, after GME, and further along the lifespan, when greater proportions of GME leavers have started families of their own. Generally speaking, however, the research discussed in this chapter provides clear evidence for the first time of longer-term social and linguistic outcomes of bilingual education among adults who received GME. This evidence should be of value for the development of policy in relation both to the provision of GME as an education system, and for creating new spaces for the use of Gaelic in the home, community, and in Scottish society at large.

Notes

1. This overarching finding is perhaps unsurprising, particularly in light of the empir-ical evidence concerning language use and socialisation outwith education provided by authors such as Ó Riagáin and Ó Gliasáin (1979), Fishman (1991, 2001a), Heller (1995), Hickey (2001) and Potowski (2004). Yet its significance, and that of the sociological correlates of Gaelic use generally, has important implications for language policy priorities in Scotland.

2. This constituted a sharp diminution in the rate of decline from ten years previously, when the equivalent loss was 11.1 per cent from the 1991 figure. In total 57,602 people over the age of three were reported to be able to speak Gaelic in 2011, approximating to 1.1 per cent of the total population of Scotland (NRS 2013a).

3. Notably, the Education (Scotland) Act 2016 established a statutory process to assess parental demand for GME in any local authority in Scotland, with the expectation that authorities provide access to GME where reasonable demand is found to exist. Crucially, however, and in contrast to recommendations the Scottish Government had received in its consultation, the Act only addresses GME provision at the primary school level. This oversight is particularly regrettable in light of findings presented in the current chapter concerning the importance of GME availability at the secondary level for continued use of Gaelic in adulthood.

4. Indeed, my own investigation of language use, ideologies and attitudes among a sample of 130 Gaelic-educated adults makes no claims of representativeness within the context of GME in Scotland. Rather, its generalisability among the relatively small universe of adults who started within the system during the first ten to fifteen years of its availability in Scotland (see MacKinnon 2005) allows for further in-depth scrutiny of the sociological, ideological and (socio)linguistic profiles of speakers in that context.

5. Through this multi-platform approach to accessing the informant pool, it is likely that dozens of other potential informants, in addition to the 210 I contacted personally, received information about the research and were provided with my contact details. A further 117 invitations were also distributed to former-GME students by an acquaintance of the author who was involved in the organisation of GME during the early years of its availability, and had been employed in the Gaelic education sector since then.

6. In line with the typology employed by the NS-SeC, reported occupations such as 'doctor', 'solicitor' and 'senior engineer' were ranked in the first, 'traditional professional' class category. Occupations such as 'broadcast journalist', 'teacher', 'nurse' and 'clerical officer' ranked in the second bracket as 'modern professional'. Routine manual and retail occupations such as bar staff, hospitality and shop assistants were classed in the third category, while respondents who are currently in education or training were ranked in the fourth category. Finally, respondents who indicated they were currently unemployed and not in education or training were grouped in the fifth category.

Bibliography

Baker, Colin. 2011. *Foundations of Bilingual Education and Bilingualism*, 5th edition. Bristol: Multilingual Matters.

Bòrd na Gàidhlig. 2012. *The National Gaelic Language Plan, 2012–2017*. Inverness: Bòrd na Gàidhlig.

Bòrd na Gàidhlig. 2014. *Gaelic Education Helps Reverse Decline of the Gaelic Language*. Available at www.gaidhlig.org.uk/bord/en/news/article.php?ID=474 (laccessed 9 July 2014).

Campbell, Iain, Marsaili MacLeod, Mike Danson and Douglas Chalmers. 2008. *Measuring the Gaelic Labour Market: Current and Future Potential – Final Report, Stage 2*. Inverness: Hecla Consulting.

Dorian, Nancy. 1981. *Language Death: The Life Cycle of a Scottish Gaelic Dialect*. Philadelphia: University of Pennsylvania Press.

Dunmore, Stuart S. 2015. Bilingual Life after School? Language Use, Ideologies and Attitudes among Gaelic-medium Educated Adults. University of Edinburgh: unpublished PhD thesis.

Dunmore, Stuart S. 2018. New Gaelic Speakers, New Gaels? Language Ideologies and Ethnolinguistic Continuity among Gaelic-medium Educated Adults. In Cassie Smith-Christmas, Noel P. Ó Murchadha, Michael Hornsby and Máiréad Moriarty (eds), *New Speakers of Minority Languages: Linguistic Ideologies and Practices*, 23–41. Basingstoke: Palgrave Macmillan.

Edwards, John. R. (ed.). 1984a. *Linguistic Minorities, Policies and Pluralism*. London: Academic Press.

Edwards, John. R. 1984b. Language, Diversity and Identity. In John R. Edwards (ed.), *Linguistic Minorities, Policies and Pluralism*, 277–310. London: Academic Press.

Edwards, John. R. 2009. *Language and Identity*. Cambridge: Cambridge University Press.

Edwards, John. R. 2010a. *Language Diversity in the Classroom*. Bristol: Multilingual Matters.

Edwards, John. R. 2010b. *Minority Languages and Group Identity: Cases and Categories*. Amsterdam: John Benjamins.

Fishman, Joshua A. 1991. *Reversing Language Shift: Theoretical and Empirical Foundations of Assistance to Threatened Languages*. Clevedon: Multilingual Matters.

Fishman, Joshua A. (ed.). 2001a. *Can Threatened Languages Be Saved? Reversing Language Shift Revisited: A 21st Century Perspective*. Clevedon: Multilingual Matters.

Fishman, Joshua A. 2001b. From Theory to Practice (and Vice Versa): Review, Reconsideration, and Reiteration. In Joshua A. Fishman (ed.), *Can Threatened Languages Be Saved? Reversing Language Shift Revisited: A 21st Century Perspective*, 451–483, Clevedon: Multilingual Matters.

García, Ofélia. 2009. *Bilingual Education in the 21st Century: A Global Perspective*. Oxford: Blackwell.

Harley, Birgit. 1994. After Immersion: Maintaining the Momentum. *Journal of Multilingual and Multicultural Development* 15, 229–244.

Heller, Monica. 1995. Language Choice, Social Institutions and Symbolic Domination. *Language in Society* 24, 373–405.

Heller, Monica. 2006. *Linguistic Minorities and Modernity: A Sociolinguistic Ethnography*, 2nd edition. London: Continuum.

Heller, Monica. 2010. *Paths to Postnationalism: A Critical Ethnography of Language and Identity*. Oxford: Oxford University Press.

Hickey, Tina. 2001. Mixing Beginners and Native Speakers in Irish Immersion: Who is Immersing Whom? *The Canadian Modern Language Review* 57, 443–474.

Hodges, Rhian. 2009. Welsh Language use among Young People in the Rhymney Valley. *Contemporary Wales* 22, 16–35.

Hymes, Dell. 1974. *Foundations in Sociolinguistics: An Ethnographic Approach.* London: Tavistock Publications.

Jaffe, Alexandra. 2007a. Discourses of Endangerment: Contexts and Consequences of Essentializing Discourses. In Alexandre Duchêne and Monica Heller (eds), *Discourses of Endangerment: Ideology and Interest in the Defence of Languages,* 57–75. London: Continuum.

Jaffe, Alexandra. 2007b. Minority Language Movements. In Monica Heller (ed.), *Bilingualism: A Social Approach,* 50–95. London: Palgrave Macmillan.

Johnstone, Richard. 2001. *Immersion in a Second or Additional Language at School: Evidence from International Research.* Stirling: Scottish Centre for Teaching and Research.

Lambert, Wallace, E. and G. Richard Tucker 1972. *Bilingual Education of Children: The St. Lambert Experiment.* Rowley, MA: Newbury House.

MacFarlane, Alina and Marjorie Wesche 1995. Immersion Outcomes: Beyond Language Proficiency. *The Canadian Modern Language Review* 51, 250–274.

MacLeod, Marsaili. 2008. The Meaning of Work in the Gaelic Labour Market in the Highlands and Islands of Scotland. University of Aberdeen: unpublished PhD thesis.

MacKinnon, Kenneth. 1994. *Gaelic in 1994: Report to the EU Euromosaic Project.* Ferintosh, Black Isle: SGRUD Research.

MacKinnon, Kenneth. 2005. *Gaelic-medium Education 1985–2007.* Available online at www.cnag.org.uk/munghaidhlig/ stats/ (last accessed 10 February 2012).

McLeod, Wilson, Bernadette O'Rourke and Stuart Dunmore. 2014. *New Speakers of Gaelic in Edinburgh and Glasgow.* Soillse Research Report. Sleat, Isle of Skye: Soillse.

Murtagh, Leila. 2003. Retention and Attrition of Irish as a Second Language. University of Groningen: unpublished PhD thesis. Available online at http://diss ertations.ub.rug.nl/faculties/arts/2003/ l.murtagh/ (last accessed 20 September 2013).

Murtagh, Lelia. 2008. Out-of-school Use of Irish, Motivation and Proficiency in Immersion and Subject-only Post-primary Programmes. *International Journal of Bilingual Education and Bilingualism* 10(4), 428–453. doi:10.2167/beb453.0

National Records of Scotland. 2013a. *2011 Census: Statistical Bulletin Release 2A.* Available at www.scotlandscensus.gov.uk/documents/censusresults/release2a/ StatsBulletin2A.pdf (last accessed 26 September 2013).

National Records of Scotland. 2013b. *2011 Census: Table LC6604SC – Occupation by Industry.* Available at http://www.scotlandscensus.gov.uk/ods-analyser/jsf/ tableView/tableView.xhtml (last accessed 1 February 2014).

National Records of Scotland. 2015. *Scotland's Census 2011: Gaelic Report (Part 1).* (Online) Available online at http://www.scotlandscensus.gov.uk/documents/analy tical_reports/Report_part%201.pdf (last accessed 2 November 2015).

Nettle, Daniel and Suzanne Romaine. 2000. *Vanishing Voices: The Extinction of the World's Languages.* Oxford: Oxford University Press.

Office for National Statistics. 2017. *The National Statistics Socio-economic Classification* (NS-SEC). Available online at https://www.ons.gov.uk/methodology/classification sandstandards/otherclassifications/thenationalstatisticssocioeconomicclassification nssecrebasedonsoc2010 (last accessed 1 January 2017).

O'Hanlon, Fiona. 2012. Lost in Transition? Celtic Language Revitalization in Scotland and Wales: The Primary to Secondary School Stage. University of Edinburgh: unpublished PhD thesis.

O'Hanlon, Fiona, Wilson McLeod and Lindsay Paterson. 2010. *Gaelic-medium Education in Scotland: Choice and Attainment at the Primary and Early Secondary School Stages.* Report for Bòrd na Gàidhlig. Available online at http://www.gaid hlig.org.uk/Downloads/CR09-005%20GME%20Choice%20and%20 Attainment %202010.pdf (last accessed 19 November 2010).

Ó Riagáin, Pádraig and Mícheál Ó Gliasáin, M. 1979. *All-Irish Primary Schools in the Dublin Area: A Sociological and Spatial Analysis of the Impact of All-Irish Schools on Home and Social Use of Irish.* Dublin: Institiúid Teangeolaíochta Éireann.

Potowski, Kim. 2004. Student Spanish Use and Investment in a Dual Immersion Classroom: Implications for Second Language Acquisition and Heritage Language Maintenance. *The Modern Language Journal* 88, 75–101.

Pujolar, Joan and Isaac Gonzalez. 2013. Linguistic 'Mudes' and the De-ethnicization of Language Choice in Catalonia. *International Journal of Bilingual Education and Bilingualism* 16, 138–152.

Romaine, Suzanne. 2000. *Language in Society: An Introduction to Sociolinguistics,* 2nd edition. Oxford: Oxford University Press.

Romaine, Suzanne. 2006. Planning for the Survival of Linguistic Diversity. *Language Policy* 5, 441–473.

Scottish Funding Council. 2007. *Gaelic Education Provision in Scotland.* Edinburgh: Scottish Funding Council.

Scottish Government. 2014. *Consultation Paper on a Gaelic Medium Education Bill. Edinburgh: Scottish Government.* Available online at http://www.scotland.gov.uk/ Publications/2014/07/5849 (last accessed 8 August 2014).

Welsh Language Board. 2008. *The Welsh Language Surveys of 2004–06.* Cardiff: Welsh Language Board.

Woolard, Kathryn. 2011. Is there Linguistic Life after High School? Longitudinal Changes in the Bilingual Repertoire in Metropolitan Barcelona. *Language in Society* 40, 617–648.

6

New Speakers of Gaelic: A Historical and Policy Perspective

Wilson McLeod

In recent decades, and especially in the twenty-first century, 'new speakers' of Gaelic have become more numerous and prominent within the Gaelic-speaking community and the Gaelic professional world in Scotland (MacCaluim 2007a; McLeod et al. 2014). The national census does not distinguish between new and traditional, first language (L1) and second language (L2) Gaelic speakers, however, and there are no other authoritative data that show the number or proportion of new speakers within the overall Gaelic-speaking community. The term 'new speaker' has become increasingly widely used in contemporary sociolinguistics (O'Rourke et al. 2015); although operative definitions vary somewhat, the key factor is the absence of inter-generational, home-based language transmission. Some definitions are more exacting than others in terms of the degree of language ability and active use that is required for an individual to be properly classified as a 'speaker', or more accepting of lesser degrees of 'newness' in terms of the timeline of individuals' learning trajectories (i.e. the age at which they began to acquire the language) and socio-cultural distance from the traditional speech community (Armstrong 2013; McLeod et al. 2014: 22). The term 'new' may also be misinterpreted so as to posit newness in a historical sense, i.e. to imply that such speakers did not exist at an earlier point in time, so that their emergence is to be understood as an unprecedented sociolinguistic phenomenon. In the Gaelic case, it is true that until recently (until the 1990s or indeed the 2000s) new speakers were relatively few. Yet on closer examination, new speakers can be seen to have made important contributions to Gaelic cultural and political initiatives since the middle of the nineteenth century, even if new speakers were rarely valorised and the importance of producing new speakers rarely prioritised by policy-makers or activists. This chapter will review the evolving role of new speakers since the late nineteenth century and analyse the principal sociolinguistic issues and policy challenges that have come to the fore today.

Two interrelated factors acted to constrain the number of such new speakers in earlier decades. First, the limited provision for Gaelic that existed within Scotland's public school system from the 1870s onwards was aimed almost entirely at native speakers of the language. Second, the cultural imperatives and material incentives to learn Gaelic were limited and attracted few outsiders, and language organisations, notably An Comunn Gàidhealach, the principal Gaelic promotional body (established in 1891), made very little effort to teach Gaelic to non-native speakers. To a substantial extent, this pattern of provision and endeavour reflected the prevailing assumptions about the territoriality and cultural significance of Gaelic in Scotland; although some activists endeavoured to construct the ideal of Gaelic as the true national language of Scotland (e.g. MacNeacail 1920), most Gaelic speakers tended to conceive of the language in more limited regional and ethnic terms, as something belonging properly only to the Gaelic minority within Scotland (and its traditional geographical heartland in the *Gàidhealtachd* or Highlands) rather than to the Scottish population as a whole (McEwan-Fujita 2010).

In recent decades, the pattern of educational provision has changed very substantially, as Gaelic-medium immersion programmes in schools, which began in 1985, have come to cater very largely for children whose parents do not speak the language and are offered in parts of Scotland in which Gaelic has not been widely spoken for centuries. At the same time, however, developing adult education programmes that would bring adult learners to fluency in the language has never been a major priority for Gaelic policy-makers, in contrast, for example, to the situation of Basque (Azkue and Perales 2005). There remains an unresolved ambiguity within Gaelic circles about the ownership of the language and the role of new speakers, debates which tend to revolve around the issue of whether new speakers of Gaelic (can) acquire an appropriate knowledge of 'Gaelic culture' or (can) become 'Gaels' (terms whose meanings are contested and rarely clearly defined) (Glaser 2007). This article will assess the ways in which questions of identity and ideology intersect with language policy strategy in relation to the challenge of producing new speakers of Gaelic.

One issue that has confounded analysis of these issues, and perhaps practical action as well, is that of terminology and definition. The term 'new speaker' has been introduced into Gaelic academic circles in recent years, but as yet has gained very little currency in the wider Gaelic community (McLeod et al. 2014: 2). The term 'learner' remains the most widely used label, as it has been since the late nineteenth century, even though it is arguably not accurate in relation to people who have reached a high level of competence and are no longer engaged in programmatic learning activities (McLeod et al. 2014: 2). Similarly, attempts to introduce the inclusive, Welsh-derived concept of 'Gaelic for Adults' (McLeod et al. 2010; MacLean 2016) as an overarching label for adult learning activity and acquisition planning have not yet gained significant purchase. At the same time, there is no simple, widely circulated Gaelic phrase for 'native speaker' or indeed the underlying term 'speaker'. Various terms and circumlocutions are in use, including *duine aig a bheil a' Ghàidhlig bhon ghlùin/bho dhùthchas* ('someone who has Gaelic from the knee/from inherited tradition') or the simple *fileantach* ('fluent one') (MacAulay 1994: 43; McLeod et al. 2014: 2). When basic terms and concepts are unfamiliar, cumbersome or contested, consensus and progress (both intellectual and practical) can be difficult to achieve.

The contribution and experience of new speakers, 1860–1940

Although native speakers of Gaelic have always been heavily predominant in Gaelic movements and organisations, from the nineteenth century up to the present, a number of new speakers played important roles in various aspects of Gaelic culture and activism in the revival period that began in the late nineteenth century. These included folklorists, journalists, editors, lexicographers and political and cultural activists of different kinds.

One fundamental challenge for would-be new speakers of Gaelic in this period was the dearth of mechanisms for acquiring the language. Adults who endeavoured to learn Gaelic used a range of strategies, as discussed below, but several prominent new speakers actually acquired Gaelic at a much earlier stage of life; these were aristocrats who learned Gaelic in their childhood from domestic servants, often through the proactive initiative of their parents (e.g. MacKenzie 1921: 34–36). Perhaps the best-known example is the family of the seventh Duke of Atholl (1840–1917), who insisted that all his children learn Gaelic (Robertson and Dilworth 2009: 27–29). One of them, Lady Evelyn Stuart-Murray (1868–1940), went on to become a prominent folklorist and two others become high-ranking office-bearers in An Comunn Gàidhealach. This practice was a revivalist one, for all the aristocratic families in the Highlands had come to abandon Gaelic over the course of the seventeenth or eighteenth centuries. James Alexander [Lovat Fraser], scion of a prominent family, wrote in 1917:

> It is a source of gratification for Highlanders that during the last thirty or forty years there has been a considerable change in the attitude of the principal Highland families to the spirit and traditions of the Gael. Fifty years ago most of the representatives of the houses that once led the clans were indifferent to those things that are especially associated with the Highlanders . . . Happily a change has taken place within the last half-century. The representatives of the old Highland houses now pride themselves on their descent and exhibit a ready sympathy with the language and outlook of the Highlander. They habitually wear the Highland dress and are ready to help movements that aim at helping and retaining Gaelic ideals. ([Lovat Fraser] 1917: 1–2)

Other prominent aristocrats who learned Gaelic in this fashion included the pioneering folklorist John Francis Campbell (1821–1885) and the journalist and editor Ruaraidh Erskine of Marr (1869–1960), probably the most militant Gaelic activist of the early twentieth century (Thompson 1984–6; Thomson 2004).

Adults who endeavoured to learn Gaelic during this period were able to draw on a considerable range of instructional books that began to emerge from the 1870s onwards. For example, Lachlan Macbean's *Elementary Lessons in Gaelic* went through six editions between 1876 and 1908, John Whyte and Alexander MacBain's *How to Learn Gaelic* went through four editions between 1897 and 1906, and Duncan Reid's *Elementary Course of Gaelic* went through nine editions in all, beginning in 1895. The *Oban Times*, the leading newspaper in the West Highlands, ran a series of twenty-one columns on 'How to Learn Gaelic' in 1882. The evidence of such publications demonstrates that there must have been at least a moderate level of public interest in learning the language at this time.

Adult learners also needed to access the spoken language, of course. Some of them, such as the minister and scholar George Calder (1859–1941), learned Gaelic while working in Gaelic-speaking areas. Others arranged extended visits to Gaelic districts for the express purpose of learning Gaelic; for example, Margaret Burnley Campbell (1857–1938), a leading activist in An Comunn Gàidhealach (Scott 2013: 27–65), spent time on the islands of Eriskay and Tiree, as she described in a 1905 essay entitled 'The Difficulties I Encountered in Learning Gaelic' (Campbell 1905). Sometimes, as for the journalist-activist William Gillies (1865–1932), accessing the language required strenuous efforts to 'assiduously cultivate opportunities of speaking Gaelic whenever' possible (Gillies 1988–90: 508), a difficulty still reported by Gaelic learners in the early twenty-first century (McLeod et al. 2014: 8–9). The prominent lexicographer Edward Dwelly (1864–1939) described his frustrations in this connection:

No one who has always spoken a language like Gaelic from the cradle can ever realize the extraordinary difficulties presented to a stranger who wishes to acquire it. First, the majority of Gaelic speakers only a very few years ago could neither read nor write it, so when one heard an unfamiliar word or phrase and the first instinct was of course to write it down lest it should be forgotten, the question was how to spell it – of course the speaker could not tell! I was baulked in this way times without number, and my progress with the language immensely retarded in consequence. Next, the great difficulty of inducing a Gael to engage in a Gaelic conversation if he thinks he can make himself understood at all by means of indifferent English, or even if there is anyone present who cannot understand Gaelic, makes the acquisition of a knowledge of colloquial Gaelic much more difficult than is the case with other modern tongues, for it is only by posing as a Highlander and one who knows Gaelic that one can ever hope to hear it spoken habitually and without restraint. These are real difficulties, but they may be overcome by scheming and perseverance as I have proved. (Dwelly 1918: iv)

There were few classes, courses or structured learning opportunities for adults, partly because this area of activity was not seen as a high priority by Gaelic organisations, especially An Comunn Gàidhealach. Indeed, at An Comunn's inaugural meeting in 1891, the interim secretary, John Campbell, announced that 'they did not want to teach people who could not speak Gaelic' (*Oban Times* 1891). Although another Gaelic organisation, the Edinburgh-based Celtic Union, began to offer Gaelic classes for learners in 1904, An Comunn's provision for adult learners only developed from 1909 onwards, when it began to run a summer school in different parts of the Highlands, at Roy Bridge in the first instance. This approach was very different to the situation in Ireland, where Conradh na Gaeilge (the Gaelic League, founded in 1891) organised hundreds of classes across the country, imparting a basic knowledge of Irish to many thousands of pupils, and where a number of Irish summer colleges were established at the turn of the century (McMahon 2008).

In 1930, a new organisation was established, the Glasgow-based Gaelic League of Scotland (Dionnasg Gàidhlig na h-Alba), which had a more politicised, revivalist view of Gaelic and a clear commitment to teaching Gaelic to adults as part of this vision. The League's principal objective, as stated in its constitution, was 'the restoration of Gaelic as the national language of Scotland' (Glasgow University 1934: 156–157). A key priority was to make 'an attempt to amend a lamentable situation in the country today – the lack of any facilities for the bulk of the people of Scotland to acquire a speaking knowledge of the language of their ancestors'. By 1935 the League was running five weekly Gaelic classes in Glasgow; it expressed the goal of establishing branches 'throughout the country to afford the same opportunities to the rest of Scotland', but never succeeded in doing so (Gaelic League of Scotland 1935). The League also established a Gaelic rambling club, held summer camps in the West Highlands (Mac a' Ghobhainn 1973: 4), and produced Gaelic learning materials, notably *Gaelic Made Easy*, a series of instructional booklets written by the organisation's founder, John M. Paterson. In the post-war decades, however, the League's influence began to wane slowly.

From the 1960s onwards adult learners of Gaelic began to become more numerous, to the extent that the increased number of Gaelic speakers recorded in Lowland areas in the national census of 1971 caused some to question the accuracy of the data (Thomson 1981: 10). In part this increase resulted from growing interest in community classes offered by local authorities and other bodies, in part from new courses for learners with the school system, as discussed below. Although new speakers were not prominent in the key Gaelic initiatives of the 1950s (including the hugely important periodical *Gairm*, founded in 1952), new speakers such as Seumas Mac a' Ghobhainn (1930–1987), William Neill (1922–2010) and Frank Thompson (1930–2012) became important advocates for Gaelic from the mid-1960s onwards. At a deeper level, the growing interest in Gaelic in the last third of the twentieth century was related to wider social and political changes in Scotland and the growing role of political and cultural nationalism, a shift which contributed significantly to the so-called 'Gaelic renaissance' that began to gather pace in the 1970s and 1980s (MacLeòid 2011).

Gaelic provision in the schools from 1872

Efforts to improve the position of Gaelic in the school system have been the principal objective of Gaelic campaigners from the 1870s onwards. In the early decades of state education in Scotland (i.e. from 1872), down to the 1920s and arguably the 1940s and beyond, these demands were directed toward provision for 'mother tongue' speakers of Gaelic only. There were no attempts to introduce Gaelic teaching for children who did not already know the language, whether in the Gàidhealtachd (much of which was already undergoing substantial language shift by the late nineteenth century) or in other parts of Scotland. An Comunn Gàidhealach identified Gaelic education as a key priority in its founding manifesto of 1891, but limited the scope of its ambition to 'children, to whom Gaelic is the mother tongue' (An Comunn Gàidhealach 1891: 2).

From 1878 the education authorities granted a series of limited 'concessions', authorising the teaching and use of Gaelic in various contexts (O'Hanlon and Paterson 2014), but all of these related to mother tongue speakers. The principal policy achievement of An Comunn in its early decades was the so-called 'Gaelic clause' in the Education

(Scotland) Act 1918, which required education authorities to prepare schemes of work that made 'adequate provision . . . for teaching Gaelic in Gaelic-speaking areas' (s. 6(1)). The Act did not define the term 'Gaelic-speaking areas', an omission that critics have often highlighted, but less attention was given to the explication of the term 'adequate provision'; in particular, there was no attempt to benchmark 'adequacy' in terms of pupils' oral and written language skills at different curricular stages or in relation to other educational outcomes. Education authorities were given substantial leeway to apply the 'Gaelic clause' as they saw fit, and in most cases this meant that Gaelic was only taught in areas where all, or almost all, the pupils were mother-tongue Gaelic speakers, and typically for only about an hour a week, usually beginning only in the upper stage of primary school (An Comunn Gàidhealach 1936: 4). When An Comunn conducted a national survey on the provision of Gaelic education in 1936, it noted that 'with very few exceptions most schools report that Gaelic is not taught to pupils ignorant of the language' and '[t]he reports from several schools . . . generate the suspicion that the presence in a class of even a few children who know English only is made the pretext for neglecting instruction in Gaelic altogether' (An Comunn Gàidhealach 1936: 5, 6). An Comunn made eighteen recommendations in its 1936 report, some of them relating to non-native speakers, such as extending the teaching of the language to non-native speakers and strengthening provision at secondary level, 'even outwith the Highlands' (An Comunn Gàidhealach 1936: 9–11).

In 1943, An Comunn followed up this report with a memorandum of recommendations to the Advisory Council that had been established to consider reforms to primary and secondary education in Scotland (An Comunn Gàidhealach 1943). In relation to the possibility of extending the teaching of Gaelic to schools in the Lowlands, it suggested that such courses should be aimed not only at Highlanders but at descendants of Highlanders, thereby implying that provision should not be limited to mother-tongue speakers, but still conceptualising Gaelic as something relevant and appropriate only to the Gaelic minority in Scotland and not the wider Scottish population. An Comunn also made a somewhat vague proposal that Gaelic 'should be given equal status with any other [modern European] language in the curriculum' (An Comunn Gàidhealach 1943). While the Advisory Council on Secondary Education accepted the proposal to introduce Gaelic in Lowland schools to a limited extent, it firmly rejected the concept of 'equal status', asserting that Gaelic is 'much harder than the romance languages', that the 'utility value of Gaelic is not high' and that '[w]hile Gaelic literature is rich in appeal for those to whom it is native, it could hardly be claimed that it has either the sustained greatness or the immense range and volume of the European Literatures' (Advisory Council on Education in Scotland 1947: 92). These dismissive views from the Scottish educational establishment demonstrated how marginal Gaelic remained within the system as a whole, and how formidable was the resistance to attempts to improve its status significantly.

Limited secondary provision in Glasgow did begin in 1947, following a campaign by An Comunn and the Gaelic League of Scotland (Glasgow Corporation Education Department 1947a), and schools in Edinburgh and Greenock followed shortly thereafter. Notwithstanding the view that provision should be offered only to 'Highlanders' and 'descendants of Highlanders', by 1957 fifty-six of the eighty-nine first-year secondary pupils studying Gaelic in Lowland schools (including thirty of the thirty-one Edinburgh pupils) did not have a Gaelic-speaking parent (Scottish Council for Research in Education 1961: 76). Yet despite the potentially large pool of students, there was no great expansion of Gaelic provision in Lowland schools after the 1950s; in 1966 only eighteen secondary schools in Scotland, the great majority of them in the Highlands, were teaching the language (Hansard 1966).

The prospect of teaching Gaelic to non-native speakers emerged as an increasingly significant issue in Gaelic education policy through the 1960s. In 1966, the prominent poet and educationalist Sorley MacLean characterised this as 'the most urgent question in Gaelic education today' and argued that 'it has always been the real touchstone of sincerity and genuine seriousness in Gaelic education' (MacLean 1969: 21). Although MacLean did not explicate his argument in detail, it is clear that provision for Gaelic learners had the potential to produce significant numbers of new speakers and thus contribute to the reversal of language shift, whereas provision for native speakers alone could at best achieve language maintenance. Even language maintenance was unlikely, given the intensity of Gaelic-English language shift in the twentieth century; the number of Gaelic speakers in Scotland dropped by more than two thirds between 1891 and 1961. Following campaigning efforts by MacLean and other Gaelic educationalists (MacNeacail 1986), new examinations designed for Gaelic learners were introduced at the newly created Ordinary grade in 1962 (for fourth-year secondary school pupils) and then Higher grade (for school leavers) in 1968. The numbers of pupils sitting Gaelic examinations rose considerably in the years thereafter, even if only a tiny proportion (much less than 1 per cent of the total) of Scottish pupils were involved. Down to the present day, provision for Gaelic learners in secondary schools remains limited and patchy, and this aspect of Gaelic education continues to receive relatively little attention (Milligan 2010). In 2014–2015, only 3,020 pupils were studying on Gaelic learners' programmes and only thirty-one secondary schools offered such programmes; these figures represent 1.06 per cent of secondary pupils and 8.6 per cent of secondary schools in Scotland (Bòrd na Gàidhlig 2015a: 5; Scottish Government 2015: 2).

Since the 1960s there has been greatly increased provision for Gaelic learners in primary schools (Hansard 1970), especially through the system of Gaelic-medium immersion education that has developed since 1985. The pioneering Bilingual Education Project in the Western Isles, which ran from 1975–1981, was originally conceived as a programme to develop children's learning by using their mother tongue, but it became apparent over the years of the project's operation that an increasing proportion of children had only limited skills in Gaelic, even in this 'heartland' area (Murray and Morrison 1984). Provision thus needed to address the needs of non-mother tongue speakers, including children with no Gaelic at all. The strategy adopted was to move away from a 'bilingual' model, which involved extensive use of English alongside Gaelic, to 'Gaelic-medium education' (GME), i.e. a system of immersion in which all teaching is delivered through Gaelic, at least in the early phases (typically the first three years of primary school) (O'Hanlon et al. 2012). GME began not in the Western Isles heartland but in the cities of Glasgow and Inverness, in 1985. From the outset a large proportion of children enrolled in GME did not speak Gaelic at home, and in the thirty years following this proportion appears to have increased steadily (cf. MacLeòid 2011: 32); although data concerning pupils' language backgrounds is not gathered in any formal manner, it is clear that the overwhelming majority of today's Gaelic-medium pupils do not speak Gaelic at home, a pattern that is increasingly apparent even in traditionally Gaelic-speaking areas in the Western Isles (Lamb 2011). GME is promoted and 'marketed' to everyone in Scotland, with a clear message that parents do not have to speak the language themselves or have any familial connection to the language (Bòrd na Gàidhlig 2015b; Education Scotland 2015).

An interesting marker of this shift was the substitution of the term 'fluent speakers' (fileantaich) for the earlier 'native speakers' in relation to school examinations; for this purpose, all children who pass through Gaelic-medium primary education are deemed 'fluent speakers' irrespective of their home background and actual linguistic competence. At the same time, as noted above, in colloquial Gaelic fileantach is often used with the meaning 'native speaker' in the absence of a more explicit term for this purpose.

The growth of GME is consistently identified as the most important success of the so-called 'Gaelic renaissance' that began in the mid-1980s (MacLeòid 2011). Over the last thirty years several thousand children have passed through the immersion system and acquired a substantial knowledge of Gaelic. Whether graduates of GME (which still remains much less developed at secondary level than primary) will remain 'new speakers' of Gaelic over the course of their adult lives is a key question for the sustainability of the language. There is evidence of attrition of language skills and in particular a lack of active use on the part of individuals who went through GME but do not have other ties (especially family connections) to the language (Dunmore 2015). In addition, there are questions concerning identity, acceptance and group membership in relation to individuals who have acquired Gaelic by means of immersion education, as discussed below.

Increasing the numbers of pupils enrolled in GME has been identified as the single most important aim of Gaelic revitalisation policy (as in the *National Gaelic Language Plan 2012–2017* (Bòrd na Gàidhlig 2012: 22)), and it is clear, given general demographic decline in core Gaelic areas and the recent pattern of enrolment growth, that progress towards this goal can only be achieved by targeting non-Gaelic families in urban areas. Creating new speakers lies at the heart of current Gaelic development policy, even if this (distinctly controversial) emphasis is rarely articulated.

Adult learners and Gaelic policy

From the early 1980s adult learners of Gaelic have also been identified as an important group who may contribute to the sustainability of Gaelic in Scotland, although this sector has received much less attention – and much less funding – than Gaelic education in school. The first major step was the creation in 1984 of a dedicated organisation, Comunn an Luchd-Ionnsachaidh, to promote the learning of Gaelic by adults (Comunn an Luchd-Ionnsachaidh 1984). The proposal originally came from An Comunn Gàidhealach, and three-year initial funding was then approved by the Highlands and Islands Development Board, one of a range of new measures in the early/mid-1980s that helped build the infrastructure for the modern era of Gaelic development (McLeod 2010; MacLeòid 2011: 30–40). Roughly at the same time, the three universities that offered Gaelic (Aberdeen, Edinburgh and Glasgow) began to develop new pathways that allowed students to begin Gaelic degree courses as *ab initio* learners of the language, and the Gaelic college Sabhal Mòr Ostaig also began to develop new long-term courses for Gaelic learners. These various initiatives have been an important mechanism for creating new speakers, even if the overall numbers of students involved have been small (Scottish Funding Council 2007).

Comunn an Luchd-Ionnsachaidh and the new national development organisation Comunn na Gàidhlig (itself also established in 1984) commissioned a major report on the needs of learners in 1992 (Comunn na Gàidhlig and Comann an Luchd-Ionnsachaidh 1992). Since that time the strategic potential of adult learners has been repeatedly noted in research studies of different kinds (e.g. MacCaluim 2007a, 2007b; McLeod et al. 2010; Tkm Consulting 2015; MacLean 2016), but this field of activity has never attracted the attention nor the resources committed to school education. Certainly there is nothing comparable to the mass uptake of Basque adult education from the 1970s onwards (Azkue and Perales 2005). There has been a lack of coordination in provision and a lack of viable learning pathways that might bring adult learners to fluency. One significant casualty has been the loss of the full-time, year-long immersion courses that developed in Scottish colleges in the 1990s (Robertson 2001).

In 2010 Bòrd na Gàidhlig commissioned a study of adult learners (McLeod et al. 2010) but most of the recommendations in the report (which drew on the 'language centre' model developed in Wales (Gruffudd and Morris 2012)) were not implemented. Instead, the Bòrd chose to invest heavily in the Ùlpan courses developed by Deiseal Ltd (and originally based on the Israeli model for rapid acquisition of Hebrew), as these offered the possibility of a structured learning pathway which could be implemented in multiple locations, and with administration devolved to a private company (see Chapter 7 in this volume for further information about this course). A review of Ùlpan completed in 2015 identified a number of problems in relation to course management and delivery, course impacts, course design and course quality (MacLeod et al. 2015), however, and the Bòrd has since withdrawn its funding from Deiseal Ltd.

In early 2016, the Bòrd published a new strategy for Gaelic learners, the outcome of a working group chaired by the broadcaster Ruairidh MacLean (MacLean 2016). This strategy identified six ambitions, including a 43 per cent increase of the number of adults engaged in Gaelic learning, a significant increase in the proportion of GfA (Gaelic for Adults) learners who advance to fluency, and the 'achievement of a broad understanding and use of individual learning pathways, based on a national scale of competencies, to map and record progress' (MacLean 2016: 2). Work on the development of a national scale of learner competencies is currently being carried out through a Bòrd project on Comasan Labhairt ann an Gàidhlig/Gaelic Adult Proficiency at the universities of Glasgow and Aberdeen. Amidst these developments, however, the Bòrd terminated its funding of Comunn an Luchd-Ionnsachaidh (since renamed Clì Gàidhlig) and as a result the organisation decided in 2016 to wind up its operations (*Hebrides News* 2016). This was widely perceived as a significant setback for the promotion of adult Gaelic learning.

New speakers and questions of identity

Over recent decades, as Gaelic has come to enjoy steadily increasing levels of structured institutional support, Gaelic revitalisation initiatives have tended to become
more 'linguicentric' in their approach, emphasising and prioritising the use of the
Gaelic language in a wide range of fields rather than other kinds of non-linguistic culturally marked activities or behaviours (Glaser 2006: 182). One manifestation of this
shift is the increasing use of language-based terms for group membership in place of
traditional ethnonyms; thus for many purposes terms like *luchd na Gàidhlig* (literally
'people of the Gaelic language') are employed instead of *Gàidheil* ('Gaels') (McLeod
2014). When language becomes the defining criterion, the terms of membership and
belonging are arguably less ambiguous and can be understood as more inclusive, as
language acquisition is open to all, while 'ethnic' understandings of group membership depend on ancestral and territorial connections which (for better or worse) are
immutable and inherently exclusionary. A now-substantial body of research (e.g.
McEwan-Fujita 2003; Oliver 2005, 2006; Glaser 2006, 2007; Dunmore 2015) demonstrates that the significance and cultural valence of the term 'Gael' has been eroded
to a substantial extent; participants in research studies express increasing uncertainty
about the meaning of the term, and mutually exclusive understandings are in circulation. To some extent, the term 'Gael' has become a 'hollow category', so that 'when
Gaels are spoken of, no one is quite sure what one is and few claim to be one' (Oliver
2005: 21).

The issue of language ability brings the issue into sharp relief. Given ongoing language
shift in traditional Gaelic communities, are people from Gaelic family backgrounds
who have lived all their lives in Gaelic areas, but cannot speak Gaelic, to be characterised as Gaels, and, conversely, do people who can speak Gaelic, but have no familial
connections to Gaelic and have never lived in a Gaelic area, count as Gaels (Bechhofer
and McCrone 2014)? Considering the matter from another perspective, some new
speakers of Gaelic make clear that they do not consider themselves to be Gaels, or do
not want to become or be identified as Gaels, and that there is a risk that the 'Gael'
label (and perhaps an associated identity) may be imposed on those who learn the language (Zall 2002; Klevenhaus 2015). Using language-based terms such as 'Gaelic
speaker' sidesteps these difficulties in relation to the label 'Gael', but only throws up a
new set of questions and judgements about what kind of 'Gaelic' people are speaking
– whether it is authentic enough, 'natural' enough, good enough (McLeod et al. 2014:
33–44; McLeod 2017), with perceptions of authenticity and naturalness often serving
as a proxy for a familial link to the language. In this sense, using linguistic rather than
'ethnic' criteria to assess group membership simply creates a new set of boundaries.
At the same time, however, 'nativeness' may be seen to be losing some of its linguistic
significance, as most young 'native' speakers are English-dominant, with reduced
linguistic confidence and competence compared to those born before c.1960 (Bell et
al. 2014), and their linguistic formation may depend to a substantial extent on school-
based input. As such, in linguistic terms the divergence between native and new
speakers may be diminishing.

Conclusion

Gaelic has been spoken in Scotland for over 1,500 years and through this period, especially until c.1400, has assimilated waves of new speakers as it spread into different parts of the country, including the formerly Norse-speaking Hebrides (Clancy 2011). Considering the issue of new speakers in the twenty-first century, leading Gaelic linguist Roibeard Ó Maolalaigh emphasised that these various new speakers have had a profound impact on the development of the language in Scotland from earliest times (BBC 2015). In that sense, new speakers of Gaelic are nothing new, and their emergence can be seen as a sign of health. The problem is that the new speaker phenomenon has become prominent at the current juncture because 'traditional' communities and intergenerational language transmission are weakening so dramatically, a development that is anything but healthy.

References

Advisory Council on Education in Scotland. 1947. *Secondary Education: A Report of the Advisory Council on Education in Scotland.* Edinburgh: HMSO.

An Comunn Gàidhealach. 1891. *Manifesto.* Oban: An Comunn Gàidhealach.

An Comunn Gàidhealach. 1936. *Report of the Special Committee on the Teaching of Gaelic in Schools and Colleges.* Glasgow: An Comunn Gàidhealach.

An Comunn Gàidhealach. 1943. Memorandum for the Advisory Council on Education for Scotland by the Education Committee of An Comunn Gàidhealach. *An Gaidheal* 38, 66.

Armstrong, Timothy Currie. 2013. 'Why Won't you Speak to me in Gaelic?' Authenticity, Integration and the Heritage Language Learning Project. *Journal of Language, Identity and Education* 12, 340–356.

Azkue, Jokin and Josu Perales. 2005. The Teaching of Basque to Adults. *International Journal of the Sociology of Language* 174, 73–83.

BBC. 2015. *Dual-chainntean Ghàidhlig ùra.* Available online at http://learngaelic.net/watch/news.jsp?v=20150101_01 (last accessed 1 March 2017).

Bechhofer, Frank and David McCrone. 2014. What Makes a Gael? Identity, Language and Ancestry in the Scottish Gàidhealtachd. *Identities: Global Studies in Culture and Power* 21, 113–133.

Bell, Susan, Mark McConville, Wilson McLeod and Roibeard Ó Maolalaigh. 2014. *Dlùth is Inneach – Final Project Report: Linguistic and Institutional Foundations for Gaelic Corpus Planning.* Glasgow: Soillse.

Bòrd na Gàidhlig. 2012. *Plana Nàiseanta na Gàidhlig 2012–2107/National Gaelic Language Plan 2012–2017.* Inverness: Bòrd na Gàidhlig.

Bòrd na Gàidhlig. 2015a. *Dàta Foghlaim Gàidhlig/Gaelic Education Data 2014–15.* Inverness: Bòrd na Gàidhlig.

Bòrd na Gàidhlig. 2015b. *Fiosrachadh do Phàrantan – Frequently Asked Questions.* Available online at http://www.gaidhlig.org.uk/fdp/en/information/frequently-asked-questions/ (last accessed 1 March 2017).

Campbell, Margaret Burnley. 1905. The Difficulties I Encountered in Learning Gaelic. *An Deò-Ghréine* 1, 43–45.

Clancy, Thomas Owen. 2011. Gaelic in Medieval Scotland: Advent and Expansion. *Proceedings of the British Academy* 167, 349–392.

Comunn an Luchd-Ionnsachaidh. 1984. *Cuairt Litir Ionnsachaidh*, 1. Inverness: Comunn an Luchd-Ionnsachaidh.

Comunn na Gàidhlig and Comann an Luchd-Ionnsachaidh. 1992. *Feumalachdan Luchd-Ionnsachaidh – Rannsachadh Nàiseanta / Provision for Gaelic Learners: A National Survey*. Inverness: Comunn na Gàidhlig.

Dunmore, Stuart. 2015. Bilingual Life after School? Language Use, Ideologies and Attitudes among Gaelic-medium Educated Adults. University of Edinburgh: unpublished PhD thesis.

Dwelly, Edward. 1918 [1901–11]. *The Illustrated Gaelic Dictionary, Specially Designed for Beginners and for Use in Schools*. Fleet: Edward Dwelly.

Education Scotland. 2015. *Gaelic Medium Education (Foghlam tro Mheadhan na Gàidhlig)*. Available online at http://www.educationscotland.gov.uk/parentzone/myschool/choosingaschool/gaelicmediumeducation/ (last accessed 1 March 2017).

Gaelic League of Scotland. 1935. *Circular Letter Soliciting Donations*, from Jean Douglas, Honorary Treasurer, 5 January (NLS MS Acc. 4721, file 474).

Gillies, William. 1988–90. Liam MacGill'Ìosa: A Friend of the Gael. *Transactions of the Gaelic Society of Inverness* 56, 503–533.

Glaser, Konstanze. 2006. Reimagining the Gaelic Community: Ethnicity, Hybridity, Politics and Communication. In Wilson McLeod (ed.), *Revitalising Gaelic in Scotland: Policy, Planning and Public Discourse*, 169–184. Edinburgh: Dunedin Academic Press.

Glaser, Konstanze. 2007. *Minority Languages and Cultural Diversity in Europe: Gaelic and Sorbian Perspectives*. Clevedon: Multilingual Matters.

Glasgow Corporation Education Department. 1947a. *Note for Director, 'Gaelic'* (JD/ABB), 16 January (Glasgow City Archives (Mitchell Library) D-ED 11.1.191).

Glasgow University. 1934. *Glasgow University Students' Handbook 1934–1935*. Glasgow: Glasgow University.

Gruffudd, Heini and Steve Morris. 2012. *Canolfannau Cymraeg and Social Networks of Adult Learners of Welsh: Efforts to Reverse Language Shift in Comparatively Non-Welsh-speaking Communities*. Swansea: South West Wales Welsh for Adults Centre/Academi Hywel Teifi.

Hansard. 1966. *Reply from William Ross MP, Secretary of State for Scotland, to Written Question from Russell Johnston MP*, House of Commons Debates, 2 February, vol. 723, col. 245W.

Hansard. 1970. *Reply from William Ross MP, Secretary of State for Scotland, to Written Question from Malcolm MacMillan MP*, House of Commons Debates, 21 April, vol. 800, col. 81W.

Hebrides News. 2016. *Gaelic Learners' Association to Fold*. 13 November. Available online at http://www.hebrides-news.com/cli-to-fold-141116.html (last accessed 1 March 2017).

Klevenhaus, Mìcheal. 2015. ''S muladach mi 's mi air m' aineol' no Wanderlust eadar Dà Shaoghal: Beachdan mu Dhearbh-aithne Ghàidhealach. In Kevin MacNeil (ed.), *Struileag: Shore to Shore/Cladach gu Cladach*, 93–104. Edinburgh: Polygon.

Lamb, William. 2011. Is There a Future for Regional Dialects in Scottish Gaelic? Paper presented to the FRLSU Colloquium, 3 December. Available online at https://www.academia.edu/1136136/Is_there_a_future_for_regional_dialects_in_Scottish_Gaelic (last accessed 1 March 2017).

[Lovat Fraser], J. A. 1917. The Duke of Argyll. *The Celtic Monthly*, 1–2.

Mac a' Ghobhainn, Seumas. 1973. Iain MacPheadruis and the Gaelic League of Scotland. *A' Bhratach Ùr* 3(1), 4–5.

MacAulay, Donald. 1994. Canons, myths and cannon fodder. *Scotlands* 1, 35–54.

MacCaluim, Alasdair. 2007a. *Reversing Language Shift: The Social Identity and Role of Adult Learners of Scottish Gaelic*. Belfast: Cló Ollscoil na Banríona.

MacCaluim, Alasdair. 2007b. 'More than Interesting': a' Ghàidhlig sa Bhaile Mhòr. In Wilson McLeod (ed.), *Gàidhealtachdan Ùra: Leasachadh na Gàidhlig agus na Gaeilge sa Bhaile Mhòr /Nua-Ghaeltachtaí: Cur Chun Cinn na Gàidhlig agus na Gaeilge sa Chathair*, 19–30. Edinburgh: Celtic and Scottish Studies, University of Edinburgh.

McEwan-Fujita, Emily. 2003. Gaelic in Scotland, Scotland in Europe: Minority Language Revitalization in the Age of Neoliberalism. Chicago: University of Chicago PhD thesis.

McEwan-Fujita, Emily. 2010. Ideologies and Experiences of Literacy in Interactions between Adult Gaelic Learners and First-language Gaelic Speakers in Scotland. *Scottish Gaelic Studies* 26, 87–114.

MacKenzie, Osgood. 1921. *A Hundred Years in the Highlands*. London: Edward Arnold.

MacLean, Ruairidh. 2016. *Ar Slighe gu Fileantas: Gaelic for Adults – A Learning Strategy for Adult Gaelic Learners in Scotland*. Inverness: Bòrd na Gàidhlig.

MacLean, Sam [Sorley]. 1969. Problems of Gaelic Education [I]. *Catalyst* 2(4), 21–22.

MacLeod, Marsaili, Michelle Macleod, Lindsay Milligan Dombrowski and Kathryn Jones. 2015. *Lìbhrigeadh Gàidhlig do dh'Inbhich tro Ùlpan/Delivery of Gaelic to Adults through Ùlpan*. Inverness: Bòrd na Gàidhlig.

McLeod, Wilson. 2010. Leasachadh na Gàidhlig: paradaim ùr? In Gillian Munro and Iain Mac an Tàilleir (eds), *Coimhearsnachdan Gàidhlig An-diugh/Gaelic Communities Today*, 1–17. Edinburgh: Dunedin Academic Press.

McLeod, Wilson. 2014. Luchd na Gàidhlig and the 'detritus of a nation'. *Scottish Studies* 36 [= *Craobh nan Ubhall: A Festschrift for John MacInnes*, ed. by Virginia Blankenhorn], 149–154.

McLeod, Wilson. 2017. Dialectal Diversity in Contemporary Gaelic: Perceptions, Discourses and Responses. In Janet Cruickshank and Robert McColl Millar (eds), *Before the Storm: Papers from the Forum for Research on the Languages of Scotland and Ulster Triennial Meeting, Ayr 2015*, 183–211. Aberdeen: Forum for Research on the Languages of Scotland and Ireland.

McLeod, Wilson, Alasdair MacCaluim and Irene Pollock. 2010. *Adult Gaelic Learning in Scotland: Opportunities, Motivations and Challenges: A Research Report for Bòrd na Gàidhlig*. Edinburgh: Celtic and Scottish Studies, University of Edinburgh.

McLeod, Wilson, Bernadette O'Rourke and Stuart Dunmore. 2014. *New Speakers of Gaelic in Edinburgh and Glasgow*. Edinburgh: Soillse.

MacLeòid, Dòmhnall Iain. 2011. *Dualchas an aghaidh nan creag: The Gaelic Revival 1890–2020*. Inverness: Clò-bheag.

McMahon, Timothy G. 2008. *Grand Opportunity: The Gaelic League and Irish Society, 1893–1910*. Syracuse, NY: Syracuse University Press.

MacNeacail, Aonghas. 1986. Questions of Prestige: Sorley MacLean and the Campaign for Equal Status for Gaelic in Scottish Education. In Raymond J. Ross and Joy Hendry, *Sorley MacLean: Critical Essays*, 201–210. Edinburgh: Scottish Academic Press.

MacNeacail, H. C. 1920. The Scottish Language. *The Scottish Review* 43, part 97, 59–68.

Milligan, Lindsay. 2010. The Role of Gaelic (Learners) Education in Reversing Language Shift for Gaelic in Scotland. Aberdeen: University of Aberdeen PhD thesis.

Murray, John and Catherine Morrison. 1984. *Bilingual Primary Education in the Western Isles, Scotland: Report of the Bilingual Education Project, 1975–81*. Stornoway: Acair.

Oban Times. 1891. *An Comunn Gàidhealach – Meeting at Oban*. 2 May, 2.

O'Hanlon, Fiona and Lindsay Paterson. 2014. Gaelic Education Since 1872. In Robert D. Anderson, Mark Freeman and Lindsay Paterson (eds), *The Edinburgh History of Education in Scotland*, 304–325. Edinburgh: Edinburgh University Press.

O'Hanlon, Fiona, Lindsay Paterson and Wilson McLeod. 2012. *Language Models in Gaelic-medium Pre-school, Primary and Secondary Education*. Edinburgh: Soillse.

Oliver, James. 2005. Scottish Gaelic Identities: Contexts and Contingencies. *Scottish Affairs* 51, 1–24.

Oliver, James. 2006. Where is Gaelic? Revitalisation, Language, Culture and Identity. In Wilson McLeod (ed.), *Revitalising Gaelic in Scotland: Policy, Planning and Public Discourse*, 155–168. Edinburgh: Dunedin Academic Press.

O'Rourke, Bernadette, Joan Pujolar and Fernando Ramallo. 2015. New Speakers of Minority Languages: The Challenging Opportunity. *International Journal of the Sociology of Language* 231, 1–20.

Robertson, Boyd. 2001. *Aithisg air Solarachadh Chùrsaichean Bogaidh Gàidhlig an Alba / Report on Gaelic Immersion Course Provision in Scotland*. Edinburgh: Scottish Qualifications Authority.

Robertson, Sylvia and Tony Dilworth. 2009. *Tales from Highland Perthshire Collected by Lady Evelyn Stuart Murray*. Edinburgh: Scottish Gaelic Texts Society.

Scott, Priscilla. 2013. 'With Heart and Voice ever Devoted to the Cause': Women in the Gaelic Movement, 1886–1914. Edinburgh: University of Edinburgh PhD thesis.

Scottish Council for Research in Education. 1961. *Gaelic-Speaking Children in Highland Schools*. London: University of London Press.

Scottish Funding Council. 2007. *Gaelic Education Provision in Scotland*. Edinburgh: Scottish Funding Council.

The Scottish Government. 2015. *Summary Statistics for Schools in Scotland*, no. 5 (2014 edition). Edinburgh: The Scottish Government. Available online at http://www.gov.scot/Resource/0047/00471917.pdf (last accessed 1 March 2017).

Thompson, Frank. 1984–6. John Francis Campbell. *Transactions of the Gaelic Society of Inverness* 54, 1–57.

Thomson, Derick S. 1981. Gaelic in Scotland: Assessment and Prognosis. In Einar Haugen, J. Derrick McClure and Derick S. Thomson (eds), *Minority Languages Today: A Selection from the Papers Read at the First International Conference on Minority Languages*, 10–20. Edinburgh: Edinburgh University Press.

Thomson, Derick S. 2004. Erskine, Stuart Richard (1869–1960). *Oxford Dictionary of National Biography*. Oxford University Press. Available online at http://www.oxforddnb.com/view/article/40311 (last accessed 28 February 2017).

Tkm Consulting. 2015. *Census Survey of Adult Learners of Gaelic 2014*. Kyle of Lochalsh: Tkm Consulting.

Zall, Carol. 2002. Barrachd an luib gnè na dìreach cànain. *An Gàidheal Ùr*, An t-Samhain (November), 4.

7

Learning Gaelic in Adulthood: Second Language Learning in Minority Language Contexts

Marsaili MacLeod

Introduction

This chapter examines the learning experiences and linguistic practices of adult second language (L2) learners of Gaelic in Scotland and reflects on this group's possible contribution to Gaelic revitalisation. O'Rourke and Walsh (2015: 15) argue that L2 speakers 'are a necessary part of reversing language shift', though are often overlooked in sociolinguistic models of language revitalisation and in practice. Whereas this might have held true in the past, in Gaelic Scotland there is now a strategic imperative to ensure greater numbers of adults learning Gaelic achieve fluency in order to help meet target increases in the crude number of Gaelic speakers in Scotland. Current Gaelic language-in-education policy aims to motivate adults to learn the language and, ultimately, to become active members of the Gaelic speech community (see Bòrd na Gàidhlig 2012). Making the transition from being an adult L2 learner to a user, or speaker, of a target language is known, however, to be a complex and non-linear process (O'Rourke and Walsh 2015; Nic Fhlannchadha and Hickey 2018). Since interaction with target language speakers is a desirable condition for adult second language acquisition (SLA), it is argued that opportunities to practise using the language in and outside the classroom are fundamental (Norton 2013). Yet, even when the classroom experience is positive and individual motivation sustained, achieving high proficiency levels is particularly challenging in a social context which does not necessarily afford opportunities to practise the target language beyond the classroom.

This chapter reports the results from an online survey of 282 L2 learners as part of a wider study exploring the effectiveness of a classroom learning programme for Gaelic, called Ùlpan (MacLeod et al. 2015). The focus of this chapter is to understand Gaelic learner pathways and to explore their potential contribution to Gaelic language revitalisation. The results offer fresh insights into the disjuncture between the aspirations of minority language policy and the social realities of adults learning a minority language in the context of diminished place-based speaker communities. The findings also highlight the liminal space which minority language learners occupy both in practice and in contemporary theorising over adult language learning; their learner situation neither replicates the foreign language social context – despite the target language not being the typical language of communication in their immediate environment – nor the immersion learning context, in which naturalistic learning of the target language can complement classroom learning.

The international context

The social turn in L2 research (Block 2003) has shown that adult learners are situated in a dynamic social learning environment, both in and beyond the classroom. Indeed, many immigrants acquire knowledge of their linguistic environment in the process of everyday communication, without ever attending classes. Block's research on international adult immigrant language learners demonstrates how naturalistic contexts provide input as well as at least the *possibility* of language learning through conversational interactions. Yet the work of Broeder et al. (1996) and Norton (2013) debunk many of the previously-held assumptions on the problem-free nature of implicit, naturalistic and immersive learning (for example, that learners and speakers of the target language are on a level playing field, and are both mutually seeking understanding in communicative practice), by unpacking how matters of class, ethnicity and gender are bound up with differential axes of power which can determine an immigrant's legitimacy to speak the target language. In the case of Gaelic, which shows some parallels with a number of other minority language situations internationally, the needs of adult language learners, and their interactions with speakers, are distinguished by a further contextual factor: all speakers are bilingual in the majority language. This has consequences in terms of sustained input for L2 learners (Meisel 2011), the attitudes which 'native' speakers hold towards new speakers (O'Rourke and Walsh 2015) and the negotiation of use (Nic Fhlannchadha and Hickey 2018). Research on L2 learners of Celtic languages has foregrounded the difficulties learners face in gaining access to the target community and on gaining legitimacy to speak in a context where the norm is to use the dominant language with outsiders, and the minority language in informal and intimate social contexts only (cf. Pritchard Newcombe 2007; McEwan-Fujita 2010a; Rothach et al. 2011; Armstrong 2013; Smith-Christmas and Armstrong 2014).

In common with foreign language learning, the institutional classroom setting is, therefore, the most significant mediator of second language activity for adult L2 learners of minority languages. With limited use of Gaelic outside the classroom, the identity transformations associated with naturalistic contexts are difficult to experience (Block 2014: 7). Instead, the learner has to create the context. Thus, just as for international adult migrant language learners, the language teacher needs to prepare Gaelic learners to speak the target language in their everyday social context. That is, adult L2 learners of Gaelic need to know both the structure of the language and the practice, and only through regular practice speaking in the classroom will confidence be gained for interacting with target language speakers outside.

This chapter builds on previous research on adult Gaelic learners (MacCaluim 2007; McEwan-Fujita 2010a, 2010b; McLeod et al. 2010; Milligan et al. 2011; Armstrong

2013; Carty 2014; Smith-Christmas and Armstrong 2014), through exploring the avenues through which L2 Gaelic learners create, resist and respond to opportunities to use Gaelic outwith the classroom, before concluding to what extent L2 learners are invested in learning, and in the Gaelic-speaking community, through language practice. The findings highlight that becoming a social user of Gaelic is not necessarily a goal nor an outcome of learning.

An introduction to learning Gaelic in adulthood

A recent 'census', commissioned by Bòrd na Gàidhlig, estimates there to be some 3,495 individuals in Scotland who would describe themselves as adult learners of Gaelic (Tkm Consulting 2015). The figure is consistent with earlier estimates (Comunn na Gàidhlig and Comunn Luchd-Ionnsachaidh 1992, cited in MacCaluim 2007), suggesting that the absolute number has remained constant since the 1980s.

The *National Gaelic Language Plan 2012–2017* (Bòrd na Gàidhlig 2012) outlined a short-term target to increase the number of adult learners progressing to fluency, with a view to increasing the total number of Gaelic speakers to 65,000 by 2021. The significance of adult L2 speakers to the reproduction of the Gaelic speech community arises due to the near cessation of intergenerational transmission and the decline in use in what were formerly Gaelic-speaking communities (see Chapter 1). Yet previous research has highlighted the gulf between the policy aspirations for, and the outcomes of, Gaelic adult learner provision. Studies have found only a small proportion of learners ever achieve a high level of competency, even when motivated to do so (for example, MacCaluim 2007; McLeod et al. 2010; Milligan et al. 2011). A recent study highlighted that successful 'new speakers' are often language elites who are highly educated and urban based (McLeod et al. 2014). For the majority of adult learners, Gaelic language learning has been found, therefore, to be a long and protracted process which, until very recently, usually commenced in adulthood (see McLeod, this volume, for an historical analysis).

One significant barrier has been the underdeveloped and under-resourced learning infrastructure. Gaelic language learning for adults has been long characterised by a 'traditional' evening class structure, in which individual tutors work in isolation to produce syllabi and coursework to meet the needs of teaching and learning preferences. The primary rationale for public investment in the development of the Ùlpan course was, therefore, the lack of a national curriculum and limited pathways for learning Gaelic to fluency as an adult. Between 2006 and 2014, over £1.3 million of public funds were invested in the course, representing an unprecedented level of investment in Gaelic adult education (for a full description of the course, see MacLeod et al. 2015).

Ùlpan is the only nationally available classroom course for learning Gaelic as an adult. The course aims to provide an accessible, accelerated and effective route to achieving oral/aural fluency in Gaelic in adulthood. It was first introduced in Scotland in 2007 by its author and owner, Deiseal, and at the time of the research it had been accessed by 2,586 learners across Scotland. The word 'ulpan' is borrowed from an approach to language learning first introduced in Israel for Hebrew, in a context in which it was crucial that adult learners learned a lingua franca with speed. The ulpan approach was subsequently adapted for Welsh through the 'Wlpan' programme (see Newcombe and Newcombe 2001), as well as for Breton and other small languages (cf. Dolève-Gandelman 1989). These approaches share in common an emphasis on achieving basic oral skills in a second language in a short time through intensive learning. The Gaelic model has been designed to be delivered for a minimum of three hours of tuition per week, or two units of one-and-a-half hours' duration, supported by self-directed learning. At this level of intensity, a student can potentially complete all 144 units in around two years.

After years of frustrated learning, plagued by fragmented course delivery, often untrained tutors, and piecemeal materials, this course was seen as a panacea by policy-makers, course providers and frustrated learners alike. So, is it the case that adult learners of Gaelic today will be the new speakers of the future?

Methodological Approach

Data presented in this article were collected as part of a wider study investigating the effectiveness of the Ùlpan programme from a practical, pedagogical and linguistic perspective. An online survey was selected as the most cost-effective method of eliciting information on learners' motivations for, and experiences of, learning Gaelic. The survey elicited information on learners' social-demographic characteristics, their participation in Ùlpan and other Gaelic courses, their evaluation of their learning experiences, their Gaelic language practices and, finally, their self-assessed language ability. The dimensions and concepts under exploration were derived from a thorough review of the literature on L2 socialisation and motivation in language learning. Thereafter, the questions and associated measures were developed and informed by a review of research conducted in other minority language contexts (for example, in Wales, Baker et al. 2011; Newcombe and Newcombe 2001; in the Basque Country, Langabaster 2001; Perales and Cenoz 2002). The survey also utilised some of the measurements used in the first published survey of adult learners of Gaelic conducted in 1993–4 (MacCaluim 2007) and in McLeod et al.'s (2010) survey of adult learners, thus enabling the identification of any change in learner characteristics and expectations over time.

The survey was piloted with a sample of learners, and then revised prior to being subject to expert review. A random sample of 1,200 learners was generated from the database of students, stratified according to region, and 282 valid responses were received, representing a response rate of 25 per cent. The survey data were imported into IBM SPSS v22 for data management and analysis. The survey also invited respondents to add comments at the end, which 127 respondents (45 per cent) elected to do. These data were imported into NVivo, a qualitative data management software package, for thematic analysis. In addition to providing a valuable insight into the experiences of these learners, the comments together with the initial quantitative findings informed the design of the subsequent stage of the research: case studies of cohorts of learners, and their teachers and course providers, in three regions of Scotland. The case-study research was designed to capture students at different stages of their Gaelic language learning and to represent a variety of sociolinguistic communities, including the Isle of Lewis in the Gaelic heartlands, Inverness, the capital of the Gàidhealtachd, and Glasgow. This chapter draws on learner data from the student survey and single and group learner interviews, which were analysed using the 'framework' research process (Spencer et al. 2003). All interviews were recorded, with the consent of the participants, and quotes are reported verbatim, with biographical details of interviewees used alongside in the format (learner status, gender, course level, geographical area). Randomly allocated pseudonyms have been used to protect the anonymity of the participants.

Learner pathways

From a language planning perspective, it is important that investment in additional language courses for adults reflects the needs of that community, as identified in language policy. As such, the level and type of proficiency needs of the community should directly inform the learning objectives, teaching materials and classroom methods. The Gaelic policy aim is to produce new speakers of Gaelic, thus, appropriately, biliteracy is not an aim of the Ulpan course. In contrast to other intensive courses for Gaelic, assessment is not built into the course design and the course aims to make learning accessible to people from all educational backgrounds. It is aimed at learners whose goal is to become active Gaelic users in the home or the workplace (who are, therefore, not of retirement age); and it is designed to attract learners who aim for oral fluency in Gaelic. The socio-demographic profile of the sample is given in Table 7.1. The data reveal that, contrary to the course aims, the learner population is generally older, better educated and less likely to use Gaelic at work or with family than Gaelic learners surveyed previously (MacCaluim 2007; McLeod et al. 2010) or subsequently (Tkm Consulting 2015).

One contributing factor is that a significant proportion of learners (44 per cent) are continuing on their language learning trajectory having attended other kinds of Gaelic classes in the past (henceforth referred to as 'continuing learners'). This course is often replacing, therefore, other Gaelic courses in what continues to be a chequered pattern of provision in parts of Scotland. Indeed, for nearly half (47 per cent) the choice to learn Gaelic with Ulpan was guided by availability. Some learners are recommencing on their language learning journey after a break, and a significant minority (34 per cent) are using Ulpan to complement other methods of learning. The course targets entry-level learners to the course, which is divided into six levels of twenty-four units each, beginning at Level 1. At the time of the survey the majority of respondents were part-way through the course, with only 27.4 per cent having reached Level 4 or above, and, of those, 7.5 per cent having completed all 144 units. While only a small proportion of respondents (10.7 per cent) were enrolled in an Ulpan class at the time of the survey, the majority (65 per cent) of those part-way through the course planned to continue to complete all 144 units. This suggests that learners are motivated to continue to learn Gaelic through Ulpan, but that, for many, learning Gaelic is not a continuous process. This is further substantiated by analysis of prior experience of learning Gaelic.

Table 7.1 Background profile of the sample of adult learners of Gaelic

	Percentage (%)
Age group	
20–24	1.1
25–34	8.3
35–44	17.4
45–54	24.3
55–64	26.8
65+	22.1
Highest qualification	
'O' or Standard Grade, GCSE	2.5
Highers, 'A' level or equivalent	6.1
Vocational/trade qualification	3.2
HNC, HND or equivalent	12.6
University/college first degree	26.6
Postgraduate qualification/professional qualification	47.8
None of the above	1.1
Prior experience of learning Gaelic	
New Gaelic learner	55.6
Lapsed Gaelic learner	27.2
Active Gaelic learner	16.1
Lapsed native Gaelic speaker	1.1
Economic status	
Employed or self-employed	61.7
Looking after family	2.6
Long-term sick or disabled	1.1
Unemployed	0.7
Retired	31.4
Student	2.6

n = 282

Most continuing learners began at Level 1; only a handful of providers have offered entry at other levels on the course. Few were dissatisfied with doing so, however, reflecting discontinuity in their Gaelic learning to this point and concomitant low self-evaluation of their language skills. Of those who had already learnt some Gaelic prior to commencing this entry-level course, 63 per cent had been learning for three or more years and 34 per cent for more than ten years. Continuing learners were asked what their main method of learning Gaelic had been prior to commencing Ùlpan: 37 per cent had attended evening classes, 13 per cent had engaged in distance learning, and 11 per cent had self-taught. Only six per cent had selected 'school' as the main method, and informal learning in the community or in the home/family was negligible. Six per cent had also studied Gaelic at college or at university degree level. Yet, when asked to self-evaluate their language skills on commencing the course, only 13 per cent believed they had lower intermediate or higher level of proficiency in their

Table 7.2 Main reason for learning Gaelic

	No.	Valid %	Not applicable
To speak Gaelic with my grandchildren	30	54.5	202
To speak Gaelic with my spouse/partner	33	34.4	159
To help children with their homework	43	64.2	190
To speak Gaelic with my children	57	67.1	173
To speak Gaelic with other family members	59	57.3	152
To advance my professional life	69	48.3	107
To speak Gaelic in the workplace	83	62.4	124
To participate in my local community	105	56.5	72
To speak Gaelic with friends	138	66.0	53
To understand Gaelic literature	169	69.3	18
To understand Gaelic music & other arts	217	83.1	9
To understand Gaelic radio & TV	229	86.4	6
For personal growth and development	246	92.8	0

n = 282.

Note: the responses 'very important' and 'important' have been combined.

spoken Gaelic. Unsurprisingly, respondents' a priori Gaelic skills were, on average, stronger in reading and comprehending spoken Gaelic than in the productive skills of speaking and writing Gaelic. These figures highlight the weaknesses in course provision historically, which this course is seeking to address.

To ascertain the potential contribution of this group of adult learners to Gaelic language planning goals in Scotland, and to understand whether the course was attracting the groups it aimed to, the survey asked respondents, 'How important to you are the following reasons for learning Gaelic?', and presented them with thirteen motivations (see Table 7.2). While recognising that motivations for learning a language are not static, the survey found that 'personal growth and development' is rated the most important factor, followed by factors which might be described as passively experiencing Gaelic in the media, the arts and Gaelic literature. Instrumental motivations, such as 'to advance my professional life' or 'to speak Gaelic in the workplace', were particularly weak, whereas as integrative motivations, such as 'to speak Gaelic with friends' and 'to participate in my local community', were relatively stronger. The findings suggest too that the key groups of 'vocational learners' being targeted by the course authors account for less than half of learners: only 30 per cent of learners identify 'to speak Gaelic at work' or 'to advance my professional life' as important motivations for learning Gaelic, and only 12 per cent of learners identify 'to speak Gaelic with my children' or 'to help my children with their homework' as important motivations. The weak influence of domestic and familial domains reflects the low proportion of learners with Gaelic-speaking family. 'Heritage' learners, as defined by Montrul (2016) as learners who were exposed to the minority language in the home in childhood, account for a minority: only 20.9 per cent of respondents stated that speaking Gaelic to a family member, excluding their spouse, children or grandchildren, was an important motivation.

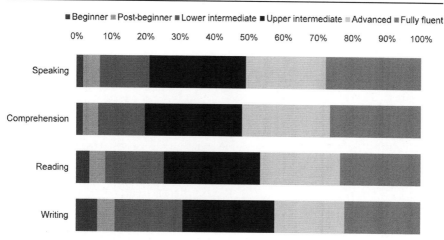

Figure 7.1 Gaelic proficiency goals

In a context where all of the target community are proficient English language speakers, reasons for learning Gaelic in adulthood have previously been found to be commonly guided by ideologies of Gaelic language revival (MacCaluim, 2007; McLeod et al. 2010; Tkm Consulting 2015). It is often assumed, therefore, that adults start learning Gaelic with the expectation of becoming active members of an endangered speech community through becoming 'proficient' speakers. This was not the case amongst this sample of learners. The survey asked learners to identify their ultimate proficiency goals, representing their goals at that particular point in time on their learning trajectory (Figure 7.1). The survey found that only 28 per cent of adult learners aim to become fluent speakers. Surprisingly, given the course aims to attract learners who prioritise oracy skills, the majority of learners want to ultimately achieve literacy as well as oracy skills. Since students are typically following a once-weekly class schedule (only 18.8 per cent attend twice-weekly classes), progression towards this fluency goal is likely to be relatively slow. Given, however, that the learners in this group are on a progressive, structured language learning pathway, they are, potentially, more likely to produce new speakers than the 'patchy, uncoordinated, poorly promoted, inadequately funded and often lacking in professional rigour' provision of the past (McLeod et al. 2010: vi).

Using Gaelic beyond the classroom

The policy expectation, and course aim, is that Ùlpan prepares students for real-world use of Gaelic. Accordingly, the course is taught based on the principle of authenticity: teaching strategies involve the tutor providing modelling, while the learner is responsible for repetition to form habits that result in high phonological and prosodic accuracy. The importance given to achievement of 'accurate and natural pronunciation' is not simply a matter of intelligibility; it is to help towards being accepted as a Gaelic speaker by native speakers, who are liable to switch to English if they find a learner's speech difficult to follow (see McEwan-Fujita 2010a). One of the positive outcomes of this teaching approach is the confidence which the course gives learners to speak:

> When I started Ùlpan I gained a lot of confidence on the pronunciation and flow of the language.
>
> (Continuing Learner, F, Level 3, Midlothian)

> I have tried many different night classes for Gaelic in the past and was far more impressed with Ulpan [sic] than with any other. I also believe that I got my pronunciations correct for the first time ever!!
>
> (Continuing Learner, F, Level 1, Highland)

On the other hand, the prescriptive nature of the course materials means there is little freedom of choice of topics, such as personal or family matters and, until Level 6, very limited opportunities for 'free talk'. As such, there is little scope to relate the language being learned to 'real' events which students can personalise in the exchange of genuine information. Since interaction with target language speakers is a desirable condition for adult SLA (Mackey and Goo 2007), and important in a course that does not include many activities based on genuine, personalised conversations, the study sought to ascertain what opportunities for spoken interaction exist outside the class-room, and which students were invested in their Gaelic learning through practice, and therefore most likely to become new speakers.

In order to explore the opportunities learners had to practise speaking or using Gaelic, the survey asked learners about the types of language reinforcement they used when enrolled on an Ùlpan course as reported in Figure 7.2. Students were most

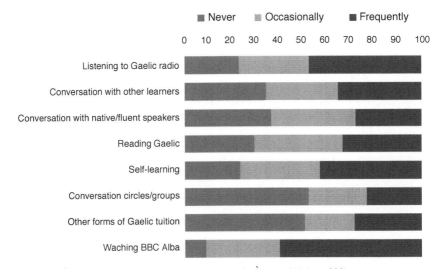

Figure 7.2 Additional learning methods used alongside Ùlpan (%) (n = 282)

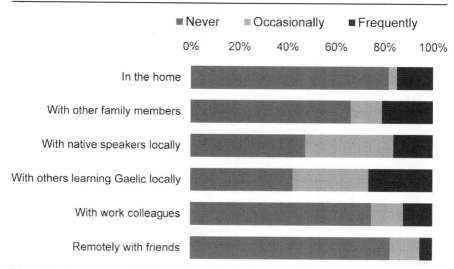

Figure 7.3 Current use of Gaelic outside of Gaelic classroom (%)
Note: 'In the home' was only offered as a category to those who live with other Gaelic speakers.

likely to engage in activities to develop their receptive skills, with listening to Gaelic radio or watching the Gaelic television channel, BBC Alba, the most common forms of language reinforcement. Self-study through consulting dictionaries or vocabulary learning was undertaken regularly by 43 per cent, but a significant minority of 23 per cent never engage in self-study. Learners at Levels 1 or 2 undertake the least; but there is no statistically significant relationship between course level and use of self-study learning strategies. The effort expended in practising speaking Gaelic outside the classroom was even less; taking into account all types of interactions measured, only 40 per cent of participants interacted with other Gaelic speakers at least weekly outside of class in unstructured and informal settings.

In order to explore with whom learners used Gaelic outside of the classroom, the survey examined three types of interlocutors for frequency of interaction, as broken down in Table 7.3: learners or non-fluent speakers, native or fluent speakers, and conversation circles. The regularity of Gaelic use is highest with learners or non-fluent Gaelic speakers. Conversing with native or fluent speakers was the least common reinforcement activity. Strikingly, over a third of respondents had no access to native or fluent Gaelic speakers outside of the formal learning environment while learning Gaelic through Ùlpan.

Bearing in mind that only 10.7 per cent of respondents (or thirty students) were enrolled in an Ùlpan class at the time of the survey, the survey also asked respondents about their current use of Gaelic, exploring in more detail their Gaelic-speaking networks. To report these findings, daily and weekly categories were combined into 'frequent', monthly or less than monthly into 'occasional', and, not at all into 'never'. The results given in Figure 7.3 further substantiate the finding that adult learners encounter barriers to using Gaelic on a frequent basis outside the Gaelic classroom, and are most likely to use Gaelic with other learners who live locally. The mean

Table 7.3 Respondents' interactional use of Gaelic as an Ùlpan student (%)

	Learners/ non-fluent speakers	Native or fluent speakers	Conversation circles
Daily	5.6	6.5	2.6
Weekly	29.6	21.4	20.5
Monthly	11.6	14.4	11.4
Less than monthly	19.4	21.4	13.5
Not at all	33.8	36.3	52.0
Total	100	100	100
n	216	201	229

number of interlocutor types is 0.9; 44 per cent of those who speak Gaelic at least weekly regularly speak to only one type of interlocutor. The findings suggest that most learners are reliant on one social context for their Gaelic practice, regardless of their course level.

The barriers small language learners face in becoming a speaker outside of the classroom are well documented in the literature (cf. Prichard Newcombe 2007; McEwan-Fujita 2010a; Gruffudd and Morris 2012). As Morris (2005 161–162, cited in Gruffudd and Morris 2012: 3) has found in the case of Welsh learners, many tend to 'stay in the educational system for too long, depending on it not only to increase and improve their knowledge of the language but also – and this is a cause for concern – to provide opportunities to use the language'.

The level of regular use of Gaelic with family members, native speakers and, most notably, other learners appears to be significantly lower for the learners in this survey than found by McLeod et al. (2010): 45 per cent of learners as compared to 77 per cent in McLeod et al. (ibid.). This might be explained by the relatively high proportion of 'new learners', who had no prior experience of learning Gaelic and, consequently, have had less time over which to develop a social network of Gaelic speakers. When the proportion of learners who use Gaelic frequently is compared for continuing and new learners, a statistically significant difference is found between the two groups ($x^2 = 11.48$, df = 2, p = 0.001): 57 per cent of continuing Gaelic learners use Gaelic daily or weekly, whereas only 36 per cent of new learners do.[1] This suggests that new learners do not have the same level of Gaelic-speaking social networks, and therefore opportunities, to speak Gaelic. In interview, new learners like Mac explained his frustration in developing social Gaelic-speaking networks:

> I tried a conversation group in Dingwall last Wednesday and it was of no use to me because I'm surrounded by four learners who trip over every third word and look around to other people who don't know how to finish the sentence for what the gap is. And I just thought, 'I'm going to pick up bad habits, if anything, here.'
>
> I seek out conversations. I spent Saturday walking halfway across Glasgow to find the Gaelic-speaking pubs. I found the Park Inn, I asked the barmaid if Gaelic was spoken there and she said, 'Yes, it is sometimes.' I couldn't find anyone speaking it but naturally I don't want to interrupt English conversations with strangers and say, 'Excuse me . . .'. . . . Then

we went to the Islay, which is the other one [pub] which is supposed to have it just up the road, no conversation there either. And that's the problem. Since my friend Rhoda died I've lost the one place in Inverness I know I can go and speak Gaelic.

(New learner, M, Level 6, Inverness)

Mac is typical of learners who are motivated to initiate speaking Gaelic in order to develop their own proficiency and who have no a priori connections to the Gaelic language. Without proximity to communities of speakers, or without ways in which to integrate into existing place-based communities, these motivated learners often need to actively seek opportunities for Gaelic's use through new social networks, and often through learner networks. Their experiences contrast with learners whose learning is predicated on integrating into existing Gaelic-speaking networks – including family, friends and colleagues – and involves negotiating a change in the normative language used. One such learner, Donnie, who had been learning Gaelic for over fifty years, explained:

I'm just finding in the last year or two that the people whom I know who can speak Gaelic will now speak Gaelic to me. In the old days they might have said a few words and then laughed and continued in English or carried on, you know, but nowadays I can actually get a conversation, a wee conversation going which is very encouraging for me.

(Continuing learner, M, Level 6, Isle of Lewis)

This he attributed to the course developing his oral skills and confidence to speak. Heritage learners, who have Gaelic-speaking family, are often perceived as having an advantage in becoming active speakers by non-heritage learners, who find it difficult to create opportunities for using Gaelic. Yet, as these learners articulate, initiating a conversation in Gaelic can be a face-threatening act with a language preference to use Gaelic being denied to them, and, in doing so, their social identity as a local Gaelic speaker also denied. Anne, who lives in the Isle of Lewis, saw speaker legitimacy as linked to notions of localness:

Anne: And if you try to use Gaelic and you are a poor Gaelic speaker people will often deliberately switch into English. There's a slight territoriality sometimes, I don't know if you've come across that. But it does happen, it really does happen . . . It is complicated politically and culturally. And there is this sort of 'Oh, you are a learner.'

And you find that even with the connection to Lewis and the croft?

Anne: I'm sure I wouldn't find it amongst my cousins but, yes, probably, I have bumped into it occasionally. People who are in my situation . . . a kind of half-way house people, you know; not quite Lewis and not quite not!

(Continuing learner, F, Level 6, Isle of Lewis)

The fear of being ridiculed or corrected could affect learners' willingness to take the risk and initiate a conversation, as Lisa explained:

I don't know whether it's because we're in Lewis and people do speak it but you get that – there's sometimes a reluctance to put yourself out there because there are so many experts around you and if you are not at that certain level then they can be critical.

(Continuing learner, F, Level 3, Isle of Lewis)

As such, one of the hurdles facing the Gaelic learner regardless of their background is to initiate or sustain conversations with 'native' or 'traditional' speakers of the language, who for conflicting ideological or practical reasons can often prefer to use the dominant language in which both speakers are fluent (cf. MacCaluim 2007; McEwan-Fujita 2010a; Wells 2011). A recurring experience relayed through the qualitative survey comments and interviews was that, as an adult L2 learner, one has to typically rely on other learners and teachers to practise speaking Gaelic until such time as spoken proficiency is achieved. The following section explores whether this is reflected in learners' self-assessment of their spoken proficiency in Gaelic and discusses the perceived barriers to progressing further.

Learning outcomes

To explore the progress this cohort of adult learners is making towards becoming proficient speakers of Gaelic, the survey used the Common European Framework of Reference (CEFR) for languages' self-assessment scale, which is based on can-do descriptors for spoken language. Scottish Gaelic has yet to be mapped onto the CEFR, thus there is no estimate of the cumulative hours of instruction that would be required to reach each level. However, well-designed self-assessment scales have been shown to be very accurate in terms of predicting language proficiency, as tested for through face-to-face language elicitation techniques (Perales and Cenoz 2002; Alderson 2005).

The scales describe L2 language proficiency at six levels, where Level A represents a 'basic user', Level B an 'independent user' and Level C a 'proficient user'.[2] Survey respondents were asked to rate their spoken production (Table 7.4) and spoken

Table 7.4 Spoken production skills by Ùlpan level (%)

	Current or Last Ùlpan Level						
	L1	L2	L3	L4	L5	L6	All
Basic user: A1	36.8	33.9	19.6	13.3		8.8	25.1
Basic user: A2	32.2	44.1	44.6	40.0	53.8	38.2	39.8
Independent user: B1	11.5	15.3	28.6	30.0	23.1	32.4	20.8
Independent user: B2	1.1	1.7		6.7	23.1	11.8	3.9
Proficient user: C1						5.9	.7
Proficient user: C2	1.1						.4
None of the above	17.2	5.1	7.1	10.0		2.9	9.3
n	87	59	56	30	13	34	279

n=279, Missing=3

Table 7.5 Spoken interaction skills by Ùlpan level (%)

	Current or Last Ùlpan Level						
	L1	L2	L3	L4	L5	L6	All
Basic user: A1	35.7	40.7	30.4	27.6	8.3	18.2	31.5
Basic user: A2	38.1	45.8	48.2	34.5	58.3	45.5	43.2
Independent user: B1	7.1	6.8	14.3	24.1	16.7	24.2	12.8
Independent user: B2				6.9	16.7	3.0	1.8
Proficient user: C1		1.7					.4
Proficient user: C2						6.1	.7
None of the above	19.0	5.1	7.1	6.9		3.0	9.5
n	84	59	56	29	12	33	273

N=273, Missing = 9

interaction skills (Table 7.5) using the CEFR scales. Overall, 65 per cent of respondents rate their spoken production at Level A, a 'basic user' of Gaelic, and 75 per cent rate their spoken interaction at Level A. The level of proficiency is correlated with level of study, yet interestingly the data illustrate a wide range of language skills on completion of each level of the course. Such a range of proficiency can reflect that learners' perceptions of their skills is relative and is likely to change as their Gaelic language skills develop. The findings also suggest that individual factors, including previous knowledge of Gaelic, are having an effect on the level of proficiency that can be expected for each level: of the seventy-two respondents who assessed their spoken production skills as B1 or above, the majority (72 per cent) were 'continuing learners' and, of the forty-three respondents who rated their spoken interaction skills as B1 or above, just under three-quarters had previous knowledge of Gaelic.

So what level of spoken proficiency might be expected by those completing this 216-hour course? If we examine learners at Level 6 (thirty-three respondents, of which twenty-one have completed the course), we find once again there is considerable variation in learners' self-assessment of both their spoken production and spoken interaction skills. For spoken production, just over half of Level 6 learners considered themselves to be 'independent users', whereas the majority (64 per cent) categorised themselves as 'basic users' for spoken interaction. In general, learners rate their spoken production skills relatively higher than their spoken interaction skills, which require more active, spontaneous participation in conversation. The use of an L2 in interactional settings is known to be affected by the competency-confidence nexus (Clément 1980) because entering into conversations unprepared requires a higher degree of fluency and self-confidence: this holds true of this group of learners. The survey found respondents' use of Gaelic outside of class to be positively associated with learners' self-assessment of their own Gaelic language skills.

While only 28 per cent of respondents aspire to achieve fluency in Gaelic, when the reasons for learning Gaelic are aggregated (Table 7.2), 75 per cent of learners surveyed are motivated to learn Gaelic in order to speak it with family, friends or colleagues or to participate in the local community. That is, they aspire to become active

Gaelic speakers, albeit it not fluent. Not all learners felt they were making the progress they hoped or expected with learning Gaelic. At the course level, in response to the question, 'Compared with what you expected, how would you rate the course in teaching you to speak Gaelic', 35 per cent were disappointed in their learning outcomes from this course. While the Ùlpan course advertises that, on completion of the course, students might expect to be 'functionally fluent' in Gaelic, the course is taught over only 216 class contact hours; substantially less when compared to the 1,500 contact hours expected to learn Welsh, or 1,715 hours to learn Basque to fluency. The term 'functionally fluent' is used to describe, in the words of the course director: 'that state of being solo and capable in a normal Gaelic-using environment, where you're driving your own learning through experience, without too much reference now to any kind of course'. This suggests that learners will have a level of independence in being able to speak and learn Gaelic by the end of the course. The use of the term 'fluent' means different things to different people, however, and some respondents to the survey revealed that they held expectations of proficiency outcomes which are way above what would normally be expected of a course of 216 teacher contact hours. One respondent explained:

> I am generally positive about ulpan [sic] although I do not see it as a method of getting me fully fluent in Gaelic. I have completed units 1–72 and I thought i [sic] would be a lot better at speaking Gaelic by this level . . . I started ulpan [sic] as it was hailed as this fantastic way of getting people to fluency in Gaelic. I am now half way through ulpan [sic] and I would struggle to hold a basic conversation.
>
> (88: New Learner, M, Level 3, South Lanarkshire)

Twenty-nine per cent are frustrated by the pace at which they are progressing through the course, which points to the rate of provision and discontinuity in provision as perceived barriers.

Aside from issues of course accessibility, analysis of qualitative comments found that learners who were dissatisfied with their attainment to date most commonly understand their own progress to be limited by, first, opportunities for using Gaelic outside of class, and, second, by their preparedness for entering or initiating conversations in Gaelic where opportunities are, theoretically at least, present. While most learners enjoy learning through Ùlpan, many explained that they did not have sufficient opportunity to practise speaking Gaelic out of class and, as such, felt they were not making the progress they expected towards becoming active speakers:

> I think Ùlpan is the best classroom option to learn Gaelic but far more needs to be done to ensure that those taking part are given decent opportunities to then converse in Gaelic in social terms.
>
> (New learner, M, Level 4, North Lanarkshire)

> I had a brilliant Tutor and the course was excellent, but without the chance to use Gaelic anywhere, it just all slowly faded away from me. There has to be reinforcement throughout

the course by actually using what you have learned in real time rather than just having banks of phrases.

(New learner, M, Level 4, Glasgow)

Given this commonly shared experience, coupled with the reliance on practising with other learners, the need to develop communicative competence in Gaelic through formal learning environments is heightened; something this course does not facilitate. One of the consequences articulated in interview and in the survey comments was that learners felt they often did not have the grammatical understanding to transform patterns being taught through drilling and activities into novel contexts. The word-strings rehearsed in drills, in theory, should help to achieve fluency by providing a reusable sentence framework for real communicative contexts. Yet without an adequate understanding of how to transform a paradigm, some students found themselves struggling to construct sentences in conversation with other speakers:

Whilst I learnt the set phrases easily enough, I didn't find it easy to apply the little grammar we learnt to building on this, so I couldn't have carried on a conversation . . . I like to understand the structure of a language, and Ùlpan doesn't teach this.

(New learner, F, Level 3, Highland)

The information in the courses is excellent but trying to adapt it into conversations is extremely difficult, especially in my case where there was no real opportunity to converse with the other students during the weekly interval between classes.

(New learner, M, Level 2, Dumfries and Galloway)

After 72 units I have opted not to continue with the Ùlpan method. I realised that I was unable to work out how to ask for a cup of coffee but I could say 'I liked it', 'you like it', 'she likes it'. Practical real-life application of the language is not supported by the Ùlpan method.

(New Learner, F, Level 3, Highland)

Recent literature on L2 learning in adulthood (Norton 2013; Ushioda 2011) argues that L2 courses need to enable the lived experiences of learners to be reflected in the curriculum and in teacher pedagogy. This has the practical benefit of giving learners the opportunity to develop vocabulary relevant to them and to develop autonomy to 'speak as themselves' (Ushioda 2011: 22). Without ancillary courses or structured learning opportunities, such learners are unlikely to become new speakers. On the other hand, for learners who were building on their understanding of the language and who were already well connected to Gaelic speakers, a course which prioritises oral practice could be transformative. One survey respondent explained that he now has self-belief in his ability to speak Gaelic beyond the classroom:

Bha Ulpan [sic] uamhasach misneachail airson fear le Gaidhlig lapach mar mi-fhin. Ro'n Ulpan [sic] cha robh mi deonach a bruidhinn facal ri duine sam bith anns an canan ged bha mi g'a ionnsachadh o chionn leth chiad bliadhna (le bearnan mora eadar oidhirpean) gun buaidh! As deidh Ulpan [sic] bha mi nas dana [sic] a bhruidhinn ach tha mi a dol slighe fada fhathast a bhith fileanta.

(Ulpan [sic] was really encouraging for someone with feeble Gaelic like me. Before Ulpan [sic] I wasn't willing to speak a word to anyone in the language although I was learning for 50 years (with big gaps between efforts) without effect! After Ulpan [sic] I was bolder in speaking although I have a long way to go to being fluent.)

(Continuing Learner, M, Level 6, Eilean Siar)

These research findings highlight the compromises made when using a teaching approach that avoids teaching grammar explicitly and that has limited conversational practice embedded within it. In minority language contexts, which do not typically afford many opportunities for using the language socially, this can have the effect of diminishing the plausibility of becoming a fluent Gaelic speaker to L2 learners. This could explain why only 28 per cent of the L2 learners surveyed aim for fluency in spoken Gaelic. This is despite the fact that a significant proportion of L2 learners of Gaelic hope to complete all six levels of the course, and having completed the course the majority (67 per cent) believe they will need further classes in order to reach their current goals. Yet, without any successor course for adult learners in the community, Gaelic learning options available to these seemingly motivated learners are limited.

Conclusions

Based on experiences to date, the majority of the learners surveyed do not aim to achieve fluency in Gaelic, despite many being motivated to learn Gaelic in order to speak it with friends, colleagues or family or to integrate into their local community. This suggests that it is difficult for L2 learners of Gaelic to envision achieving fluency in light of their current individual learning circumstances. The survey has found that, despite the policy aspirations for speakers to follow a progressive course to fluency, the pathways for learning Gaelic continue to be multifarious and the learner outcomes are likely to be variable. This reflects the limitations of a 216-hour taught course, the challenge of continuity of provision and the social realities of learners. For many, multiple learning options are the norm, and extensive rather than intensive learning typical, as they fit Gaelic language learning around family and working life and course accessibility.

The safe learning environment of the Ùlpan classroom, with its emphasis on repetition of phrases and memorisation, contrasts with the reality of using Gaelic conversationally in natural contexts in the local community. While learner-for-learner networks are identified as the most common source of out-of-classroom oral practice, there are many 'new learners' of Gaelic who have not, as yet, invested in out-of-classroom use – often because there are no forms of informal learning activities or networks supported in their locality. This highlights the need for Gaelic language provision to include informal learning activities which connect all types of learners, and which connects learners with speakers with native-like competence. While a course which aims for oral skills is fitting with policy objectives, it is at odds with a proportion of learners' own literacy goals; not only is writing a tool they can use to support language learning, social online communication gives access to a virtual community that transcends proximity and in which the learner is a 'locus of control' (Norton Peirce et al. 1993).

In this sociolinguistic context, completion of the Ùlpan course is, in itself, a poor predictor of proficiency or of a learner becoming an active Gaelic speaker. Without investment in follow-on courses, and/or more intensive models of Gaelic language learning in adulthood, the possibility of even the motivated classroom learners becoming new speakers is significantly diminished.

Acknowledgements

The author wishes to acknowledge the significant contribution to this research made by Dr Michelle Macleod and Dr Lindsay Milligan Dombrowski, who conducted some of the interviews upon which this analysis is based, and Dr Kathryn Jones who also collaborated on the project. I would also like to extend my gratitude to all the research participants, who were so generous with their time and volunteered their experiences so freely. Finally, the author gratefully acknowledges the support and assistance of Bòrd na Gàidhlig, Highlands and Islands Enterprise, Skills Development Scotland and Deiseal Ltd.

Notes

1. Continuing learners are classified as respondents who identified as 'lapsed native speakers', 'lapsed learners' and 'active learners' at the time of the survey.
2. For information on the Common European Framework of Reference for Languages and the descriptive scales for self-assessment of spoken production and spoken interaction, see Council of Europe (date unkown) Common European Framework of Reference for Languages: Learning, Teaching, Assessment. Available online at https://www.coe.int/t/dg4/linguistic/Source/Framework_EN.pdf (last accessed 22 August 2017).

References

Alderson, J. Charles. 2005. *Diagnosing Foreign Language Proficiency: The Interface between Learning and Assessment*. New York: Continuum.

Armstrong, Timothy C. 2013. 'Why Won't you Speak to me in Gaelic?': Authenticity, Integration and the Heritage Language Learning Project. *Journal of Language, Identity and Education* 12(5), 340–356. doi:10.1080/15348458.2013.835585

Baker, Colin Andrews, Ifor Hunydd Gruffydd and Gwyn Lewis. 2011. Adult Language Learning: A survey of Welsh for Adults in the Context of Language Planning. *Evaluation & Research in Education* 24(1), 41–59.

Block, David. 2003. *The Social Turn in Second Language Acquisition*. Washington, DC: Georgetown University Press.

Block, David. 2014. *Second Language Identities*. 2nd edition. New York: Bloomsbury Academic.

Bòrd na Gàidhlig. 2012. *National Gaelic Language Plan 2012–2017: Growth & Improvement/Plana Cànain Nàiseanta Gàidhlig 2012–2017: Fàs & Feabhas*. Inverness/Inbhir Nis: Bòrd na Gàidhlig.

Broeder, Peter, Kathrina Bremer, Celia Roberts, Marie-Thérèse Vasseur and Margret Simonot. 1996. *Achieving Understanding: Discourse in Intercultural Encounters.* Longman: London.

Carty, Nicola. 2014. The Adult Learner in Gaelic Language-in-Education Policy: Language Revitalisation and the CEFR. *European Journal of Language Policy* 6(2), 195–217. Available online at https://doi.org/10.3828/ejlp.2014.11

Clément, Richard. 1980. Ethnicity, Contact and Communicative Competence in a Second Language. In Howard Giles, W. Peter Robinson and Phillip M. Smith (eds), *Language: Social Psychological Perspectives*, 147–154. Oxford: Pergamon.

Dolève-Gandelman, Tsili. 1989. 'Ulpan' is not 'Berlitz': Adult Education and the Ethiopian Jews in Israel. *Social Science Information* 28(1), 121–143.

Gruffudd, Huw and Morris, Steven. 2012. *Canolfannau Cymraeg and Social Networks of Adult Learners of Welsh: An Executive Summary.* Aberystwyth: Academi Hywel Teifi.

Langabaster, David. 2001. Bilingualism, Immersion Programmes and Language Learning in the Basque Country, *Journal of Multilingual and Multicultural Development* 22(5), 401–425.

MacCaluim, Alasdair. 2007. *Reversing Language Shift: The Social Identity and Role of Scottish Gaelic Learners.* Belfast: Cló Ollscoil na Banríona.

McEwan-Fujita, Emily. 2010a. Ideology, Affect, and Socialization in Language Shift and Revitalization: The Experiences of Adults Learning Gaelic in the Western Isles of Scotland. *Language in Society* 39(1), 27–64.

McEwan-Fujita, Emily. 2010b. Ideologies and Experiences of Literacy in Interactions between Adult Gaelic Learners and First-language Gaelic Speakers in Scotland, *Scottish Gaelic Studies* 26, 87–114.

Mackey, Alison and Jaemyung Goo. 2007. Interaction Research in SLA: A Meta-analysis and Research Synthesis. In Alison Mackey (ed.), *Conversational Interaction in Second Language Acquisition*, 249–308. Hillsdale, NJ: Lawrence Erlbaum.

MacLeod, Marsaili, Michelle Macleod, Kathryn Jones and Lindsay Milligan-Dombrowski. 2015. *Lìbhrigeadh Gàidhlig do dh'Inbhich tro Ùlpan/Delivery of Gaelic to Adults through Ùlpan. Report for Bòrd na Gàidhlig.* Inbhir Nis/Inverness: Bòrd na Gàidhlig.

McLeod, Wilson, Irene Pollock and Alasdair MacCaluim. 2010. *Adult Gaelic Learning in Scotland: Opportunities, Motivations and Challenges. A Research Report for Bòrd na Gàidhlig.* Available online at http://www.gaidhlig.org.uk/bord/wp-content/uploads/sites/2/CR09-04-GfA-Gaelic-for-Adults-2010-English.pdf (last accessed 16 September 2016).

McLeod, Wilson, Bernadette O'Rourke and Stuart Dunmore. 2014. *New Speakers of Gaelic in Edinburgh and Glasgow.* Report to Soillse. Sleat, Isle of Skye: Soillse. (Online.) Available online at http://www.soillse.ac.uk/foillseachaidhean/coimhearsnachdan/ (last accessed 7 January 2015).

Meisel, Jürgen M. 2011. *First and Second Language Acquisition Parallels and Differences.* Cambridge: Cambridge University Press.

Milligan, Lindsey, Douglas Chalmers and Mike Danson. 2011. *Gaelic Language*

Development Strategy. Report to Glasgow City Council. Glasgow: Glasgow City Council.

Montrul, Silvina. 2016. *The Acquisition of Heritage Languages.* Cambridge: Cambridge University Press.

Newcombe, Lynda P. and Robert G. Newcombe. 2001. Adult Language Learning: The Effect of Background, Motivation and Practice on Perseverance. *International Journal of Bilingual Education and Bilingualism* 4(5), 332–354. Available online at http://dx.doi.org/10.1080/13670050108667736

Nic Fhlannchadha, Siobhán and Tina M. Hickey. 2018. Minority Language Ownership and Authority: Perspectives of Native Speakers and New Speakers. *International Journal of Bilingual Education and Bilingualism* 21(1), 38–53.

Norton, Bonny. 2013. *Identity and Language Learning: Extending the Conversation.* Bristol: Multilingual Matters.

Norton Peirce, Bonny, Merrill Swain and Doug Hart. 1993. Self-assessment, French Immersion, and Locus of Control. *Applied Linguistics* 14(1), 25–42.

O'Rourke, Bernadette and John Walsh. 2015. New Speakers of Irish: Shifting Boundaries across Time and Space, *International Journal of the Sociology of Language* 231, 63–83.

Perales, Josu and Jasone Cenoz. 2002. The Effect of Individual and Contextual Factors in Adult Second-language Acquisition in the Basque Country. *Language, Culture and Curriculum* 15(1), 1–15.

Pritchard Newcombe, Lynda. 2007. *Social Context and Fluency in L2 Learners: The Case of Wales.* Bristol: Multilingual Matters.

Rothach, Gillian, Iain Mac an Tàilleir and Timothy Armstrong. 2011. *The State of Gaelic in Shawbost: Language Attitudes and Abilities in Shawbost.* Report for Bòrd na Gàidhlig. Sleat, Isle of Skye: Sabhal Mòr Ostaig.

Smith-Christmas, Cassie and Timothy C. Armstrong. 2014. Complementary Reversing Language Strategies in Education: The Importance of Adult Heritage Learners of Threatened Minority Languages. *Current Issues in Language Planning.* doi:10.1080/14664208.2014.915460

Spencer, Liz, Jane Ritchie and William O'Connor. 2003. Analysis: Practices, Principles and Processes. In Jane Ritchie and Jane Lewis (eds), *Qualitative Research Practice: A Guide for Social Science Students and Researchers,* 199–218. London: SAGE.

Tkm Consulting. 2015. *Census Survey of Adult Learners of Gaelic 2014.* Kyle of Lochalsh: Tkm Consulting.

Ushioda, Ema. 2011. Motivating Learners to Speak as Themselves. In Garold Murray, Xuesong Gao and Terry Lamb (eds), *Identity, Motivation and Autonomy in Language Learning,* 11–24. Bristol: Multilingual Matters.

Wells, Gordon. 2011. *Perceptions of Gaelic Learning and Use in a Bilingual Island Community: An Exploratory Study.* Ormacleit: Cothrom Ltd. Available online at http://www.soillse.ac.uk/wp-content/uploads/Perceptions-of-Gaelic-Learning-and-Use-in-a-Bilingual-Island-Community.pdf (last accessed 15 January 2015).

8

Dlùth is Inneach: Charting Language Ideology in the Contemporary Gaelic World

Susan Bell and Mark McConville

McLeod (2004a) argued persuasively that the post-1970s renaissance in Gaelic language development had been neglecting issues related to corpus planning, with the result that codification and elaboration of the language had seriously fallen behind the status planning ambitions of the Gaelic community. He concluded that corpus planning should become a 'key priority' for the new statutory language body, Bòrd na Gàidhlig, created as a result of the Gaelic Language (Scotland) Act 2005, and that 'a dedicated unit focused on corpus planning, including both the ongoing creation of new terms and specific projects such as dictionaries, thesauruses and style guidebooks, should be created without delay and made a top priority'. When the Bòrd published its first five-year National Plan for Gaelic in 2007, it included a commitment that 'Bòrd na Gàidhlig, consulting with key partners, will investigate the most suitable structure for a Gaelic language academy in order to ensure the relevance and consistency of Gaelic, including place-names' (BnaG 2007: 35). The need for a Gaelic language academy to deliver codification and elaboration was given further impetus by Bauer et al. (2009) in a Bòrd-commissioned survey of the prospects for Gaelic language technology.

By March 2011, Bòrd na Gàidhlig was reporting that 'progress on [the Gaelic language academy] has been slower than expected and it is now anticipated that the public consultation will take place as part of the National Gaelic Language Plan 2012/17 consultations' (BnaG 2011: 39). In an attempt to break the apparent deadlock, in late 2011 a group of Soillse-affiliated academics from the Universities of Glasgow and Edinburgh drafted a discussion paper for the Bòrd's Gaelic Academy Working Group, recommending 'a twelve-month investigative survey into corpus planning for Gaelic, aimed at establishing an appropriate linguistic foundation, and surveying and evaluating the work that has already been done' (McConville et al. 2011). This recommendation was largely accepted in late 2012, and in January 2013 Soillse commenced work on the Dlùth is Inneach public consultation project,[1] commissioned by Bòrd na Gàidhlig to answer the following questions:

- What corpus planning principles, or linguistic foundations, are appropriate for the strengthening and promotion of Scottish Gaelic?
- What effective coordination, or institutional framework, would result in their implementation?

One of the key guiding principles for the Dlùth is Inneach project was Joshua Fishman's (1991: chapter 11) notion of 'risk-free corpus planning'. Distinguishing between 'corpus planning that helps' and 'corpus planning that hinders', Fishman argues in essence that: (1) not all corpus planning activities are helpful to language revitalisation; (2) in some cases, corpus planning has actively hindered the process; (3) bad corpus planning can alienate speakers and accelerate language shift away from the minority language; and (4) language planners should tread very carefully, and focus on not alienating people. With this in mind, any development of the Gaelic corpus should be undertaken carefully, with a linguistic foundation based on an in-depth understanding of the community's dominant language ideology, and with their consensus and approval.

In this chapter, we report on the methodology and results of the Dlùth is Inneach project. The project used a methodological approach that was innovative in two ways: to conceptualise language ideology as a multi-dimensional space, and to introduce the 'Focused Conversation' methodology to language policy research.

Multi-dimensional language-ideological space

The novel approach of conceptualising language ideology as a multi-dimensional space was inspired by the similar approach taken in Fishman (2006), but heavily elaborated and contextualised according to previous academic work on Gaelic corpus ideologies (Gillies 1980; MacAulay 1982a, 1982b, 1986; McLeod 2004b, 2008).

We chose to interpret each ideological dimension as involving contrasting positive and negative attitudes towards particular kinds of Gaelic linguistic usage (whether at the level of words, idioms, constructions, pronunciations, etc.):

- anglicisms – borrowings and influences from English
- neologisms – unfamiliar, new usages of any kind
- hibernianisms – borrowings and influences from (modern) Irish
- archaisms – antiquated usages which are no longer part of vernacular Gaelic

Based on these four kinds of usage, we identified four ideological dimensions, each of which has both a positive and a negative pole, and we assigned each pole a semi-technical term as a designator. Thus, for the anglicisms dimension we envisage a continuum between the following two poles:

- anglophilia – We should just speak English like everyone else, and perhaps look to express our Gaelic cultural heritage and traditions in other, non-linguistic ways.
- anglophobia – We should take pride in, and remain faithful to, our Gaelic cultural heritage and traditions by using Gaelic rather than English.

The neologisms dimension runs between the following poles:

- neophilia – We should cultivate the expansion and modernisation of Gaelic beyond its traditional boundaries, to suit the exigencies of the twenty-first-century world.
- neophobia – We should keep Gaelic the way it was in the time of our grand-parents, and reject attempts to modernise it in any way.

The hibernianisms dimension has the following poles:

- hibernophilia – We should make Scottish Gaelic more like Irish Gaelic in order to draw on our common strengths for language revitalisation and/or rebuild our common cultural heritage.
- hibernophobia – We should emphasise the uniqueness of Scottish Gaelic by making it less like Irish Gaelic.

And the archaisms dimension runs between the following poles:

- retrophilia – We should actively revert to the Gaelic language practices of the past.
- retrophobia – We should avoid archaisms when speaking and writing Gaelic.

It should be noted in passing that retrophilia is theoretically distinct from neophobia, and retrophobia from neophilia, since attachment to the old does not necessarily entail dislike of the new, and vice versa.

The four dimensions of Gaelic language ideological space should all be considered to be theoretically independent of each other. In addition, each dimension is a continuum from negative to positive, and thus can be assumed to have a middle point of ideological neutrality, which could be termed anglo-neutral, neo-neutral, hiberno-neutral or retro-neutral.

In the context of the Dlùth is Inneach project, we interpreted 'linguistic foundations' for Gaelic corpus planning in terms of this multi-dimensional language-ideological space. Hence, one of the aims of the consultation was to identify the location in this space which represents the dominant language-ideological consensus of the Gaelic language community (defined straightforwardly as speakers of Scottish Gaelic).

Focused conversation methodology

The second main innovation of the Dlùth is Inneach consultation project involved introducing the 'focused conversation' methodology to language policy research, as a useful way of approaching what Fishman (2001) calls 'ideological clarification', a necessary precursor to any attempt to influence and alter language practices. This approach meant that many kinds of users of contemporary Gaelic (i.e. not simply academics) were given the chance to have a voice in corpus planning at the crucial stage of building an ideological strategy that is actually helpful for the community's goals.

The focused conversation method (Stanfield 2000) is a structured group dialogue aimed at building a consensus about future action through a discussion of experiences, reactions and interpretations. The method was designed by the Institute of Cultural Affairs (ICA), based on the values of a culture of participation, collaboration and ownership. The focused conversation method has four distinct phases:

- objective: What are your experiences of the topic under investigation?
- reflective: What are your feelings about these experiences?
- interpretive: What can we learn from these feelings and experiences?
- decisional: What do we need to do to move on from here?

The focused conversation is designed and led by a facilitator whose role is to create an environment in which the participants feel comfortable and in which their knowledge and experience is respected and valued. The facilitator asks questions to lead the participants through each of the above phases, giving the opportunity for reflection and moving towards understanding the values that lie beneath opinions. Carrying out the conversations in groups allows peer-to-peer sharing of experiences and the establishment of consensus, not necessarily as unanimous agreement, but as an ability to move forwards together. Because of the interactive nature of the conversation, where participants listen to each other rather than individually completing a survey, the method also has the effect of allowing each participant to come away from the conversation with a greater understanding of, and insight into, their community.

Focused conversation appeared to us to be a useful methodology for engaging with the theme of Gaelic corpus development, a topic which arouses strong opinions in many people. It allows people not only to share their experiences and have their feelings about these experiences recognised and validated, but also gives them an opportunity to situate these experiences and feelings in the wider context of Gaelic language development, and then to reach some kind of resolution. It was in the last of these that we hoped to see a majority consensus emerging as to what kind of linguistic foundation and institutional support is appropriate for Gaelic corpus development.

Two conversation schemas for the Dlùth is Inneach project were created as structured 'road maps' for the conversations to follow, so as to allow the facilitator to apply the four stages described above to discussion of corpus development. Each focused conversation ran over a 50-minute session, with a short break in between, with the first session covering linguistic foundations, and the second corpus resources and institutional frameworks.

The schema for the linguistic foundations session involved a series of activities based on some interesting instance of lexical or grammatical usage variation, for example Gaelic translational equivalents for the English terms 'fridge', 'chemotherapy' or 'referendum', or different ways of expressing the proposition 'the weather was better than I had expected'. Participants were presented with a range of different ideological alternatives for each example, including anglicisms, neologisms, archaisms and hibernianisms, and asked to consider the relative merits of each of these, working through the four phases (objective, reflective, interpretive, decisional) in each case.

The conversation schema for the second session involved two phases. First of all, participants were asked to consider the current state of the resource landscape for Gaelic learners and users, with a particular emphasis on identifying 'missing' resources, i.e. those which really should be available but as yet are not. The theme of the final activity involved asking the group to design an appropriate institutional framework within which these missing resources could realistically be developed, making decisions about duties, priorities, staff and contributors, location, independence, structure, funding, legitimacy and nomenclature.

Between September and December 2013, we conducted thirty-nine focused conversations, in various locations in Scotland, involving a total of 184 participants. Participants from a wide variety of backgrounds and ages were encouraged to attend with the only stipulation that their Gaelic language proficiency was enough for them to be comfortable participating in a Gaelic-medium discussion. Groups ranged in size from one to fifteen participants, and involved a combination of public meetings, visits to workplaces (schools, Gaelic agencies, local authorities, broadcasting studios), local history societies and arts groups. Participants ranged in age from fourteen to eighty-four, with 134 describing themselves as 'native speakers' and twenty-eight as 'learners', with the remaining participants defining themselves in other ways.[2] The focused conversations were primarily conducted through the medium of Gaelic. All focused conversations were facilitated and audio-recorded by the first author, who then transcribed the data. Subsequent to this data collection phase, both authors were involved in a process of recursive abstraction of the conversations, gradually identifying the most significant themes that had emerged, and that could be said to constitute the dominant language ideology from the sample of the Gaelic community we surveyed.

The focused conversation methodology was notably successful in at least three ways. First, the open and fluid dynamic of the conversation allowed participants to drive the discussion and to determine what was important for them to discuss, allowing factors which the research team had not anticipated to surface. Second, our conversation schema proved useful at giving those who rarely think about meta-linguistic issues a path into the discussions. And, finally, the group dynamic allowed participants to exchange knowledge and sometimes challenge each other's approaches and beliefs about the language.

One problem we came across was the difficulty of engaging members of the public (i.e. Gaelic speakers who are not professionally involved with the language), by getting them to come along to public meetings. For this reason, twelve of the conversations took place as one-to-one interviews, in order to secure the opinions of a wider range of people than would otherwise have been the case. Although these lacked the benefits of the group dynamic, the method was still successful in eliciting discussion and the facilitator could make reference to the viewpoints of previous participants to reflect on diverse perspectives. Although they were not planned in the design of the project, these individual sessions often allowed participants to go into more detail, and speak honestly about deep concerns in a way that they might be reluctant to do with colleagues or friends in a group setting. Thus, our final analysis was able to draw on the positives of both group and individual conversations.

While we have gone into more detail here than might be expected, we believe the success of the methodology in foregrounding the needs and wishes of Gaelic speakers is fundamental to subsequent success in corpus planning (or even language development efforts generally). This is the first time, that we are aware of, that an established methodology from the fields of community building and engagement has been applied in language policy.

The remainder of this chapter discusses the results of the Dlùth is Inneach consultation project, in terms of linguistic foundations, language resources and institutional framework.

Linguistic foundations

The first part of each focused conversation was concerned with identifying the dominant language ideology among Gaelic speakers with respect to the corpus of their language – vocabulary, grammar, pronunciation, orthography – in relation to the multi-dimensional model of language ideology discussed above.

First, it is clear that participants confer linguistic authority (the model of 'best' Gaelic speakers) on fluent speakers belonging to the generations who were born before 1960 and are still alive. Both native speakers and learners largely see this generation as the source of authority and legitimacy on what is acceptable, natural and 'good' Gaelic. These 'model speakers' grew up during the last era when there were strong Gaelic-speaking communities in the Highlands and Islands, with three generations of Gaelic-dominant bilinguals all living together and interacting with each other through the medium of Gaelic, before the arrival of television. In this respect, the main aspect of the dominant ideology among contemporary Gaelic speakers appears to be a form of retrophilia, defined in this case as an attachment to the traditional form of the language still in use by typically older, fluent speakers, and often manifested as grammatical and lexical neophobia.

> Ma tha sibh a' bruidhinn air a' bhliadhna 2013 far a bheil sinn an-dràsta [. . .] tha mi a' smaointinn gur e na daoine as sine, bu chòir dhuinn a bhith ag amas orra. Nam biodh sibh a' dèanamh seo an ceann leth-cheud bliadhna – chan eil fhios 'am. Ach an-dràsta, cha-nainn, no anns na beagan bhliadhnaichean a tha romhainn gur e na daoine as sine anns a' Ghàidhealtachd, a thogadh le Gàidhlig 's a tha ga bruidhinn, gur e sin – slat-tomhais.
>
> (If you are talking about the year 2013 where we are just now [. . .] I think that we should be aiming for the oldest people. If you're doing this in 50 years' time – I don't know. But right now, I'd say, or in the next few years that it is the oldest people in the Highlands, who were raised with Gaelic and who use it, that that's the – standard.)
>
> (P172, 40s, Native, Broadcasting)

Second, when participants were asked about which sources of linguistic authority were most influential for them, it became clear that oral sources (such as everyday vernacular speech, folk tales, radio broadcasts and sermons) carry more weight than written sources or existing dictionaries and grammars. Thus, we concluded that the dominant language ideology is more accurately described as 'retro-vernacular' as it places the highest linguistic value on the vernacular language of older speakers as opposed to the tradition of formal written Gaelic of previous centuries.

Third, participants are not overly concerned about the use of borrowed English terminology in Gaelic speech and writing. In general, people appear to be significantly more neophobic than anglophobic, in the sense that they are much less accepting of Gaelic neologisms, and more accepting of anglicisms, than might have been expected. Even the minority of participants who most strongly espoused the principle that ideally there should be a 'Gaelic word for everything' felt just as keenly that Gaelic terminology development has occasionally 'gone too far'. Participants place much more importance on the production of 'good, plain Gaelic' with appropriate use of familiar English terminology, in opposition to what is perceived to be an opaque, artificially intellectualised calque of formal English, as one native speaker in their 50s, who works in Gaelic broadcasting, commented, "'S e an rud a tha gu diofar 's e far a bheil an dòigh-labhairt agus an syntax gu tur air seòl na Beurla [. . .] Rudan mar "Tha mi a' dèanamh e". Eisimpleir bitheanta.' (The thing that matters is when the way of speaking and the syntax are totally in the English way [. . .] Things like, "Tha mi a' dèanamh e". A common example.)

On the other hand, participants are by no means hostile to all lexical innovation, and it is recognised that there may well be a place for deliberate vocabulary development when driven by reasonable demand as new concepts and objects gain currency in everyday language. Such terminology should be ideologically sound (i.e. authentic sounding, and semantically transparent to older Gaelic speakers), and aesthetically attractive. However, beyond a small minority of participants, the overriding opinion is that large-scale, committee-driven terminology creation is not of primary importance for contemporary Gaelic corpus planning. This finding is not particularly surprising given the similar experience in the Irish Gaelic context (see Ní Ghearáin 2011). However, it presents a challenge for professional language users who require terminological development to meet their needs but who do not want to be become estranged from the wider community.

Fourth, although participants are relatively anglo-neutral in terms of the lexicon, they are significantly more anglophobic when it comes to the grammatical and idiomatic structure of the language. Many participants feel that the characteristic syntactic and semantic foundations of traditional Gaelic (the speech of the model Gaelic speakers mentioned above) are breaking down under the influence of English-dominant bilingualism and the lack of effective reinforcement of traditional Gaelic norms. From the examples cited by participants, this erosion is felt most strikingly at the levels of word order, choice of grammatical function words, lexical distinctions and traditional Gaelic idiom. Although the structure of the focused conversations was not designed to specifically address Gaelic-medium education (GME), the topic was raised by some participants and inevitably underlined most of the discussions with education groups. There was concern at the ability of teachers to shoulder the burden of responsibility of preventing the erosion of traditional Gaelic. Staff and those involved in education expressed frustration at the limitations of resources and time to specifically address language development on top of the requirements of curriculum delivery. There is a fear that, should the government be successful in increasing the quantity of Gaelic speakers, this would come at the cost of undermining the quality of the language, leaving a reduced blend of Gaelic vocabulary and English grammar, of little social or cultural value to the community. Respondents used a range of pejorative terminology to describe this 'mixed' language, for example *Beurla tro mheadhan na Gàidhlig* 'English through the medium of Gaelic', or *Beurlachas* (a term which could be loosely translated into English as 'Gaelglish').

> Tha sinn a' call tòrr de na gnàthasan-cainnte nàdarrach. Tha a' Ghàidhlig a tha a' tighinn tron sgoil, tro fhoghlam, gu math tric chan fhaigh thu gnàthas-cainnte ann idir. 'S e rud sìmplidh sìmplidh a th' ann. Chan eil a' Ghàidhlig agamsa cho math ri sin [. . .] ach cluinnidh mo chluas droch Ghàidhlig no Gàidhlig a tha dìreach mar bhrochan tana mar gum biodh.

> (We are losing lots of the natural idioms. The Gaelic that comes through the schools, through education, often you don't get idioms at all. It just a simple simple thing. My Gaelic is not that great [. . .] but my ear can hear bad Gaelic or Gaelic that's just like a thin porridge.)
> (P172, 40s, Native, Broadcasting)

In addition, we considered the question as to whether contemporary grammatical standards for use particularly in education should be updated to include the innovative, anglophilic usages of the younger generation (cf. Bateman 2010). However, we found no evidence of any popular desire for a neophilic standard modelled on this evolving Gaelic usage. Rather, younger speakers expressed a clear desire to acquire the retro-vernacular Gaelic standards of the model speakers. It should be noted that many aspects of existing grammatical description remain to be updated in the literature from nineteenth-century norms.

Finally, Scottish Gaelic speakers do not appear to be particularly interested in their language's common heritage with Irish Gaelic, even when explicitly asked to consider the potential for a closer relationship between, or even unification of, the two languages. The dominant language ideology appears to be neutral between hibernophilia and hibernophobia (cf. McLeod 2008). Perhaps unsurprisingly, the small number of participants who did express a preference for hibernophilia were Irish learners of Scottish Gaelic.

Whereas a typical approach of corpus planning is to develop a formal register for a language where none has previously existed, our participants were clear in their belief that an accepted (and acceptable) standard language and grammar already exist and that they do not wish to see major change in this respect. However, they are aware of a lack of appropriate guidance, gaps in provision and a lack of consistency and reinforcement of the relevant norms, and wish to have a greater understanding of, access to, and confidence in, using the formal registers.

A less predictable outcome of the consultation was that many Gaelic speakers want access to advice and guidance about informal, vernacular and dialectal usage. This view was expressed by adult learners, by people who had gone through GME without Gaelic at home, and by younger native speakers who wished to enrich their language and develop idiomatic usage. There is a fear that informal, vernacular, traditional Gaelic (the variety that is valued as the linguistic foundation) is dying out, since it is not receiving enough reinforcement within families or communities. Moreover, participants are concerned that deliberate Gaelic corpus development will only accelerate this process, by encouraging the overuse of puristic formal usages to the neglect of non-puristic informal ones. What people want is for 'good' Gaelic usage to be supported at both formal and informal levels, so that younger speakers can familiarise themselves with the many appropriate modes of speaking (including dialects), and do not end up using formal Gaelic in informal contexts.

Language resources

The second part of each focused conversation included discussion of Gaelic language resources, in particular those that participants feel are currently missing from the Gaelic development environment.

First, participants reported on a wide range of existing linguistic resources that they turn to when they have questions about vocabulary and grammatical usage.[3] However, it was frequently commented that the Gaelic resource landscape is fragmented and uncoordinated. Many participants were unaware of some important resources available, while others regretted having to invest considerable amounts of time consulting a range of different, often inconsistent, sources in order to try and find answers to linguistic questions. A clear desire was expressed for a 'one-stop shop' for online Gaelic linguistic resources – a single website where people could go for fast, authoritative, trustworthy, detailed advice on advanced lexical and grammatical usage. It was suggested, for example, that such a site could consolidate, in one place, the new vocabulary being proposed by the main Gaelic terminology providers, thus allowing for a greater degree of consistency. This site would not necessarily decide or select for the community, but if users could see which forms were 'approved' by particular agencies, they could then make their own informed choices.

Second, less confident users often expressed a desire for clear, accessible, unambiguous guidance on what is, and what is not, good traditional Gaelic, along with clear explanations as to why certain usages are ungrammatical. There is considerable demand for a comprehensive, up-to-date, online reference grammar for Gaelic, based on the vernacular usage of the remaining traditional Gaelic speakers, for use by learners and speakers at all levels of ability.

Third, a priority for some of the younger, less confident Gaelic speakers is learning how to speak what they consider to be more authentic, natural and stylistically appropriate Gaelic, avoiding some of the more obvious examples of *Beurlachas*. It was suggested that a particularly useful resource would be a guide to good Gaelic stylistic usage, including a list of commonly perceived unacceptable usages, along with suggested, more acceptable alternatives.

Fourth, concern was expressed that existing dictionaries of Gaelic do not contain enough information to decide what is the right word to use in particular contexts. It was felt that a good dictionary should not just list words with their English equivalents, but should be much more systematic in explaining distinctions relating to shades of meaning, context, dialects, colloquial versus formal usage, marked versus unmarked usage, and contemporary versus archaic usage. (While the inter-university *Faclair na*

Gàidhlig historical dictionary project will provide a partial solution to this problem, it will not be available until 2035, at the very earliest.)

Fifth, although participants are generally wary of neologisms (as they have frequently encountered unsuitable or unacceptable ones), they understand the need for new coinages to be made in particular circumstances, where there is reasonable demand. In such cases, most professional users (for example, broadcasters, translators and teachers) have a clear preference for there to be a single agreed Gaelic term rather than a range of competing synonyms created by different organisations. It should be noted that attitudes to neologisms differ markedly in this respect compared to already established vocabulary, where people are happy dealing with a wider range of stylistic and dialectal variants.

Finally, when talking to some older, highly fluent and confident Gaelic speakers, it seems that there is to a certain extent a mismatch between the corpus resources that they assume exist to support younger less confident speakers become fluent, and the resources that actually do exist. One native speaker, who works in education, told us, 'Tha mi smaointinn gu bheil gu leòr a-muigh a sin fhad 's a tha ùidh aig daoine ionnsachadh agus ionnsachadh ceart' (I think there's enough out there as long as people are interested in learning and learning properly). Older fluent speakers have a strong intuitive sense that there already exists a well-understood, accepted, supra-dialectal formal register of Gaelic. If younger speakers want to familiarise themselves with this kind of Gaelic, then all they have to do is consult the authoritative grammar books, dictionaries and textbooks of the language, and these resources will answer all the questions that they have. However, these kinds of accessible and detailed language resource do not exist for Scottish Gaelic. There is no comprehensive, descriptive or prescriptive grammar of the modern language that adequately covers the needs of users and teachers. Existing grammatical resources are either restricted in scope (being textbooks), are too old-fashioned in style or content, or are too specialised to be easily understood without a study of linguistics. While useful descriptions and materials exist, they are spread out in various publications in a way that makes them inaccessible to the average Gaelic speaker. The full codification and consolidation of modern Gaelic grammar, in the sense of being described and explained in a clear, detailed and accessible way, has yet to be carried out.

Institutional framework

The aim of the final section of each focused conversation was to canvass opinions and ideas on the most desirable institutional framework for future Gaelic corpus development.

First, when participants were explicitly asked how they envisaged themselves as contributing to or participating in future Gaelic corpus development initiatives, there emerged three distinct groups: end-users, decision-makers and contributors. The *end-users* emphasised that they would be happy to put into practice the corpus development policies formulated by the *decision-makers*, as long as they felt that the framework had legitimacy and majority buy-in. However, there were also a significant number of potential *contributors*, who expressed a desire to be actively involved in the corpus development process itself. These were typically expert language practitioners (translators, language teachers, creative writers, academics), who feel that they have a lot of Gaelic expertise to offer, and want to be involved and consulted during the corpus development process, particularly if it involves recommendations on usage. One point that this suggests is that the preferred model for a Gaelic corpus development framework would be one that is highly participatory and democratic, allowing people to get involved at a number of different levels. A possible model in this respect is Wenger's (1998) 'communities of practice', with its guiding principle of 'legitimate peripheral participation'.

Second, when asked what would make a Gaelic corpus development framework legitimate for them, participants identified three main sources of legitimacy: popular, scientific and political. Some emphasised the importance of *popular* legitimacy, i.e. having people involved who are widely recognised as being excellent traditional Gaelic speakers, who are not necessarily academic experts or managers of Gaelic agencies, but who are accepted by the community as representing authenticity and cultural continuity. Others raised the importance of *scientific* legitimacy, i.e. having expert linguists (grammarians, lexicographers, sociolinguists and phoneticians) involved in the corpus development framework, in order to ensure that decisions are made on the basis of expert, verifiable evidence. A third source of legitimacy, less commonly cited yet also important, is *political* legitimacy, i.e. the importance of involving people from Gaelic status development agencies who can bring strategic and project managerial expertise to the process, and who can ensure that corpus and status development activities remain 'in sync' with each other.

Third, from the content of the discussions, we perceived two distinct perspectives on the Gaelic corpus development process, which we have termed 'outsourcing/technocratic', and 'participatory/democratic'. From the perspective of Gaelic status planning managers (whose day-to-day work involves getting more people learning and using Gaelic), corpus development is often seen as an uninteresting technical task, similar to developing an IT system, which can simply be outsourced to whichever individual or organisation can do the work to a reasonable professional standard at the lowest cost. Language practitioners, on the other hand, are usually much more aware that corpus development involves making decisions that are more political than technical, and hence that a wide range of people should have a voice in the process. They are wary of an outsourcing model which has in the past led to problems of quality control, inconsistency and lack of 'buy-in', and prefer a participatory model for Gaelic corpus development, where they are themselves involved in the process.

Fourth, while recognising the importance of corpus development to the future of the Gaelic language in Scotland, focused conversation participants were reluctant to consider diverting funding from existing status, usage and acquisition activities. Most participants had little knowledge about funding arrangements or potential sources of funding for Gaelic corpus development, and hence they had difficulty recommending a funding model. Other participants named Bòrd na Gàidhlig and the Scottish Government as potential funders, in line with their existing commitments to the maintenance of the language. Finally, there is no appetite for the establishment of a Gaelic language academy as linguistic 'status symbol', on the model of the great

European language academies of the eighteenth and nineteenth centuries. Proposed names such as 'Acadamaidh na Gàidhlig' (Gaelic Academy) or 'Àrd-chomhairle na Gàidhlig' (Gaelic High Council) were rejected by many participants as reminiscent of these prescriptive institutions. Rather, the recommended corpus development framework for Gaelic should be practical, unbureaucratic, unpretentious, with potential for the community to be actively engaged.

Conclusion

The final report of the Dlùth is Inneach consultation project (Bell et al. 2014) was submitted to Bòrd na Gàidhlig in February 2014, along with the practical recommendation that they establish a tripartite quality control framework for Gaelic corpus development. This would involve recognised traditional Gaelic speakers, academic linguists and representatives of Gaelic agencies, thus ensuring popular, scientific and political legitimacy for corpus development products and processes. Many of our recommendations have now been accepted by Bòrd na Gàidhlig, and in November 2015 a seven-member 'Buidheann Stiùiridh Corpais' (corpus steering group) was launched (renamed in early 2017 as 'Comataidh Comhairleachaidh Cànain' or 'Language Advisory Committee'). This group includes seven traditional native speakers with long experience of Gaelic development and one Gaelic language expert, and it is being supported by the LEACAG project (short for 'Leasachadh Corpais na Gàidhlig' or 'Gaelic Corpus Development') – a two-year funded academic project aimed at providing linguistic and technical expertise, led by the University of Glasgow in collaboration with our Soillse colleagues at the University of Edinburgh and Sabhal Mòr Ostaig.

To this extent, the project can be seen to have been a success. By conducting an empirical, sociolinguistic investigation into the ideology of the Gaelic community, and presenting the results to policy-makers in terms of practical recommendations, we have been able to initiate a process that should result in the resolution of a problem that has been holding back progress across all sectors of Gaelic development. An important element in this success was our decision to use the focused conversation method, which, unlike other semi-structured interview methods, has the advantage of concentrating minds during the final, decisional phase. The importance of Fishman's notion of 'ideological clarification' has long been recognised in language policy research, but focused conversation can now be seen to give language planners a concrete methodology to implement ideological clarification in practice. Ní Ghearáin's research on Irish terminology suggested that official policies can have a tendency to approach speakers (in her study, the Gaeltacht community) as a tool or target for language policy rather than as 'a legitimate stakeholder in policy development' (2011: 306). The Dlùth is Inneach method of a community- and consensus-building approach has shown speakers can be placed at the centre of determining language policy. Professional and non-professional speakers are treated alike as legitimate stakeholders, creating valuable insight and direction when they are offered structures and frameworks in which they can participate.

Finally, there has long been a regrettable lack of trust in Gaelic development between academics working in university Celtic departments and language planners working for Gaelic agencies, in particular those agencies working in the statutory education sector. There is good reason to believe that these tensions were one of the obstacles that had set back progress in Gaelic corpus development during the lifetime of the first quinquennial National Plan. As one retired educationalist and activist memorably exclaimed in one of our focused conversations, when discussing the role of academics in Gaelic corpus planning, 'Dìochuimhnich na h-academics! Tha na h-academics ann an saoghal leotha fhèin. Chan eil iad ann an saoghal doirbh, practaigeach, an latha idir' (Forget the academics! The academics are in a world of their own. They're not at all in the difficult, practical, day-to-day world).

We hope that the practical, real-world outcomes of the Dlùth is Inneach consultation project will go some way to countering these views and to provide a model for how such tensions can be resolved, thereby allowing minority language academics and policy-makers to work constructively together as we attempt to find local solutions to the problem of sustainably cultivating linguistic and cultural diversity in a rapidly homogenising world.

Acknowledgements

The authors wish to acknowledge the important contribution to this research made by Professors Roibeard Ó Maolalaigh, Wilson McLeod and Robert Dunbar, who advised us during all stages of the project. We would also like to thank Dr Peadar Morgan and the other members of Bòrd na Gàidhlig's Gaelic Academy Working Group for the guidance and assistance they gave us during the project, as well as our colleagues within the Soillse research network who gave us invaluable feedback and encouragement during the early stages. In particular, we would like to recognise the invaluable contribution made by our participants, who generously gave their time to our project.

Notes

1. The name *Dlùth is Inneach* was chosen from a quote by the Rev. Donald Lamont where he specially praises writing that uses the *fìor dhlùth is inneach*, the 'real warp and weft', of Gaelic (Lamont 1960).
2. A space was available for participants to write in their own definition. Definitions included 'part native/part learner' and 'native learner'. Ten opted to enter some variation of 'fluent speaker/learner', defining themselves by their proficiency even though that was covered in the following question. For these participants, 'learner' clearly has connotations of a lack of proficiency.
3. Important examples being the *Am Faclair Beag* and *Ainmean Àite na h-Alba* websites, Colin Mark's Gaelic–English dictionary, and the Scottish Qualifications Authority's *Gaelic Orthographic Conventions* (GOC).

References

Bateman, Meg. 2010. 'Gàidhlig Ùr?'. In Gillian Munro and Iain Mac an Tàilleir (eds), *Coimhearsnachdan na Gàidhlig an-diugh*, 87–98. Edinburgh: Dunedin Academic Press.

Bauer, Michael, Roibeard Ó Maolalaigh and Rob Wherrett. 2009. *Survey of Gaelic Corpus Technology: Project Report*. Inverness: Bòrd na Gàidhlig.

Bell (Ross), Susan, Mark McConville, Wilson McLeod and Roibeard Ó Maolalaigh. 2014. *Dlùth is Inneach Final Project Report: Linguistic and Institutional Foundations for Gaelic Corpus Planning*. Inverness: Bòrd na Gàidhlig/Soillse.

BnaG. 2007. *The National Plan for Gaelic 2007–2012*. Inverness: Bòrd na Gàidhlig.

BnaG. 2011. *Annual Report 2010/2011*. Inverness: Bòrd na Gàidhlig.

Fishman, Joshua. 1991. *Reversing Language Shift*. Clevedon: Multilingual Matters.

Fishman, Joshua (ed.). 2001. *Can Threatened Languages Be Saved?* Clevedon: Multilingual Matters.

Fishman, Joshua. 2006. *Do Not Leave Your Language Alone: The Hidden Status Agendas within Corpus Planning in Language Policy*. New Jersey: Lawrence Erlbaum.

Gillies, William. 1980. 'English Influences on Contemporary Scottish Gaelic'. *Scottish Literary Studies Journal*, Supplement 12, 1–12.

Lamont, Donald. 1960. Sgrìobhadh na Gàidhlig. In T. M. Murchison (ed.), *Prose Writings of Donald Lamont 1874–1958*. Edinburgh: Scottish Gaelic Texts Society.

MacAulay, Donald. 1982a. Register Range and Choice in Scottish Gaelic. *International Journal of the Sociology of Language* 35, 25–48.

MacAulay, Donald. 1982b. Borrow, Calque and Switch: The Law of the English Frontier. In John Anderson (ed.), *Linguistic Form and Linguistic Variation*. Amsterdam Studies in the Theory and History of Linguistic Science IV, 203–37. Amsterdam: John Benjamins.

MacAulay, Donald. 1986. New Gaelic? *Scottish Language* 5, 120–125.

McConville, Mark, Wilson McLeod and Roibeard Ó Maolalaigh. 2011. *A Way Forward for Gaelic Corpus Planning and the Gaelic Language Academy*. Unpublished discussion paper, November 2011.

McLeod, Wilson. 2004a. The Challenge of Corpus Planning in Gaelic Development. *Scottish Language* 23, 68–92.

McLeod, Wilson. 2004b. Feumaidh sinn a' Ghàidhlig a chumail pure: Problems of Linguistic Purism in Scottish Gaelic. In Donall Ó Riagain and Thomas Stolz (eds), *Purism: Second Helping*, 25–45. Bochum: Brockmeyer.

McLeod, Wilson. 2008. Linguistic Pan-Gaelicism: A Dog that Wouldn't Hunt. *Journal of Celtic Linguistics* 12, 87–120.

Ní Ghearáin, Helena. 2011. The Problematic Relationship between Institutionalised Irish Terminology Development and the Gaeltacht Speech Community: Dynamics of Acceptance and Estrangement. *Language Policy* 10(4), 305–323.

Stanfield, R. Brian. 2000. *The Art of Focused Conversation*. Philadelphia: Chipping Norton.

Wenger, Etienne. 1998. *Communities of Practice: Learning, Meaning, and Identity*. Cambridge: Cambridge University Press.

9

Gaelic Language Use in Public Domains

Ingeborg Birnie

Introduction

Decennial census data from the late nineteenth century onwards has shown a sharp decrease in the number of Gaelic speakers in Scotland, in absolute terms, but also as a percentage of the population; whereas in 1891 254,415 people, 6.3 per cent of the total population of Scotland, were recorded as being 'in the habit of making colloquial use of the Gaelic language' (Census Office 1893), by 2011 this had fallen by 85 per cent to 57,375 people, 1.1 per cent of the population, self-reporting to be able to speak the language (National Records of Scotland (NRS) 2013). This decline in numbers of speakers has also been accompanied by a contraction in the geographical regions where the language is spoken by a majority of the population; whereas in 1901 Gaelic was spoken by more than 75 per cent of the population in the Inner and Outer Hebrides and, with the exception of North Mull, 'all mainland parishes in an unbroken line from Appin in the south to Farr in the North' (Mac an Tàilleir 2010: 33), in 2011 no parish remained where more than 67 per cent of the population claimed to be able to speak the language (NRS 2013). With research conducted in the Gaeltacht in Ireland by Ó Giollagáin et al. (2007) suggesting that the proportion of active, integrated minority language speakers needs to be more than 67 per cent for the use of the language in the community to be sustainable, it is therefore likely that Gaelic is continuing to yield to English as the main language used in communities, even in last remaining 'heartland' of the language, the Western Isles, where more than half the population are still able to speak Gaelic (NRS 2013).[1]

This continuing language shift from Gaelic to English should be set against various support initiatives from the early twentieth century onwards, initially aimed at supporting and developing the fragile economic status of the traditional heartland of the language, the Gàidhealtachd.[2] Although economic status has been identified by Grenoble and Whaley as 'maybe the single strongest force influencing the fate of endangered languages' (1998: 125), with Crystal (2000: 132) acknowledging that 'an endangered language will progress if its speakers increase their wealth relative to the dominant community', no official consideration was given to supporting the Gaelic language itself until the 1980s. This change in official attitude initially manifested itself through a programme of support for the public and institutional provision of the language, focused on the media, education, the arts and also through the establishment of various Gaelic language support agencies (McLeod 2011).

Fishman referred to this phase of initiatives aimed at reversing language shift as 'distant from the immediate nexus of mother tongue transmission' and a 'nigh complete reliance on the school and other higher order "props"' (1991: 379–380), with McLeod referring to the Gaelic language revival movement of this period as a 'Renaissance without planning', as

> relatively little consideration has been given to matters of language development in a more formal sense, to language planning, or to language policy. There has been a serious lack of strategy to this 'renaissance' and fundamental questions have been side stepped. Initiatives have tended to be uncoordinated and haphazard, driven without the guidance of theory or the control of planning. (McLeod 2002: 279)

Dunbar, in response to McLeod (ibid.), argued that this period was in fact a 'Renaissance without policy'. Dunbar distinguishes language planning from language policy, by defining the latter as 'the change in linguistic behaviour which language planning seeks to achieve . . . Language policy sets the goals which are sought to be achieved, and language planning is concerned with the mechanism for attaining such goals' (2010: 139).

Gaelic Language (Scotland) Act 2005

It was not until the Gaelic Language Scotland Act (hereafter referred to as 'the Gaelic Act') was ratified by the Scottish Parliament in 2005 that, according to Dunbar (2010), a clear policy with regard to Gaelic was articulated, with the Gaelic Act securing the status of Gaelic as 'an official language of Scotland commanding equal respect to the English language' (Scottish Parliament 2005). Under the provisions of the Gaelic Act, Bòrd na Gàidhlig (the Gaelic language board) was established as a statutory body 'to promote and facilitate the promotion of the use and understanding of the Gaelic language) (Bòrd na Gàidhlig 2014). As part of its remit Bòrd na Gàidhlig (BnaG) is responsible for the production of the five-yearly National Gaelic Language Plan, as well as being the public body tasked with overseeing the creation of statutory Gaelic language plans (GLPs) by public authorities in which public authorities are required to set out the measures their organisation will be taking with respect to increasing the audibility and usage of Gaelic in the provision of services to the public as well as in internal operations. Although the aim of this provision was to ensure that the public sector in Scotland plays 'a part in creating a sustainable future for Gaelic by raising its status and profile and creating practical opportunities for its use' (Scottish Government 2015), no rights or regulations have been created to facilitate the usage of the language in public domains. The Gaelic Act instead allows individual public bodies to interpret the provisions of the Act according to their own particular circumstances and this raises the question about the effectiveness of these statutory GLPs in creating a 'sustainable future for Gaelic in Scotland' at a time where 'the position of the language is extremely fragile and the declining numbers of those speaking Gaelic fluently or as a mother-tongue in the language's traditional heartlands threatens the survival of Gaelic as a living language' (Scottish Government 2015).

Research method

Although the Gaelic Act has meant that for the first time a clear policy with respect to the Gaelic language has been articulated (Dunbar 2010), Shohamy (2006: 51) has recognised that 'even when policies are stated explicitly it still does not guarantee that the language policy will in fact turn into practice'. This research project, based on Spolsky's tripartite classification of language policy, explored the language management initiatives, as articulated through the statutory GLPs of public bodies in Scotland and the linguistic ideologies and practices of Gaelic/English bilinguals in Stornoway in particular as regards the use of Gaelic in the public domains to which the statutory GLPs pertain.[3] Situated on the Isle of Lewis, Stornoway is the largest settlement in the Western Isles, the heartland of the language, and as the major commercial and administrative centre of the area (HIE 2014), home to many public spaces which fall under the auspices of a statutory GLP created under the provision of the Gaelic Act.

Unlike the data collected in the census, which relies on a self-declared ability to speak the language, or indeed speakers' estimates of frequency of language use, which can be affected by the social and political milieu, this research was based on the principles established in the 'Kale Neurkata' or street surveys of Basque language use. This research aimed to collect *in situ*, real-time data on spoken language use as:

> Oral or spoken language use is the most natural use of the language. It is the most direct kind of linguistic interaction between two or more individuals. Spoken language is also characterized by spontaneous interaction. The choice of spoken language is often a reflex action rather than a result of reflexion [sic]. (Altuna and Basurto 2013: 28)

This linguistic soundscape study allowed data on language choice, participants and purpose of the interaction to be collected, and this was further supplemented with additional information about domains of usage and ideologies from language use diaries as well as ethnographic interviews with a cross-section of bilingual Gaelic/English speakers in the parish of Stornoway.

To assess the effect of language management initiatives on *de facto* language use, linguistic soundscape observations were made in both public spaces with and without statutory GLPs and compared to the isotropic or expected language use based on the number of participants in the observed conversations and the level of bilingualism in the parish. Using the 2011 Census data as a baseline estimate for the number of bilinguals in the parish of Stornoway, 43.5 per cent (NRS 2013), coupled with a self-reported language use of 48 per cent across all domains,[4] the isotropic or statistically expected level of Gaelic language use can be calculated using Txillardegi's theory of isotropic use (Alvarez 2001):

$$P_g = m_g (w_2e_x^2 + w_3e_x^3 + w_4e_x^4 + w_5e_x^5 + w_6e_x^6 + w_7e_x^7 + w_8e_x^8)$$

Where:

P_g is the isotropic level of Gaelic use
M_g is the loyalty of Gaelic speakers to Gaelic
E_x is the proportion of bilinguals
W_{ax} weight of the group containing x participants

Based on the assumption that the relationships between the people observed in this study are randomly distributed, the statistically expected level of Gaelic use across the study would be 9.1 per cent.

Results: Gaelic language use

In the linguistic soundscape study the basic unit of observation was the conversation, defined as an interaction between two or more individuals where information was exchanged beyond an initial greeting. During each observation session a given conversation was only registered once, delimited by a change of language or of participants. Although each conversation was observed for a very short period of time, and therefore the behaviour of each member of the group as an active participant might not be able to be observed, it was assumed that if any other member of the group had been talking, the language of the interaction would have been the same.

During this study 2,000 conversations were observed and recorded in eight different public spaces, four of which were under the auspices of statutory GLPs and the other four without statutory GLPs, with a total of 4,563 participants. Across all these recorded conversations Gaelic was used as the main language in 182 interactions, involving 408 participants, as illustrated by Figure 9.1.

This means that across this study the total use of Gaelic matched Txillardegi's theoretical point of reference of 9.1 per cent, meaning that the *de facto* language use was the same as the statistically expected level of usage of the language.

To assess the effect of the language management initiatives this data was further analysed according to type of public domain, that is whether or not the public space

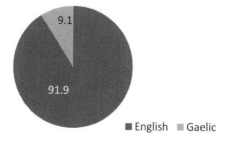

Figure 9.1 Percentage language use

Table 9.1 Language use in conversations

	English	Gaelic	Total
Public spaces with a statutory Gaelic plan	927	93	1020
Public spaces without a statutory Gaelic plan	891	89	980
Total	**1801**	**182**	**2000**

was under the auspices of an organisation with a statutory GLP (see Table 9.1 and Figure 9.2).

These results would suggest that language management initiatives to promote the usage of the language do not significantly impact on the overall level of spoken Gaelic in a public domain, with both public spaces with and without a statutory GLP recording Gaelic as the main language of the conversation in 9.1 per cent of interactions. However, it is when these Gaelic conversations are analysed by participants and purpose of the conversation that clear distinctions between the two types of public domains do start to emerge.

Participants

Although the overall number of Gaelic speakers across all public domains was similar, with 203 participants recorded in ninety-three Gaelic interactions in public spaces with statutory GLPs and 205 participants recorded in eighty-nine Gaelic interactions

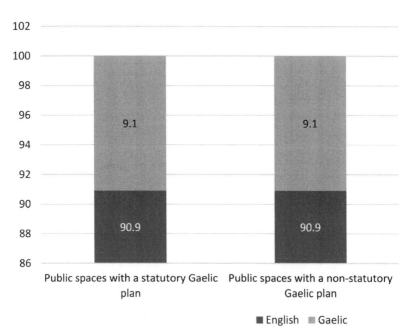

Figure 9.2 Language use in public spaces as a percentage of the observed conversations

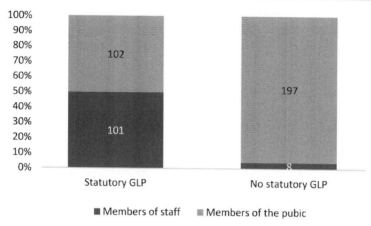

Figure 9.3 Participants in Gaelic interactions

in domains without statutory GLPs, the ratio of members of staff versus members of the public speaking the language was very different between the two types of spaces.

In public spaces with statutory GLPs the individuals participating in Gaelic conversations were evenly distributed between members of the public and members of staff; however, in public spaces without statutory GLPs only 4 per cent of those recorded in interactions using the language were members of staff, as illustrated in Figure 9.3.

However, as recognised by Altuna and Basurto (2013: 74), 'spoken use of a language is by nature a collective matter. Oral use of a language does not depend on the individual but on the group', therefore what the linguistic soundscape study measured was not so much the language of the individuals but instead the language of the conversations of the group of participants.

In this study three different types of conversations can be identified according to the groups of participants involved in the interaction; conversations involving members of public only, conversations between members of staff only, and, finally, conversations with mixed participants. When the data are analysed according to these three groups, it can be seen that the rate of Gaelic language among members of the public remained constant at around 15 per cent; however, there were large variations in the rate of Gaelic language use between the two types of domains when members of staff were involved in the interaction. Whereas in public spaces with statutory GLPs Gaelic was used in thirty-seven out of 253 – or 14.6 per cent – recorded interactions between members of staff, in public spaces without statutory GLPs the language was not used at all in this category of speakers.

This would, at the first instance, suggest that front-line staff in these public spaces were not Gaelic/English bilinguals, unlike those employed in public spaces with statutory GLPs, but evidence from conversations involving mixed participants would appear to contradict this, as, although recording a significantly lower level of Gaelic language use than those spaces with statutory GLPs, the language was used in interactions with members of the public. These results might be considered surprising as, unlike places with a statutory GLP, where the language is highly visible in the linguistic landscape and especially on corporate logos and permanent signage and where members of staff are encouraged to be involved in using the language, such language management initiatives tend not to be present in spaces without statutory GLPs. Spaces without statutory GLPs can almost exclusively be characterised by a 'tokenistic' use of the language in the public spaces, with just the occasional use of Gaelic, often using 'stock' phrases on pre-printed, non-company specific signage.

It should be noted that, despite the language being used in the linguistic landscape, none of the public domains surveyed in this study used markers to identify individual bilingual Gaelic/English staff members who were willing and able to speak the language, both with colleagues as well as members of the public:

> Bidh mi dìreach ga cleachdadh leis an teaghlach agus na co-obraichean agam san oifis . . . chan eil mi ga cleachdadh anns na bùthan – chan eil fhios agam cò leis a' chànan.

> (I just use it with my family and colleagues in the office . . . I don't use it in the shops – I don't know who speaks the language.)

> (Ethnographic interview participant 16)

This would suggest that, where Gaelic was used between members of staff and members of the public, or even between different members of staff themselves, the language would have to have been previously established as the preferred, or at least accepted, linguistic norm. This might in many instances be based on personal acquaintance between the various interlocutors in the conversation, but also on the linguistic soundscape created in the public space. In the ethnographic interviews with English/Gaelic bilinguals during this study various public spaces were identified where Gaelic was routinely spoken, either in conversations involving staff or members of the public, and it was indicated during the interviews that this made them more likely to consider using Gaelic as the initial language of the interaction.

This initial language of the interaction is a very good indicator of the language choice for future interactions between the same groups of participants, as, once established, linguistic habits tend to be of an enduring nature (Altuna and Basurto 2013). Thus where Gaelic was established as the linguistic norm, future conversations were also more likely to be conducted in the language. Conversely, where English was established between participants, even where all participants were English/Gaelic bilinguals, future conversations were likely to continue using English.[5]

Topic of the conversation

Although previous knowledge of the linguistic norms of the individuals participating in the conversations appears to be the primary driver for the initial language choice, it is evident from the language use diaries and ethnographic interviews that other factors impact on language use; this can be explained by looking at the traditional domains of usage associated with the language.

Research from the late twentieth and early twenty-first centuries has shown that the language is most frequently used in what might be considered *Gemeinschaft* domains

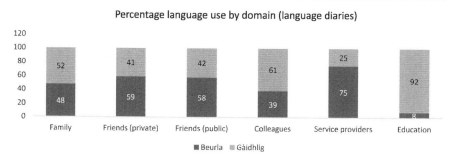

Figure 9.4 Language diary recorded conversations according to domain, participant and language used

(MacKinnon 1977, 2006; NicAoidh 2010); that is, those domains based around the principles of 'spontaneous organic participation, in which membership is self-fulfilling/self-perpetuating and often part of a long journey of tradition' (Oliver 2006: 157). Data from the language use diaries has shown this still to be the case, with the language most frequently used with family, friends and colleagues, regardless of the location of the interaction.[6]

The use of Gaelic in the domains where the participants are acquainted with the linguistic norms of their interlocutors contrasts sharply with the use of recorded Gaelic interactions with service providers, involving conversations with members of staff in organisations, with or without a statutory Gaelic plan, but not colleagues of the participant, as shown in Figure 9.4.

This distinction in language use was also seen in the linguistic soundscape data when this was analysed according to the main topic of the conversation, with two categories being identified: business transactions if the conversation related directly to the provision of goods or services of the organisation where the interaction took place, and private conversations where this was not the case. It can be seen in Figure 9.5 that the use of Gaelic was very limited across all business interactions, with the language being used in 4.3 per cent of these conversations, whereas private interactions were

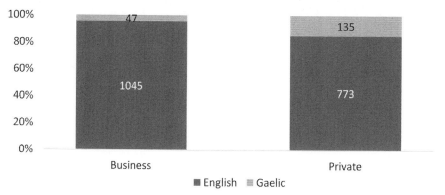

Figure 9.5 Percentage language use by purpose of the conversation

significantly more likely to be conducted in Gaelic, recording 14.9 per cent of the total conversations in the language.

Therefore, it would appear that even if Gaelic has been agreed as the linguistic norm the topic of conversation might actually determine whether or not the language is actually used. This can be exemplified by the following quotes from the ethnographic interviews:

> My dad and I always use Gaelic in the house . . . when we are discussing something complex or technical, for example linked to photography, we use English.
>
> (Participant 6, female, < 30, L1)

With another participant stating:

> Tha sinn a' cleachdadh na Gàidhlig san oifis seo, ach uaireannan . . . uaireannan tha e duilich rud teicnigeach a mhìneachadh sa Ghàidhlig – bidh e nas fhasa agus nas luaithe a' Bheurla a chleachdadh.
>
> (We use Gaelic in this office, but sometimes . . . sometimes it is difficult to explain something technical in Gaelic – it is easier and quicker to use English.)
>
> (Participant 4, male, < 30, L2)

Therefore, it is likely that when interacting with service providers, Gaelic/English bilinguals, consciously or unconsciously, prefer to use English for what they might consider business transactions, even where the members of front-line staff appear able and willing to communicate in the language.

Conclusions

Gaelic language management initiatives, especially since the ratification of the Gaelic Act in 2005 have increasingly focused on promoting and encouraging the use of Gaelic in public domains. These formal language management ideologies, as set out in language planning and policy documents prepared under the guidance of Bòrd na Gàidhlig, express explicit support for the language. In practical terms this often translates as an increased usage of the language in the linguistic landscape of the organisation, through bilingual permanent signage and a bilingual corporate identity especially. Although these language plans all make reference to an increased use of the language, these initiatives do not appear to have affected the *de facto* language use, with Gaelic still being used at the expected rate of 9.1 per cent.

It does appear, however, to have influenced who speaks the language, with members of staff in public spaces with statutory GLPs more likely to use the language, both in interactions with other members of staff as well as with members of the public compared to public spaces without statutory GLPs. However, Gaelic is more likely to be used in *Gemeinschaft* domains rather than in situations involving service providers, even where these services are available in the language. Individual speaker confidence and established linguistic norms would appear to be the main drivers for language use, rather than the management initiatives which appear to merely raise the visibility of the language in the linguistic landscape rather than drive language use as intended by the language management documents.

The real or *de facto* language policy of the Gaelic/English bilinguals in public domains in the parish of Stornoway is more dependent on the ideologies of individual speakers than on the management initiatives – people speak Gaelic to who they know, about what they know, regardless of any policy or planning initiative.

Notes

1. Where it should be noted that the Scottish census does not collect data about the levels of ability or indeed frequency of usage, making it, according to Munro (2011: 165) 'impossible to know how, and even if, those who self-report to have Gaelic are actually using Gaelic in those ten years'.
2. Where the term Gàidhealtachd is taken to refer to the areas in the modern local authorities of Argyll and Bute, Highland Council and Comhairle nan Eilean Siar.
3. Although no census data on monolingual Gaelic speakers has been collected since 1971, it is according to Dunbar (2011: 152) likely that 'aside from very small children who are being raised through the medium of Gaelic, all Gaelic speakers are bilingual in Gaelic and English'.
4. During the fieldwork study, twelve Gaelic speakers resident in the parish of Stornoway were asked to record their language use, both English and Gaelic, for a period of at least seven days in a language use diary. A total of 449 conversations were recorded, 217 (48 per cent) of which used Gaelic as the main language of the conversation.
5. A clear example of this is an interview conducted as part of this study where the researcher was interviewing a Gaelic/English bilingual in a public domain. As the initial contact had been made in English, the interview was conducted in English. The interview was interrupted by another Gaelic/English bilingual who was acquainted with both the researcher and the interview participant and had previously established Gaelic as the linguistic norm, speaking in Gaelic. The language of the conversation changed from English to Gaelic in the presence of this individual. However, when the interview continued, and despite both the interview participant and the researcher now being aware of the linguistic capabilities of the other person, the interview, and indeed further conversations, were conducted in English.
6. Where it should be noted that 'education' in almost all instances referred to some form of Gaelic learning, with the participants either taking part as a learner or as a facilitator.

Bibliography

Altuna, Olatz and Asier Basurto. 2013. *A Guide to Language Use Observation Survey Methods*. Soziolinguistika Klusterra, Vitoria-Gasteiz.

Alvarez Enparantza, José Luis. 2001. *Txillardegi, Hacia una Socio-linguistica Matemática*. Donostia: Euskal Soziolinguistika Institutua Sortzen.

An Lanntair. 2012. *Gaelic Language Plan*. Stornoway: An Lanntair.

Bòrd na Gàidhlig. 2007. *Stiùireadh air deasachadh phlanaichean Gàidhlig*. Inverness: Bòrd na Gàidhlig.

Bòrd na Gàidhlig. 2013. *Plana Cànain Nàiseanta Gàidhlig*. Available online at http://www.gaidhlig.org.uk/bord/plana-naiseanta-na-gaidhlig/index.php (last accessed 19 November 2013).

Bòrd na Gàidhlig. 2014. *The Gaelic Language (Scotland) Act 2005 and the National Gaelic Language Plan*. Available online at http://www.gaidhlig.org.uk/bord/en/the-bord/about-bord-na-gaidhlig/gaelic-language-act/ (last accessed 12 April 2015).

CalMac Ferries Ltd (Trading as Caledonian MacBrayne). 2012. *Gaelic Language Plan*. Greenock: Calmac Ferries Ltd.

Cenoz, Jasone and Durk Gorter. 2006. Linguistic Landscape and Minority Languages. In Durk Gorter (ed.), *Linguistic Landscape: A New Approach to Multilingualism*, 67–80. Clevedon: Multilingual Matters.

Census Office. 1883. *Tenth Decennial Census of the Population of Scotland*. Table 1. Scotland in Civil Counties and Parishes Showing the Number of Families, Houses, Populations, Speaking Gaelic and Rooms with Windows in 1891, and Corresponding Particulars in 1881. Edinburgh: Her Majesty's Stationary Office (HMSO).

Comhairle nan Eilean Siar. 2013. *Comhairle nan Eilean Siar Gaelic Language Plan 2013–2017*. Stornoway: Comhairle nan Eilean Siar.

Crystal, David. 2000. *Language Death*. 7th edition. Cambridge: Cambridge University Press.

Dunbar, Robert. 2010. A Research Strategy to Support Gaelic Language Policy in Scotland. In Gillian Munro and Iain Mac an Tàilleir (eds), *Coimhearsnachd na Gàidhlig an-diugh/Gaelic Communities Today*, 139–161. Edinburgh: Dunedin Academic Press.

Dunbar, Robert. 2011. Bilingualism: Conceptual Difficulties and Practical Challenges. In John M. Kirk and Dónall P. Ó Baoill (eds), *Strategies for Minority Languages: Northern Ireland, the Republic of Ireland, and Scotland*, 150–163. Beul Feirste: Cló Ollscoil na Banríona.

Fishman, Joshua. 1991. *Reversing Language Shift – Theoretical and Empirical Foundations of Assistance to Threatened Languages*. Clevedon: Multilingual Matters.

Grenoble, Lenore A. and Lindsay J. Whaley. 1998. Towards a Typology of Language Endangerment. In Lenore A. Grenoble and Lindsay J. Whaley (eds), *Endangered Languages – Current Issues and Future Prospects*, 22–55. Cambridge: Cambridge University Press.

GROS (General Registrar of Scotland). 2005. *Scotland's Census 2001 Gaelic Report*. Edinburgh: General Registrar of Scotland.

HIE (Highlands and Islands Enterprise). 2014. *Innse Gall Area Profile*. Inverness: Highlands and Islands Enterprise.

Mac an Tàilleir, Iain. 2010. A' Ghàidhlig anns a' Chunntas-shluaigh. In Gillian Munro and Iain Mac an Tàilleir (eds), *Coimhearsnachd na Gàidhlig an-diugh/Gaelic Communities Today*, 19–34. Edinburgh: Dunedin Academic Press.

MacKinnon, Kenneth. 1977. *Language, Education and Social Processes in a Gaelic Community*. London: Routledge.

MacKinnon, Kenneth. 2006. The Western Isles Language Plan: Gaelic to English Language Shift 1972–2001. In Wilson McLeod (ed.), *Revitalising Gaelic in Scotland*, 49–72. Edinburgh: Dunedin Academic Press.

McLeod, Wilson. 2002. Gaelic Scotland: A 'Renaissance' without Planning. *Hizkuntza Biziberritzeko Saoiak/Experiencias de Inversion del Cambio Linguistico/Recuperation de la Perte Linguistique/Reversing Language Shift*, 279–295.

McLeod, Wilson. 2006. Leasachadh solarachadh sheirbhisean poblach tro mhead-han na Gàidhlig: duilgheadasan idè-eòlach agus pragtaigeach. In Wilson McLeod (ed.), *Revitalising Gaelic in Scotland*, 25–48. Edinburgh: Dunedin Academic Press.

McLeod, Wilson. 2010. Poileasaidh Leasachaidh na Gàidhlig: Paradaim Ùr. In Gillian Munro and Iain Mac an Tàilleir (eds), *Coimhearsnachd na Gàidhlig an-diugh/Gaelic Communities Today*, 1–18. Edinburgh: Dunedin Academic Press.

McLeod, Wilson. 2011. Planaichean Reachdail Gàidhlig: cothroman is cnapan-starra. In Richard Cox and Timothy Armstrong (eds), *A' Cleachdadh na Gàidhlig*, 227–248. An t-Eilean Sgitheanach: Clò Ostaig.

McLeod, Wilson. 2013. *Gaelic in Contemporary Scotland: Contradictions, Challenges and Strategies*, 2nd edition. Edinburgh: University of Edinburgh.

Munro, Gillian. 2011. The Barail agus Comas Cànain Survey of Community Language Use, Ability and Attitudes: Some General Observations Regarding Future Gaelic Language Policy Planning in Scotland. In John M. Kirk and Dónall P. Ó Baoill (eds), *Strategies for Minority Languages: Northern Ireland, the Republic of Ireland, and Scotland*, 163–171. Beul Feirste: Cló Ollscoil na Banríona.

Munro, Gillian and Iain Mac an Tàilleir (eds). 2010. *Coimhearsnachd na Gàidhlig an-diugh/Gaelic Communities Today*. Edinburgh: Dunedin Academic Press.

National Records of Scotland (NRS). 2013. *Table QS211SC Gaelic Language Skills*. Edinburgh: HMSO.

NicAoidh, Magaidh. 2010. Plana Cànain nan Eilean Siar. In Gillian Munro and Iain Mac an Tàilleir (eds), *Coimhearsnachd na Gàidhlig an-diugh/Gaelic Communities Today*, 49–60. Edinburgh: Dunedin Academic Press.

Ó Giollagáin Conchúr, Seosamh Mac Donnacha, Fiona Ní Chualáin, Aoife Ní Shéaghdha and Mary O'Brien. 2007. *Comprehensive Linguistic Study of the Use of Irish in the Gaeltacht: Principal Findings and Recommendations*. Dublin: The Department of Community, Rural and Gaeltacht Affairs.

Oliver, James. 2006. Where is Gaelic? Revitalisation, Language, Culture and Identity. In Wilson McLeod (ed.), *Revitalising Gaelic in Scotland*, 155–168. Edinburgh: Dunedin Academic Press.

Oliver, James. 2010. The Predicament? Planning for Culture, Communities and Identities. In Gillian Munro and Iain Mac an Tàilleir (eds), *Coimhearsnachd na Gàidhlig an-diugh/Gaelic Communities Today*, 73–86. Edinburgh: Dunedin Academic Press.

Pròiseact Plana Cànain nan Eilean Siar/Western Isles Language Plan Project. 2004. *Rannsachadh agus toraidhean ìre 1 den Phròiseact/Research and Outcomes of Phase 1 of the Project. Aithisg Dheireannach/Final report*. Stornoway: Colaiste a' Chaisteil/Lews Castle College.

Rothach, Gillian. 2006. Gàidhlig air an Oir. In Wilson McLeod (ed.), *Revitalising Gaelic in Scotland*, 221–238. Edinburgh: Dunedin Academic Press.

Rothach Gillian, Iain Mac an Tàilleir and Timothy C. Armstrong. 2011, *Cor na Gàidhlig ann an Siabost*. A research report for Bòrd na Gàidhlig.

Scottish Government. 2015. *Gaelic Language Plan*. Available online at http://www.gov.scot/Publications/2010/07/06161418/3 (last accessed 28 August 2017).

Scottish Parliament. 2005. *Gaelic Language (Scotland) Act 2005*. Available online at http://www.legislation.gov.uk/asp/2005/7/contents (last accessed 8 May 2015).

Shohamy, Elena. 2006. *Language Policy: Hidden Agendas and New Approaches*. New York: Routledge.

Spolsky, Bernard. 2004, *Language Policy*. Cambridge: Cambridge University Press.

Spolsky, Bernard. 2009. *Language Management*. Cambridge: Cambridge University Press.

Withers, Charles W. J. 1989. On the Geography and Social History of Gaelic. In William Gillies (ed.), *Gaelic and Scotland: Alba agus a' Ghàidhlig*. Edinburgh: Edinburgh University Press.

10

Planning for Growth: The Professionalisation of the Taskforce for Gaelic Revitalisation

Michelle Macleod, Timothy C. Armstrong, Gillian Munro and Iain Taylor

Introduction

It is only relatively recently that scholars and the public have become aware of the accelerating loss of linguistic diversity around the world; consequently, the development of organised planning for survival in response to the crisis is also relatively new. Given that language planning for linguistic diversity is such a new endeavour, it is not surprising that a culture of professionalism and expertise among its practitioners is also still in the early stages of development. We have much to learn about what does and does not work when it comes to language planning in this respect, and there is also much work to be done in terms of disseminating this knowledge to those language planners, educators and activists working on the ground in indigenous communities who might use it. This chapter explores the levels of training experienced and required by individuals involved in the implementation of planning interventions in the Scottish Gaelic context.

Background

In Scotland, the development of an organised, national response to the demographic decline of Gaelic-speaking communities is very recent indeed (see, for example, Dunbar 2010 and Macleod 2008). In the last quarter of the twentieth century, as language activists became increasingly concerned about the growing crisis in Gaelic-speaking communities, various initiatives in education, in the media, and in local-government service provision, were effected aiming to re-strengthen the transmission and use of Gaelic. These early efforts, while motivated by good intentions, were nonetheless characterised by a general lack of professional expertise. In the absence of a clear understanding of the nature of the problem, and without access to state-of-the-art theory of best practice in indigenous-language education and revitalisation, these early efforts tended to be of limited efficacy (McLeod 2002). Commenting in 2001, McLeod identified a lack of professionalisation in Scottish language planning bodies as a pervasive problem:

> Despite the growing institutionalization of the Gaelic movement in Scotland – an institutionalization underpinned by millions of pounds of government investment every year – very little specialist professional expertise is brought to bear on Gaelic development, a phenomenon one activist has unkindly described as 'amateur hour'. Almost none of those steering the various Gaelic organisations have any specialist training or experience in applied linguistics or language planning, and there is relatively little awareness of theoretical and analytical advances in the field of language revitalization and language planning in general [. . .]. (McLeod 2001: 23)

The Scottish Gaelic example is typical of the need for effective interaction between the policy-maker and the policy enabler: in this case to be able to support more effective grass-roots language intervention activity.

Much has been written with regard to the importance of evaluating the efficacy of language policies, and most scholars agree that to do so is difficult, not least because of the many variables at play, as noted by Romaine (2002). This chapter explores one such variable: that of the human, and even more specifically, the training experiences and requirements. Kaplan and Baldauf (1997: 303) suggest that 'language planning is ultimately about human resource development' and that 'involving participants in the planning is therefore a critical "problem" in wider situational contexts if language planning is to be meaningful and successful'. Mac Donnacha (2000) and Macleod (2011) have also considered the importance of the human resource management in terms of successful implementation. Mac Donnacha noted the importance of human resource development in his Integrated Language Planning Model: human resource management was considered there as one of the key support activities necessary to co-exist alongside the primary intervention activities. Macleod's survey of community animateurs concluded that relevant training was necessary both for the efficacy of individual contributions in language intervention activities and for the long-term development of the human resource sector and succession planning in Gaelic organisations.

Since the implementation of the Gaelic Language (Scotland) Act 2005 there has been a considerable increase in planning and interventionist activity aimed at revitalising the language. One of the main facets of the Act tasked Bòrd na Gàidhlig (the government agency charged with directing planning for Gaelic) to require public bodies to prepare Gaelic plans for their organisations; a number of non-governmental organizations (NGOs) were similarly tasked with specific language intervention initiatives through their funding arrangements with the Bòrd, and as these plans and funding contracts were approved and implemented, a new cadre of professional language planners, professionals and policy implementers with responsibility for Gaelic plans has begun to develop in Scotland. These plans often prescribe employing a Gaelic officer for the organisation in order to progress policy recommendations, or the plans might note that an existing employee will have responsibility for enforcing the Gaelic policy; the plans themselves often include some content about offering training in Gaelic language skills or Gaelic awareness to existing staff. However, questions have been raised about the potential efficacy of these plans (Mac an Tàilleir et al. 2010: 224–225; McLeod 2011); about possible challenges of implementation due to often low levels of language fluency across various organisations (Milligan 2010); and with specific regard to the level of training and support provided to Gaelic development officers employed by 'Gaelic organisations' (Macleod 2011). It is questionable whether the swift roll-out of so many public authority plans has been matched by increased ideological awareness amongst personnel affected by these policy changes (in 2017 fifty-one public authorities have statutory languages plans, according to Bòrd na Gàidhlig).

The study and methodology

The *National Plan for Gaelic 2012–2017* lists the development of Gaelic in the workplace and community as two of its priorities for development with the intention that more Gaelic should be used in these domains. In order for these aims to have a chance of success in fulfilling the strategic direction of the *National Plan*, it is important that the human resource cohort is well trained and supported. To date there has been little research on the experiences and qualifications of those employed in the sector commonly referred to as 'Gaelic development', other than McEwan-Fujita's (2008, pre-Act) ethnography of the Gaelic workplace and Macleod's (2011) survey of the experiences of the community development workers. Other studies related to Gaelic and the labour market tend to focus on how the creation of Gaelic-related jobs can make a positive contribution to both local economies and Gaelic revitalisation (Sproull and Ashcroft, 1993; Sproull, 1996; Sproull and Chalmers, 1998; MacLeod, 2008). MacLeod (2008) has done considerable work on language use and training in the Gaelic workplace and has noted the emphasis placed on Gaelic language skills with regard to human resource development.

The new planning environment that Gaelic finds itself in since the implementation of the Gaelic Language Act is similar to the situation noted in Wales a number of years earlier: commentators there have noted that language awareness training has become an important tool in human resource management and one that needs to develop alongside language planning so that individuals' and corporate ideology about language is positively affected:

> As institutions faced the task of creating and implementing statutory language schemes, the need arose for them to rethink and revise old patterns of behaviour towards the Welsh language, types of behaviour that were long established in all aspects of their contact with the public and in all services provided to the public. (Eaves 2007: 2)

Based on the experiences noted (as above) in Wales and building on existing literature on human resources in language revitalisation cited above, this chapter explores practice related to language awareness training, theoretical language planning training, language usage and learning and community development training. These issues are explored in the context of the academic literature and the results of a survey conducted in 2013, originally commissioned by Bòrd na Gàidhlig. Our study provides a new lens through which to better perceive the developing culture of professionalism among Gaelic language planners in Scotland, as well as informing policy-makers on how to measure the need and demand for continuing professional development training in language planning and Gaelic skills among public sector and voluntary sector staff who work with the Gaelic-speaking Scottish public. The research was designed to expand on several of the questions related to the quick expansion of language planning activities, specifically:

- What is the current level of Gaelic-related and language planning training among staff working in Gaelic agencies and other bodies dealing with the Gaelic-speaking public?
- What are the currently unmet training needs of staff in this respect?
- How do key stakeholders in public organisations understand questions of professionalism, Gaelic development and service provision through the medium of Gaelic?

The 2013 survey was able to explore the experiences of a greater number of individuals than either McEwan-Fujita (2008) or Macleod (2011) and has considered a broader range of training issues than MacLeod (2008): the survey considered what the skill-base and training history of the current workforce was and what additional training needs were required. This chapter presents findings from our interview and survey data addressing these research questions and we discuss these results in the light of our understanding of best practice in language planning for strengthening transmission and use of threatened indigenous languages.

The study selected fifty organisations, ensuring a range of organisational structures: public bodies, 'Gaelic organisations' (i.e. organisations such as Comunn na Gàidhlig whose operations are solely related to Gaelic promotion in some way or another), local authorities and charity or voluntary organisations. All of the organisations either have a Gaelic policy or were in the process of preparing one at the time of writing. Each of these organisations was asked to complete a comprehensive questionnaire about their work practices. In addition to the questionnaire, semi-structured interviews were carried out with key personnel from four organisations (representative of the different organisational structures): the questions were loosely based on the ones asked on the questionnaire but encouraged the discussion of issues more broadly related to human resource management and language planning and implementation.

Thirty-eight organisations (76 per cent) returned the questionnaire and a reasonable mix of organisations of different structures took part, allowing a comparative analysis of the different experiences. The organisations which responded could be split into five main types, as shown in Table 10.1.

The organisations were also asked where their main office was located (not where they had a work locus), and the following responses indicated that there was a still a dominance of organisations with a Gaelic-related work remit based in the traditional heartland areas (Table 10.2).

Most of the organisations sampled (32/38) either had or were working on Gaelic

Table 10.1 Types of organisations and number of each type

Type	Number of organisations
Gaelic organisation	10
Public body	7
Local authority	8
Charity organisation	10
Voluntary organisation	1
Other	2
Total	**38**

Table 10.2 Location of organisations

Location	Number of organisations
Western Isles	13
Inverness	6
Highland region	5
Central Scotland	10
Argyll and Bute	1
Elsewhere in Scotland	3
Total	**38**

plans detailing how they would deliver and develop Gaelic services and develop the skills of their employees in order to deliver the plan. The types of training offered in public authorities would tend to be typical of those noted below and extracted from Comhairle nan Eilean Siar's Gaelic Language Plan 2013–17:

1. (in relation to its policy objective) . . . establish Gaelic as the administrative language for the Comhairle, by providing facilities for in-post training and to enable staff to develop their linguistic skills (p. 5)
2. . . . offer Gaelic media training (p. 30)
3. . . . provide Gaelic training for leaders of after-school or holiday clubs (p. 39)
4. . . . establish a 'Gaelic Language in the Primary School (GLPS) Training for Trainers' course (p. 49)
5. . . . ensure that every member of staff, if required, is encouraged to take up Gaelic *Ùlpan* learning opportunities, catering for all levels of fluency, and/ or written Gaelic learning opportunities for fluent speakers, provided by *Gràmar na Gàidhlig* classes (p. 49)
6. . . . organise Gaelic awareness sessions for staff, delivered by *Clì Gàidhlig* to highlight the importance of the Comhairle's bilingual identity, and to encourage uptake of Gaelic learning opportunities (p. 69)

It should be noted, however, that as a local authority with a significant number of Gaelic-speaking employees and serving the traditional Gaelic heartlands, the options expressed by Comhairle nan Eilean Siar are probably more ambitious than those of many others.

Language engagement and language usage

Clearly, and as has been established previously (for example, MacLeod 2008), the increased use of Gaelic in the workplace is a desired outcome of language policy intervention, either through effective policy facilitating existing speakers or by the active offer of language training. Of the thirty-eight organisations which took part in the survey, we were able to ascertain how many people in these organisations were involved in Gaelic development related activity, both on a paid and a voluntary basis (see Table 10.3). While this figure is in no way conclusive about the number of people actively engaged in Gaelic-related work, it does give some extent of the exponential impact of the requirement put on public bodies to implement plans and thus employ staff with a specific remit in this area: it also provides a base-line figure to compare other responses in the survey.

It is clearly important that an organisation which engages with Gaelic-related activity should be able to conduct at least part of its activity through the medium of Gaelic. Table 10.4 shows how many of the above people used Gaelic in their work activities, although we were not able to ascertain what level of language was used or how regularly Gaelic was used (this not being the central focus of the research).

It will be shown below that language training is the second most common type of training undertaken and the most widely offered across the board. Moreover, during the follow-up interviews 'improving language skills' was identified by stakeholders as the most highly valued area for future skill development. The type of language skill development ranged not only from courses for beginners but support in advanced writing (on account of the perceived weak Gaelic literacy skills amongst many employees).

Table 10.3 Number of people working in Gaelic-related activity

Number of people in the organisation who work specifically on issues directly relating to Gaelic communities and speakers

Organisation	Number of workers		Number of organisations
	Paid	Voluntary	
Gaelic organisation	63	57	10
Public body	73	0	7
Local authority	1281	9	8
Charity organisation	86	22	10
Voluntary organisation	1	6	1
Other	1	0	2
Total	1505	94	38

Table 10.4 Number of people using Gaelic

Number of people in the organisation who work through the medium of Gaelic for at least part of their time

Organisation	Number of workers		Number of organisations
	Paid	Voluntary	
Gaelic organisation	63	36	10
Public body	91	0	7
Local authority	276	7	8
Charity organisation	42	22	10
Voluntary organisation	1	6	1
Other	3	11	2
Total	476	82	38

'S e rud a tha dhìth oirnn fhathast: 's e sgilean cànain fhèin. Tha e mar thoradh air an siostam foghlaim a tha air a bhith againn san dùthaich a tha seo bho chionn grunn bhliadhnaichean nach tàinig a h-uile duine, gu dearbh cha tàinig a' mhòr-chuid againn, tro FMG. 'S dòcha gur ann aig glè bheag againn aig a bheil trèanadh foirmeil sa chànan.

(What we still need is: language skills. As a result of the education system that we have had in this country for many years not everyone, indeed not the majority, came through GME. Perhaps very few of us have formal training in the language.)

(Angus, Community Organisation)

Bhiodh e math nan robh goireasan digiteach ann air an cruthachadh le Bòrd na Gàidhlig – a' teagasg briathrachas, abairtean ('s dòcha le sound files), msaa – bhiodh sin feumail do luchd-obrach san àit-obrach. Tha goireasan ann marthà mar LearnGaelic.net, ach chan eil iad gu sònraichte airson daoine a tha ag obair ann am buidhnean poblach agus bhiodh e glè mhath nan robh rudeigin mar sin ann as urrainn dhaibh a chleachdadh san àit-obrach.

(It would be good if digital materials were created by Bòrd na Gàidhlig – teaching vocabulary, phrases (perhaps with sound files), etc. – that would be useful to workers in the workplace. There are materials already like LearnGaelic.net, but they aren't specifically for people who are working in public authorities and it would be very good if there was something like that that they could use in the workplace.)

(Iain, Rural Local Authority)

MacLeod (2008: 293) has previously identified that the lack of language training was a factor which contributed to a failure to address language confidence in the workplace:

Possible support mechanisms to address language confidence of those in employment could include a government co-ordinated scheme to support employers to identify and deliver work-related (professional, technical, administrative) Gaelic language training as part of continued professional development. Further, the continued paucity of Gaelic language training opportunities as part of vocational training schemes needs [to be] addressed.

There seems to be little real movement in this direction, particularly for those who already have some skills in the language but who wish to develop these skills further.

It can be noted from Table 10.4 above that a very high number of those using Gaelic work in local authorities: of the 276, 180 work for Comhairle nan Eilean Siar, thirty for Edinburgh City Council and thirty-one for Glasgow City Council. Of the thirty-six volunteers working for Gaelic organisations, thirty of them worked for An Comunn Gàidhealach, a membership Gaelic promotional body (established in 1891). The total number of employees in all organisations surveyed was 57,071, with an additional 257 unpaid individuals; the percentage of employees that use Gaelic is similar to the 1 per cent of the Scottish population who are Gaelic speakers.

These figures are interesting on a number of counts: they show that there are considerably more people working with Gaelic speakers than are using Gaelic as part of their daily work practice. This suggests that not everyone engaging with Gaelic speakers is themselves able or willing to speak Gaelic. Significantly again, of the 1,281 paid employees who work in Gaelic-related activity for local authorities (Table 10.3), 1,200 of these come from Comhairle nan Eilean Siar. Of the fifty-seven unpaid individuals working for Gaelic organisations, fifty of these belong to Comann nam Pàrant, the national organisation for Gaelic-medium education parents. This information begins to give some kind of indication of how many employees or unpaid volunteers are in direct contact with Gaelic speakers and have the capacity to impact either positively or negatively on language practices in the community, particularly if they themselves are not able to speak Gaelic.

Training experiences

Given the potential impact of employees who have any kind of Gaelic-related remit on the sociolinguistic situation, it is important that all of these individuals understand and receive adequate training to carry out their duties in a manner that is sensitive to nationally agreed language planning goals. While the research team identified four areas for training based on pre-existing research on the Gaelic workplace and experiences in other minority language regions (language awareness training, theoretical language planning training, language usage and learning and community development training, as indicated above), it should be noted that a number of the organisations will organise (and have organised) other types of training that they see as intrinsic to their roles in delivering their Gaelic language policies or development targets. For example, Comunn na Gàidhlig (CnaG) currently offer four training days per annum which relate specifically to their language revitalisation activities, and these training opportunities represent the diverse nature of the type of activities undertaken by CnaG employees: this is usually very practical training, rather than the type identified here (although CnaG did organise training in community language planning in 2010).

Given the diverse range of organisational structures involved in delivering Gaelic services, it is as important that the small community organisations have the same level of access to training as the national organisations. Table 10.5 groups the organisations surveyed into two super-categories: public (national) organisations and community

Table 10.5 Training already undertaken

Received training in	Number of people		
	Total	Public/nationally	Community
Language planning (paid)	30	24	6
Language planning (unpaid)	2	0	2
Language awareness (paid)	666	659	7
Language awareness (unpaid)	3	0	3
Community development (paid)	191	168	23
Community development (unpaid)	4	0	4
Gaelic language skills (paid)	619	588	31
Gaelic language skills (unpaid)	10	0	10

organisations: it shows what number of people had received training, and the totals of each of the subsections have been organised into two categories of work organisation.

It can be seen that many paid employees in the public (national) organisations have undertaken language awareness training, with 666 having done so at some point: 320 of these belong to the Scottish Government, 120 to Glasgow City Council and 100 to the Scottish Parliament. The next most common training area was in language skills, with 619 people having undertaken some kind of Gaelic tuition: of these 210 worked for Glasgow City Council, fifty for Scottish Natural Heritage and seventy-five for Comhairle nan Eilean Siar. In comparison, the number of unpaid workers who had undertaken any training was low and they were most likely to have completed training in language skills: in fact, from the figures here, it should be noted that all the unpaid workers taking part in language training belong to one organisation, Fèisean nan Gàidheal, the national umbrella organisation for community-based Gaelic arts tuitition festivals.

It is particularly striking that only thirty employees were reported as having received training in language planning out of a total of 57,071 employees working for the organisations surveyed. This represents strong objective evidence that professional language planning remains a marginal concern in most of these organisations, a conclusion that is discussed further in light of the interview data below. When examined in more detail it was evident that very few of the community groups had undertaken or offered their employees opportunities to develop skills in language planning: a fact which could be counter-productive to the aims of Bòrd na Gàidhlig's *National Language Plan 2012–2017*.

In addition to looking at the existing skill levels of the sector, the survey also undertook to examine what training opportunities were currently available. While there is much academic discourse about the aims and successes of delivering continuing professional development (CPD) training in various employment sectors, there is at the core an acceptance that CPD is a mainstay of the learning society. CPD may 'deliver strategies of learning that will be of benefit to individuals, foster personal development, and produce professionals who are flexible, self-reflective and empowered to take control of their own learning' and may concurrently be 'a means of training professionals to fulfil specific work roles and as a guarantee of individual, professional

Table 10.6 Training currently available by type of organisation

Type of training	Total (38)	Public/ national (21)	Community/ local (17)
Training available now in Language Planning, Language Awareness, Community Development, or Gaelic language skills	20	14	6
No mention of any current training	18	7	11
Training available now in Language Planning (paid)	5	5	0
Training available now in Language Planning (unpaid)	0	0	0
Training available now in Language Awareness (paid)	4	4	0
Training available now in Language Awareness (unpaid)	0	0	0
Training available now in Community Development (paid)	5	2	3
Training available now in Community Development (unpaid)	0	0	0
Training available now in Gaelic language skills (paid)	17	14	3
Training available now in Gaelic language skills (unpaid)	1	0	1

competence' (Friedman and Phillips 2010: 362–363). We are predominantly interested in the second of these two purposes.

Of all the organisations surveyed, only twenty organisations currently offer any training in the four skills identified: significantly, an employee is more likely to have an offer of training if working for a public body rather than a community organisation. In the sample, two-thirds of the public organisations offer some kind of training, whereas only one-third of the community groups do this (see Table 10.6). The type of training most commonly offered is in Gaelic language skills, with the majority of the national/public organisations (fourteen out of eighteen) offering training in this. At the time of the survey five public bodies offered training in Language Planning and Community Development and four public bodies offer training in Language Awareness.

The provision of training may relate to the provisions made in any training policy and, with that in mind, we further explored whether the different groups had any kind of specific training policies and, if so, how these might take cognisance of the skills identified as necessary for successful implementation of Gaelic language policy. Out of the thirty-seven groups with paid employees which answered that question approximately three-quarters have a training policy. With regard to unpaid workers, seventeen organisations answered and of these ten have a training policy and seven do not. Given the overall paucity of policy on the issue of in-work training, it is perhaps not surprising that when asked about the compulsory nature of training the results were as presented in Table 10.7.

In both cases fewer than half of the organisations which responded made training compulsory. Of course, it would not be realistic to expect that all of the organisations surveyed here would be in a position to offer comprehensive training on the topics associated with Gaelic language policy implementation and we postulated whether there was a need for coordinated national training opportunities. A question about the need for more coordination was put on the questionnaire: out of the thirty-five groups which responded to the question, only two were of the opinion that there was not a

Table 10.7 Training essential

Is training essential?	Organisations' paid workers	Organisations' unpaid workers
Yes	16	4
No	19	14
Total	**35**	**18**

Table 10.8 Need for annual training event

There is a need for a common, annual training programme for organisations contributing to Gaelic revitalisation

	Completely against	Against	No opinion	Agree	Strongly agree	**Total**
			Number of groups			
Total	1	2	4	21	8	36
Public organisations	0	1	1	11	6	19
Community groups	1	1	3	10	2	17

need for more coordinated training opportunities (see Table 10.8). When this issue was explored a little further, twenty-nine out of thirty-six groups agreed that there was a need for an annual training event open to all organisations that participate in Gaelic revitalisation; this demand was particularly strongly expressed amongst public bodies.

The interviews with key stakeholders demonstrated that they too thought there was a greater need for national coordination amongst the groups that are involved in implementing Gaelic policy.

> Bhiodh e math nan robh prògram ann airson Oifigearan Gàidhlig mar mi fhìn (agus feadhainn eile aig comhairlean eile) trèanadh a dhèanamh – ach dh'fheumadh cuideigin sin a chur air dòigh agus an uair sin 's e ùine agus airgead a dh'fheumas sinn airson pàirt a ghabhail.

> (It would good if there was a training programme for Gaelic Officers like myself (and others at the other councils) – but someone would have to facilitate that and then there's the [issue of] of time and money need to take part.)

> (Andrew, City Local Authority)

When explored a little further, on the questionnaire and in interview, it was noticeable that people were also open to the possibility of receiving training using various technologies.

In addition to identifying a need for more training in language skills, the main themes which came out of the discussions concerned the diversity of skills required to work in the community and also the lack of networking opportunities available when it comes to Gaelic policy implementation. For those working directly with the community, 'soft' skills such as 'being good with people', 'enthusiasm for the job', 'confidence' and 'diplomacy' were mentioned as being necessary, although it was recognised that these would be difficult to teach. In a similar vein, it was noted how isolating it could be to be either working in the community (at a distance from colleagues) or to be the sole 'Gaelic' employee in a major organisation; while no suggestion was made as to how resilience to the isolation might be countered via any kind of CPD, it was noted that some kind of networking (training or other) might have the potential to quell the feelings of isolation. Virtual and physical networking was a recurring theme in the interviews as a way to receive and deliver formal CPD and also a means of sharing good practice:

> Mar as trice tha mi nam aonar agus chan eil fhios agam a bheil mi a' dèanamh an obair agam ceart. Bhiodh e math a bhith ag obair barrachd còmhla ri daoine. Bhiodh e math barrachd chothroman coinneachadh ri Bòrd na Gàidhlig agus nach biodh againn feitheamh 's dòcha sia mìosan – bhiodh sinn a' faighinn a-mach dè bha tachairt. Seòrsa *regular communication* – a bharrachd air na naidheachdan press releases – barrachd conaltradh eadar obair agam, comhairlean eile agus Bòrd na Gàidhlig – an àite a bhith ag obair leinn fhìn. Chan eil sinn a' faighinn a-mach dè an diofar a tha an obair againn a' dèanamh.

> (Usually I am alone and I don't know whether I am doing my work effectively. It would be good to work more with people. It would good to have more opportunities to meet with Bòrd na Gàidhlig and that we would have to wait, perhaps, six months – we would be able to find out what was happening. Kind of regular communication in addition to the news, press releases – more communication between my work and the other councils and Bòrd na Gàidhlig instead of working by ourselves. We don't find out what difference our work is doing.)

> (Andrew, City Local Authority)

Conclusion

Sharing of good practice and reflective practice is, of course, an important principle in language planning theory and while the discourse on Gaelic language planning (and language planning in general) continues to grow, there is still a problem with relation to synthesising the sociolinguistic data and policy recommendations into policy implementation. Kaplan and Baldauf (1997) have discussed the dilemma of the dual role of language planner and social science researcher: to what extent can the planner become involved in policy articulation and implementation? There is growing evidence that there needs to be better interaction between the policy-maker and the policy enabler: in this case to be able to support more effective grass-roots policy implementation.

We have shown that a significant number of employees (1,505) and volunteers (ninety-four) in these organisations are working on issues directly relating to Gaelic communities and speakers. We have also shown that a subgroup of these employees (476) and volunteers (eighty-two) use Gaelic to some degree in their work day. However, very few employees (thirty) or volunteers (two) were reported to have received training in language planning specifically. Indeed, in the interviews with key stakeholders, little interest was expressed in this type of training. It is clear that there is still considerable work to do in Scotland in promoting a culture of language planning professionalism among those public-sector and voluntary-sector staff who work with threatened Gaelic communities. There is a persistent view, expressed in the interviews, that language planning theory has little relevance to the day-to-day, practical work of community development:

> 'S e buidheann practaigeach a th' annainn a-nis. Tha uallach a thaobh *strategy* is eile air cuideigin eile, chan eil sinn ach a' lìbhrigeadh cùmhnantan agus mar siud tha focas gu math practaigeach againne air an obair againn.

> (We are a practical organisation now. The responsibility for strategy is on someone else, we are only delivering contracts and therefore we have a very practical focus on our work.)

> (Angus, Community Organisation)

> Cha tàinig iarrtas sam bith thugam a' sireadh trèanadh son a bhith ag obair sa choimhearsnachd tro mheadhan na Gàidhlig

> (I have never received a request seeking training to work in the community through the medium of Gaelic.)

> (Iain, Rural Local Authority)

This false dichotomy between theory and practice is a significant impediment to promoting language planning professionalism and expertise in these organisations. From the survey data, it appears that many still understand language planning as a concern only for those working in Gaelic revitalisation directly, and that language planning has not been integrated into the work of many of these organisations generally. In the same way that all development work now takes into account the impact of development on the environment, it is critical that as part of the professionalisation of language planning in Scotland, a bilingual culture is promoted in these organisations, so that the potential impact on the vitality of Gaelic-speaking communities is considered as a taken-for-granted precondition of any development work (e.g. Gaelic proofing).

The survey showed that there was a general interest in training and a recognition of its importance, although there was clearly an issue with regard to how such training might be funded: any lack of funding presents another impediment to promoting language planning professionalism and expertise in these organisations. Macleod (2011) and MacLeod (2008) have previously shown that a lack of recognition and confidence hampers the professional development of this new cadre of language planners in Scotland. Gaelic language development in Scotland will never achieve its full potential for promoting the vitality of Gaelic-speaking communities until all government and non-government organisations working with the Gaelic-speaking public make an intentional effort to shift from a pattern of development characterised by ad hoc initiatives and anecdotal knowledge to development founded on professional expertise and on knowledge of international best practice in language planning for the survival of linguistic diversity.

Bibliography

Baldauf, Robert B. Jr. 1994. 'Unplanned' Language Policy and Planning. *Annual Review of Applied Linguistics* 14, 82–89.

Bòrd na Gàidhlig. 2012. *Plana Cànain Nàiseanta Gàidhlig 2012–2017*. Inverness: Bòrd na Gàidhlig.

Comhairle nan Eilean Siar, *Gaelic Language Plan 2013–17*. Available online at www. cne-siar.gov.uk/sgioba/documents/languageplan/plan_e.pdf (last accessed 15 April 2016).

Dunbar, Robert. 2005. The Gaelic Language (Scotland) Act 2005. *Edinburgh Law Review* 9(3), 466–479.

Dunbar, Robert. 2010. Language Planning. In Moray Watson and Michelle Macleod (eds), *The Edinburgh Companion to the Gaelic Language*, 146–171. Edinburgh: Edinburgh University Press.

Eaves, Steve. 2007. The Contribution Made by Welsh Language Awareness Training to Language Planning and the Process of Creating a New Wales. *Contemporary Wales* 20(1), 82–105.

Fishman, Joshua A. 1991. *Reversing Language Shift: Theoretical and Empirical Foundations of Assistance to Threatened Languages*. Clevedon: Multilingual Matters.

Friedman, Andrew and Mary Phillips. 2010. Continuing Professional Development: Developing a Vision. *Journal of Education and Work* 17(3), 361–376.

Grenoble, Lenore A. and Lindsay J. Whaley. 2006. *Saving Languages: An Introduction to Language Revitalization*. Cambridge: Cambridge University Press.

Henderson, Paul and Andrew Glen. 2006. From Recognition to Support: Community Development Workers in the United Kingdom. *Community Development Journal* 41(3), 277–292.

Ioan, Gareth. 2011. Waking the Dragon Within: Empowering Local Language Communities. In R. A. V. Cox and T. C. Armstrong (eds), *A' Cleachdadh na Gàidhlig: slatan-tomhais ann an dìon cànain sa choimhearsnachd*, 109–122. Ostaig: Clò Ostaig.

Jones, Kathryn and Gareth Ioan. 2000. *Venturing Onwards: Review of the Mentrau Iaith 2000. Full Report*. Castell Newydd Emlyn: Cwmni Iaith Cyf.

Kaplan, Robert B. and Richard B. Baldauf. 1997. *Language Planning from Practice to Theory*. Clevedon: Multilingual Matters.

Mac an Tàilleir, Iain, Gillian Rothach and Timothy C. Armstrong. 2010. *Barail agus Comas Cànain*. Inverness: Bòrd na Gàidhlig.

Mac Donnacha, Seosamh. 2000. An Integrated Planning Model. *Language Problems and Language Planning* 24, 11–35.

McEwan-Fujita, Emily. 2008. Working at '9–5' Gaelic: Speakers, Contexts, and Ideologies of an Emerging Minority Language Register. In A. King Kendall, Natalie Schilling-Estes, Lyn Fogle, Jia Jackie Lou and Barbara Soukup (eds), *Sustaining Linguistic Diversity Endangered and Minority Languages and Language Varieties*, 81–94. Washington, DC: Georgetown University Press.

MacLeod, Marsaili. 2008. The Meaning of Work in the Gaelic Labour Market in the Highlands and Islands of Scotland. Aberdeen: University of Aberdeen PhD thesis.

Macleod, Michelle. 2008. Measuring Gaelic Language Planning. *Scottish Language* 26, 61–78.

Macleod, Michelle. 2011. The Human Factor: Community Language Workers and National Strategies. In John M. Kirk and Dónall P. Ó Baoill (eds), *Strategies for Minority Languages: Northern Ireland, the Republic of Ireland, and Scotland*, 223–230. Beul Feirste: Cló Ollscoil na Banríona.

McLeod, Wilson. 2001. Gaelic in the New Scotland: Politics, Rhetoric and Public Discourse. *Journal of Ethnopolitics and Minority Issues in Europe* 2. Available online at http://www.ecmi.de/fileadmin/downloads/publications/JEMIE/JEMIE02MacLeod28-11-01.pdf (last accessed 18 June 2018).

McLeod, Wilson. 2002. Gaelic in Scotland: A 'Renaissance' Without Planning. Seventh International Conference on Minority Languages, Bilbao, 1–3 December 1999. Available online at www.izenpe.com (last accessed 16 September 2010).

McLeod, Wilson. 2006. Securing the Status of Gaelic? Implementing the Gaelic Language (Scotland) Act 2005. *Scottish Affairs* 57(1), 19–38.

McLeod, Wilson. 2011. Planaichean Reachdail Gàidhlig: cothroman is cnapan-starra. In R. A. V. Cox and T. C. Armstrong (eds), *A' Cleachdadh na Gàidhlig: slatan-tomhais ann an dìon cànain sa choimhearsnachd*, 227–248. Ostaig: Clò Ostaig.

Milligan, Lindsay. 2010. Gaelic in the Workplace: Helping to Create Linguistic Capacity. *Scottish Language Review* 21, 7–16.

Munro, Gillian, Michelle NicLeòid, Iain Mac an Tàilleir and Timothy C. Armstrong (Lèirsinn). 2013. *Dealbhadh Prògram CPD airson Obair Choimhearsnachd Ghàidhlig*. A research report for Bòrd na Gàidhlig.

Romaine, Suzanne. 2002. The Impact of Language Policy on Endangered Languages. *International Journal on Multicultural Societies* 4(2), 194–212.

Romaine, Suzanne. 2006. Planning for the Survival of Linguistic Diversity. *Language Policy* 5, 441–473.

Sender, Helen, Areenay Hatamian and Barbara Carlisle, B. 2009. *Survey of Community Development Workers and Managers*. London: Community Development Foundation.

Sproull, Alan. 1996. Regional Economic Development and Minority Language Use: The Case of Gaelic Scotland. *International Journal of the Sociology of Language* 121, 93–117.

Sproull, Alan and Brian Ashcroft. 1993. *The Economics of Gaelic Language Development: A Research Report for Highlands and Islands Enterprise and the Gaelic Television Committee with Comunn na Gàidhlig*. Glasgow: Glasgow Caledonian University.

Sproull, Alan and Douglas Chalmers. 1998. *The Demand for Gaelic Artistic and Cultural Products and Services: Patterns and Impacts*. Glasgow: Glasgow Caledonian University.

Tsunoda, Tasaku. 2006. *Language Endangerment and Language Revitalization*. New York: Mouton de Gruyter.

Williams, Colin. 2000. Community Empowerment through Language Planning Intervention. In Colin Williams (ed.), *Language Revitalization. Policy and Planning in Wales*, 221–246. Cardiff: University of Wales Press.

11

Organisational Language Planning: Gaelic Language Plans in the Public Sector

Robert Dunbar

The Gaelic Language (Scotland) Act 2005[1] (the 'Act') is the single most important piece of legislation to have been enacted in support of the Gaelic language. Passed by the Scottish Parliament on 21 April 2005, it received Royal Assent on 1 June of that year, and came into force on 13 February 2006.[2] The Act created a dedicated language planning body, Bòrd na Gàidhlig (the 'Bòrd'), and a mechanism, Gaelic language plans, by which potentially all Scottish public authorities – essentially, the wider public sector subject to regulation by Scotland's devolved institutions, as well as those institutions themselves – can be subjected to obligations in relation to their use of, and policy for, the Gaelic language. In this respect, the Act replicated the approach taken in Wales in the Welsh Language Act 1993 and in the Republic of Ireland in the Official Languages Act 2003, in which language plans, or 'schemes', to use the term employed in those two pieces of legislation, were central. Before the Act, public authorities in Scotland were under no obligation to use Gaelic in dealing with the public or to provide other support for the language, although a small number of such bodies, including Comhairle nan Eilean Siar (CNES), the local authority for the Outer Hebrides, the Highland Council and the Scottish Executive (as the Scottish Government was called prior to 2007), had voluntarily adopted policies on these matters.[3]

Both domestic legislation and international legal standards in relation to minority languages can have a variety of aims. In some cases, the aim is political: relations between the linguistic minority and the majority can be a source of tensions which can lead to instability, secessionist movements and, in extreme cases, violence, and in such circumstances legislation can be intended to assuage such tensions.[4] In some cases – particularly those in which significant numbers of members of the linguistic minority are unable to communicate in the majority or official language – legal measures are motivated by equality considerations: provision of minority language services facilitates equal access to such services for members of the minority who are unable to communicate effectively in the majority or official language.[5] And, often, the aim is the revitalisation of the minority language.[6]

ORGANISATIONAL LANGUAGE PLANNING

This last aim is central to the Act. In its 2003 consultation document on the Gaelic Language (Scotland) Bill – the bill which ultimately became the Act – the Scottish Executive made abundantly clear that the overarching purpose of the legislation was the revitalisation of the Gaelic language in Scotland. For example, the consultation document noted the following:

> Language legislation, as is proposed in this draft Bill, is not uncommon. From Wales to New Zealand, it is an established and proven method of protecting and supporting minority languages. This draft Bill seeks to contribute to a sustainable future for Gaelic in Scotland. The aim is to increase access to Gaelic in Scotland's public life and thus to increase the use and appreciation of Gaelic and the confidence of speakers and learners. (Scottish Executive 2003: 6)

With regard to the Gaelic language plans, the consultation document again made clear the centrality of language revitalisation, and acknowledged the inspiration in this respect provided by the earlier Welsh and Irish legislation:

> The duty to consider, and the encouragement of public bodies to have Gaelic language plans, is a practical step to increase the *use* and *profile* of Gaelic. This is similar to the approach in the Welsh Language Act 1993, and in the Republic of Ireland's more recent Official Language Equality Act 2003 [sic]. It is intended that this would redress the perceived low profile of Gaelic in Scottish public and official life which leads to its worth being questioned by speakers and non-speakers alike. Gaelic plans for public bodies will contribute to a sustainable future for Gaelic, *encouraging and stimulating opportunities for its use and raising the confidence of speakers and learners.* The purpose of a language plan would be to *facilitate increased public usage of Gaelic, improve the rights of Gaelic speakers to use the language in a wider range of contexts and promote an enhanced profile for the language.* (Scottish Executive 2003: 21; emphasis added)

In all of these references, promotion of the greater use of Gaelic is emphasised as of crucial importance; repeated reference is also made to increasing the profile of the language, and the confidence of speakers and learners. Thus, the legislation was conceived of as a means of 'status planning': modifying the functions which the language is meant to serve and enhancing its social and, one might add, its political position (Cooper 1989: 32–33).

The Gaelic language plan mechanism is set out in section 3 of the Act. It empowers Bòrd na Gàidhlig to give notice to any relevant public authority[7] to prepare a Gaelic language plan.[8] The Act indicates what the Bòrd should consider in exercising this power, and gives a right to public authorities to appeal to the Scottish Government against a notification by the Bòrd; thus far, none has done so.

With regard to the content of Gaelic language plans, the Act requires that every plan must set out the measures that the public authority will take in relation to the use of Gaelic in both its internal operations and the provision by it of any services to the public;[9] it must also set out the date by which the measures are to be taken.[10] Here, we again see the centrality in the Act and in particular in the plan mechanism of the promotion of greater use of Gaelic. In preparing its Gaelic language plan, a public authority must have regard to a number of matters, including the Bòrd's most recent National Gaelic Language Plan, the extent to which persons in relation to whom the authority provides services use Gaelic, the potential for developing the use of Gaelic in the provision of services to the public or in its internal operations, any representations made to the authority – and the authority is required to consult the public in relation to its plan[11] – and any guidance given by the Bòrd or by the Scottish Government. While the focus of this paper will be on the implications of Gaelic language plans for the use of Gaelic by public authorities in service delivery and internal operations – so-called 'Core Commitments' of the plans – the requirement of public authorities to consider the Bòrd's National Gaelic Language Plan, which the Bòrd is required to produce every five years, is also important, as it is a means of translating the Bòrd's more general policies, as reflected in the National Plan, into policies of public authorities.

Once the public authority's plan has been prepared, it must be submitted to the Bòrd for approval[12] – again, a refusal by the Bòrd to approve a plan can be appealed to the Scottish Government, though this has not yet occurred – and the plan must be renewed every five years.[13]

In 2007, the Bòrd issued its guidance on the preparation of Gaelic language plans (the '2007 Guidance') (Bòrd na Gàidhlig 2007b);[14] in February 2014 the Bòrd issued a revised version of the guidance in draft form for public consultation (the '2014 Draft Guidance'), but the final version has not yet been issued (Bòrd na Gàidhlig 2014). The centrality of language revitalisation to the Gaelic language plan mechanism is also apparent in the 2007 Guidance. In discussing the rationale for this mechanism, the Bòrd made explicit reference to key language policy and planning concepts. It noted, for example, that '[a] key element to enhancing the status, and in turn usage and acquisition, of Gaelic is the creation of conditions for its use in public life'. The Bòrd suggested that Gaelic language plans should assist members of the public who may wish to use Gaelic in conducting their business with the public body, and assist employees of the public authority who may wish to use Gaelic in their work within the organisation. By providing for the use of Gaelic, the Bòrd argued, the plans 'will increase the profile and visibility of the language, helping to increase its status'. The Bòrd also noted that in order to deliver Gaelic provision, 'Gaelic-language skills will become useful job-skills in an increasingly wide range of employments', thereby greatly enhancing the perceived utility of the language and the desire of speakers to pass it on and non-speakers to acquire it (Bòrd na Gàidhlig 2007b: 6).

The Bòrd's conception here of how Gaelic language plans may contribute to Gaelic language revitalisation calls to mind the 'Catherine Wheel', a model developed by the Catalan sociolinguist Miquel Strubell to guide minority language revitalisation. This model suggests that a greater supply of public services in Gaelic may lead to greater consumption of those services, thereby enhancing the perceived utility of the language, thereby enhancing the motivation to acquire and use it, thereby leading to more social use of Gaelic, and greater demand for yet more services, public and otherwise, creating a self-reinforcing process of expanded language acquisition and use (Walsh and McLeod 2008: 23–24; Dunbar 2010: 151, and the references therein).[15]

In the 2007 Guidance, the Bòrd provided advice on how a public authority should go about preparing its Gaelic language plan, and on how the plan should be structured. The Bòrd suggested that 'in some situations' it may be helpful for the authority to consider establishing a Gaelic Language Plan working group, which could include senior officers of the authority, to prepare and coordinate the implementation of the plan. The Bòrd did not, however, specify the situations in which such a working group would be helpful or, indeed, advisable. Given that recent research on the implementation of language legislation in Ireland, Wales and Finland has highlighted the importance of buy-in and, indeed, leadership at senior levels (Ó Flatharta et al. 2014), perhaps the establishment of such working groups should become standard practice. The Bòrd also suggested, but did not require, that public authorities undertake an 'internal language capacity audit' to determine their existing capacity to deliver services to the public and to assist in the implementation of their plan (Bòrd na Gàidhlig 2007b: 11).[16] Furthermore, the Bòrd noted that the Act requires that public authorities, in preparing their plan, take into account any representations from the public, and to comply with this requirement the Bòrd recommended that public authorities conduct a public consultation exercise on their draft plan (Bòrd na Gàidhlig 2007: 13).

The 2007 Guidance sets out how public authorities should structure their Gaelic language plans, and the Bòrd has supplemented this with Gaelic and English versions of a template.[17] The plans are required to describe the authority's 'Core Commitments', which should detail how the authority will use Gaelic in relation to its internal processes, how it will be used in any of its services to the public, and a timetable for the implementation of individual commitments. The Bòrd identifies four 'areas' that it wishes public authorities to address in this part of their plans, namely: (1) identity, encompassing the use of Gaelic in corporate identity and on external and internal signage; (2) communications, encompassing the use of Gaelic at points of contact with the public, in telephone, mail and email communications, on forms used by the public, in public meetings, and in making complaints; (3) publications, encompassing the use of Gaelic in public relations and in dealing with the media, in printed material, on websites, and in exhibitions; and (4) staffing, encompassing Gaelic language training and learning for staff, the recruitment of Gaelic-speaking staff, and the use of Gaelic advertising for staff posts.

The Bòrd's long-term vision, as set out in the 2007 Guidance, was that the level of Gaelic provision by public authorities would increase incrementally over time; in other words, the level of Gaelic use of the public body in dealing with the public and in its internal operations would increase from one Gaelic language plan to the next (Bòrd na Gàidhlig 2007b: 5). When discussing the 'internal language capacity audit', the Bòrd stressed that the purpose of developing a Gaelic language plan was to expand Gaelic language provision, and that all public authorities would be expected 'to illustrate the extent to which they will provide increased provision and services from the level they currently offer' (Bòrd na Gàidhlig 2007b: 11). However, the Bòrd also noted that the Act was designed to take into account the need for a flexible approach to Gaelic development in Scotland, and that the guidance 'will enable the development of Gaelic Language Plans that are reasonable and proportionate according to the particular circumstances of individual public authorities' (Bòrd na Gàidhlig 2007b: 11).

The need for a flexible approach is due to the demographics of the Gaelic language. Gaelic speakers comprise only slightly over one per cent of the Scottish population. In some parts of the country, such as the Outer Hebrides and some parts of the Inner Hebrides (notably in Skye, Tiree and to a lesser extent Islay), there are significant concentrations of Gaelic speakers, whereas in most other areas, both numbers and percentages of speakers are low; even in Glasgow and Edinburgh, where there are significant numbers of Gaelic speakers, they make up a tiny percentage of the population (National Records of Scotland (NRS) 2015). The ability to deliver services through the medium of Gaelic and to promote its use more generally is clearly more limited in such areas than in places such as the Outer Hebrides, both because of more limited demand for such services and opportunities for such use, and a much smaller pool of people who could provide such services and interact in Gaelic more generally. The policy challenge is to ensure that the flexibility inherent in the Act is not used to minimise the commitments of public authorities relating to their use of Gaelic.

In the 2007 Guidance, the Bòrd set out its general approach with respect to how the flexibility inherent in the Gaelic language plan mechanism should be applied. It noted that it was not possible to be precise about the specific content for individual public authorities, but that, generally,

> [i]n those geographical locations in which the percentages or numbers of Gaelic speakers is greater, the scope of the Gaelic Language Plan of the public authority will be wider and the level of commitments in it will be stronger. (Bòrd na Gàidhlig 2007b: 19)

The level of provision expected varies, therefore, according to the absolute number of Gaelic speakers in the service area, and their proportion as a total of the population.

The Bòrd then identified four 'broad categories of expected Gaelic language provision'. First, for public authorities operating wholly in areas in which people with Gaelic language skills (that is, the ability to understand, speak, read or write Gaelic) form a majority, institutions should, over the longer term, strive to achieve bilingualism and should work towards practices under which Gaelic can be used in day to day operations (Bòrd na Gàidhlig 2007a: 31). The first National Gaelic Language Plan (the 'First National Plan'), covering the period 2007 to 2012, suggested that this category would include areas such as the Western Isles, Skye and Tiree. Based on 2011 Census figures, the only council area which would fit into this category is that of Comhairle nan Eilean Siar, an area in which 61.2 per cent of the population had Gaelic language skills (NRS 2015: supporting spreadsheet, figure 1).

The second category comprises public authorities whose areas of operation include districts in which people with Gaelic language skills formed a local majority (as well as districts in which Gaelic is not the language of the majority), which, based on the 2011 Census, would appear to include some districts on Skye (NRS 2015). Such authorities are expected to work towards, again within a reasonable timescale and having regard to particular circumstances, creating conditions in which Gaelic can be used across services to the public from offices based in those Gaelic-majority districts. In such districts, the public authorities should endeavour to identify 'a broad range of commitments' to include in their plans, some of which may be at a high level (Bòrd na Gàidhlig 2007b: 20).

The third category comprises public authorities serving districts in which people with Gaelic language skills do not form a majority but are present in significant numbers or percentages, or in significant concentrations. In such cases, the public authority will work towards, within a reasonable timescale and having regard to its particular circumstances, providing services in Gaelic that local Gaelic speakers are more likely to access, such as agricultural services. The First National Plan indicated that districts covered by this category might include many parts of the Highland and Argyll and Bute council areas.

The final category comprised all other areas in Scotland, in which there are low percentages of Gaelic speakers and where significant Gaelic provision may therefore not be possible. This category would presumably include all areas outside of the Highlands and Islands, including even urban areas such as Glasgow and Edinburgh, in which absolute numbers of people with Gaelic language skills are relatively high, but in which they make up tiny percentages of the local population.[18] Even in these districts, though, public authorities should still endeavour to work towards, within a reasonable timescale and having regard to their particular circumstances, identifying service areas in which some Gaelic provision can be made available.

In its second National Gaelic Language Plan, covering the years 2012–2017 (the 'Second National Plan') (Bòrd na Gàidhlig 2012), the Bòrd signalled a somewhat different approach in relation to the flexibility provided by the Gaelic language plan mechanism than that set out in the 2007 Guidance. In particular, the Second National Plan provided the following:

> In communities where 20% or more of the population have Gaelic abilities, Gaelic's use should be strengthened by means of the provision by public authorities of bilingual services, such as education and communication with the public . . .
>
> In other areas with significant concentrations of Gaelic speakers, support will be available for a wide range of community initiatives to promote the learning and use of Gaelic. (Bòrd na Gàidhlig 2012: 30–31)

The Bòrd indicated that a similar approach would be taken to enhancing the use of Gaelic in the workplace through Gaelic language plans including an expectation that public authorities would 'offer training, as appropriate, with a view to increasing the availability of services and employment opportunities in Gaelic and promoting a positive Gaelic ethos' (Bòrd na Gàidhlig 2012: 35). The third National Gaelic Language Plan, for 2018–23, is largely silent with respect to the Bòrd's approach to statutory Gaelic Language Plans (Bòrd na Gàidhlig, 2018).

Thus, the Bòrd seems to have taken a somewhat stronger view of what is expected of public authorities operating in areas with significant concentrations of people with Gaelic abilities, making relatively unambiguous reference to a bilingual approach. They have also made clear that more is expected in terms of the use of Gaelic in the workplace, as well as in terms of service delivery to the public, in such areas. Furthermore, the Bòrd has lowered the threshold for such an approach from areas with a majority of the population having Gaelic abilities to areas in which at least 20 per cent have such abilities; as a practical matter, given that there are few communities outside the Outer Hebrides which have such percentages, these targets will not significantly increase the areas in which something approaching full bilingualism is expected, but they do ensure that areas with less than a majority of people with Gaelic abilities, which could in the near future include several districts even in the Outer Hebrides, are covered by the strongest commitments. This approach has been adopted in the 2014 Draft Guidance, but as noted above, the guidance itself still has not been made public, and therefore the 2007 Guidance still applies. This leaves public authorities – and the Bòrd itself – in a rather confusing position, as they are required in preparing their Gaelic language plans to have regard both to the Bòrd's guidance and the Bòrd's most recent National Plan.

How might the effectiveness of the Gaelic language plan mechanism be assessed? As we have seen, both the Act itself and the Gaelic language plan mechanism which it creates are overwhelmingly concerned with increasing the use of Gaelic, and the Bòrd considers that Gaelic language plans can contribute to this by increasing the level of Gaelic services provided to the public, increasing the number of jobs available to people with Gaelic language skills, and generally enhancing the status of the language so that more people are motivated to learn, transmit and use the language in daily life. A first step in assessing the effectiveness of the plan mechanism would therefore involve a textual analysis of the Gaelic language plans themselves; are the plans themselves sufficiently strong to be able to effect significant changes in practices? A second step would be to investigate the extent to which the plans are actually being implemented by public bodies; if plans are not being fully implemented, the expected impacts on behaviour of the public will be blunted. A third step would be to analyse the behavioural and attitudinal changes that plans and their implementation (or incomplete implementation) produce. There are two aspects to this. Where legal standards and other formal policies are designed to create enhanced opportunities for the language to be used in the internal workings of an organisation and in its dealings with the public, to what extent are users of the language actually taking advantage of such opportunities? And, more generally, what is the broader impact of legal standards and formal policies on the attitudes and behaviour of the public, Gaelic-speaking and otherwise?

To date, a relatively small amount of research has been done on the Gaelic language plan mechanism, and it has mainly focused on step one: analysis of the content of the plans (see Walsh and McLeod 2008, 2011; Milligan et al. 2010; MacCaluim 2011a, 2011b; McLeod 2011a, 2011b). This focus is primarily due to the lack of data relevant to steps two and three, and the costs involved in the collection of such data; by contrast, the plans themselves are in the public domain, available on the Bòrd website and, usually, the website of the public authority itself. As a result of the lack of data on steps two and three, though, only the most tentative conclusions can be offered at present on the impact and effectiveness of the mechanism.

With regard to step two, an analysis of implementation of plans, a fundamental problem relates to the design of the Act itself, as the mechanisms in the legislation for monitoring and enforcing the Gaelic language plan mechanism (and the Act more generally) are weak. There is, for example, no Language Commissioner to monitor implementation, or legal recourse to tribunals or courts, as exists, for example, in Ireland under the Irish Official Languages Act 2003 and in Wales under the Welsh Language (Wales) Measure 2011. The Act does allow the Bòrd to require public authorities to submit at least a year after adoption of a Gaelic language plan a report on the extent to which the public authority has implemented its plan, and if the Bòrd feels that the authority is failing to implement the plan the Bòrd can report this to Scottish Ministers, who may direct the authority to implement its plan.[19] It appears, however, that the Bòrd has not referred any alleged failure in implementation to Scottish Ministers.

It is understood that the Bòrd now requests all public authorities with an approved plan to submit a report on implementation, and the Bòrd has commissioned research to examine these implementation reports. Such reports and the commissioned research could well provide some valuable data with regard to implementation, but the Bòrd has not made either public. Given the importance that the Bòrd has placed on the Gaelic job creation potential of Gaelic language plans and the attitudinal and behavioural changes which the creation of such jobs could produce, up-to-date data on the numbers of such jobs that have been created as a result of Gaelic language plans would also be extremely useful.[20] A range of potential problems in implementing plans – both ideological (a suspected 'monolingual mentality' in public authorities in Scotland; a view that Gaelic is not relevant outside its Highland and Hebridean 'heartlands') and practical (small numbers of potential users of Gaelic, resulting in high costs of provision, difficulties in recruitment; deep-seated diglossic patterns that could depress demand; difficulties in relating to unfamiliar or under-developed terminology relating to the public services being provided) – have been identified (McLeod 2006). However, in the absence of any significant data on implementation, it is not clear whether or to what extent such concerns have been borne out.

With regard to step three, an analysis of the behavioural and attitudinal changes which may have been produced by the plans, we again have virtually no data that would allow us to come to any conclusions. Data on the degree to which persons with Gaelic abilities have actually taken advantage of any opportunities that have been created by Gaelic language plans to use Gaelic in dealing with public authorities would be of fundamental importance, as would an assessment of levels of satisfaction with such services. Broader attitudinal research would be useful, but involves a range of methodological issues which would require close consideration (see Birnie in this volume for one novel approach).

As of May 2017, fifty-five public authorities have had their Gaelic language plans approved by the Bòrd, although four of those public authorities have ceased to exist owing to mergers. Sixteen of those public authorities have had their second plan approved, and one, Highlands and Islands Enterprise, has had its third plan approved. The pace of approval has been rather slow; it had been anticipated that the Bòrd would approve between eight and ten plans per year, and at that pace, between eighty and one hundred should have been approved by now.

Unsurprisingly, the first public authorities required in 2007 by the Bòrd to produce a Gaelic language plan included the three councils that contained the highest percentages of Gaelic speakers and in which the strongest vestigially Gaelic-speaking communities are to be found, Comhairle nan Eilean Siar (CNES), Highland Council, and Argyll and Bute Council, as well as HIE, which has a particularly important role in relation to economic and social development in these Gaelic-speaking communities. Also included were the Scottish Government and the Scottish Parliament Corporate Body. Only two of the fifty-eight public authorities could be said to be organisations which fit into the first category set out in the 2007 Guidance, authorities whose areas of operation coincide with areas in which a majority has Gaelic abilities: CNES and NHS Eileanan Siar, the health authority for the Outer Hebrides. Perhaps ten others would fit into the second (or possibly the third): the two councils already mentioned and HIE, NHS Highland, the Crofting Commission, University of the Highlands and Islands, Sabhal Mòr Ostaig, Lews Castle College, Highlands and Islands Airports Ltd, and Caledonian Maritime Assets Ltd (which supplies the ferries used by Caledonian MacBrayne), although several other authorities, such as the Scottish Government, Police Scotland, the Scottish Ambulance Service, and Visit Scotland, have operations in Gaelic-speaking areas. While Glasgow City and Edinburgh Councils would probably be considered to fit within category four, given the numbers of Gaelic speakers in both cities, their plans are also significant ones. Twenty-three of Scotland's thirty-two councils have had their Gaelic language plans approved. Several national agencies involved in Scotland's education system have had plans approved, as have three universities that offer degrees in Celtic or Gaelic Studies – Aberdeen, Edinburgh and Glasgow. Finally, a number of national cultural institutions, such as the National Library of Scotland, the National Museum of Scotland, the National Galleries of Scotland, and Creative Scotland have had their plans approved.

Space does not permit a comprehensive review of approved plans. The plan of NHS Eileanan Siar is, however, particularly interesting. Given it is one of two public authorities operating wholly in an area in which those with Gaelic language skills form a majority, one would expect, based on the 2007 Guidance, that its plan would either reflect or aspire to a fully bilingual service. Unfortunately, based on the approved plan itself, this does not appear to be the case. The shortcomings in the NHS Eileanan Siar plan are problematic because, unlike most public authorities, even councils, it is highly likely that most people will have significant and regular contact with the health service. Some of the difficulties evident in the content of the NHS Eileanan Siar Gaelic language plan also usefully illustrate difficulties which are evident in many other of the approved plans.

NHS Eileanan Siar's first Gaelic language plan was approved by the Bòrd on 19 June 2012 (NHS Eileanan Siar 2012). One immediate issue is that the commitments are different for NHS Eileanan Siar itself and the twelve independent GP practices which form part of the NHS service in the Outer Hebrides; in respect of the latter, the plan only commits NHS Eileanan Siar to 'encouraging' the practices to take actions. This is presumably because of the semi-autonomous relationship between the NHS Eileanan Siar and such practices; however, this is highly problematic, as independent GP practices are frequently the first point of contact the public has with the health service, and if the language policies of such practices are not being effectively regulated under the plan mechanism then the possibility of providing anything approaching a fully bilingual health service in the strongest Gaelic-speaking part of the country is in effect significantly compromised.

With respect to 'identity', the NHS Eileanan Siar commitments generally reflect a bilingual approach: they commit to the general use of a bilingual logo (1.1(a), p. 14) and to the development of fully bilingual external signage (1.2(a), p. 16, though only 'as part of any upgrade' of signage), with a similar commitment to internal signage (1.2(b), p. 17). With respect to 'communications', however – a crucial area for a provider of public services – the commitments are more tentative. The plan raises the possibility of creating a logo on staff identity cards for members of staff who speak Gaelic (2.1(a), p. 18); in terms of actual service delivery, this is important, as it would alert users of NHS services to the possibility that they can use Gaelic in dealing with staff, an important aspect of what is known as 'active offer'. However, the commitment is only to 'consider' the creation of such a logo, and that it would only apply to members of staff who 'wish to indicate that they are Gaelic speakers'. Commitments to 'consider' a particular action rather than actually taking the action are very common features of Gaelic language plans, but they do not promote any certainty as to what the public can expect and may well not result in any provision at all.

With regard to telephone calls, there is no commitment to providing a bilingual service; rather, the plan merely provides that NHS Eileanan Siar 'should encourage non-Gaelic-speaking members of staff who deal with calls from the public, to acquire basic Gaelic language skills, in their own time' (2.2(a), p. 19). Gaelic-speaking members of the public are, based on this commitment, unlikely to know what sort of telephone service they are entitled to receive, and in such circumstances it is difficult to say that the use of Gaelic is being promoted. In fact, this commitment falls below others which frequently appear in Gaelic language plans, which involve the provision of a greeting in Gaelic, followed by a transfer to a Gaelic-speaking member of staff.

With regard to the NHS Eileanan Siar's 'Language Line' service, which offers an instant access interpretation facility to provide information to service users whose first language is not English, the plan commits the NHS Eileanan Siar to 'investigating' the provision of a Gaelic option (2.2(b)). The completion date for this investigation was December 2015, but it does not appear that any Gaelic option is yet available: the NHS Eileanan Siar website directs users to an NHS 24 service which offers ten languages as well as British Sign Language, but not in Gaelic.[21] This is one example of how plan commitments are not being translated into practice, and the NHS Eileanan Siar is far from unique in this although, as noted earlier, significant data on implementation of plans are not yet available.

With regard to mail and email, the plan acknowledges that there is 'no formal system in place to reply in Gaelic to any letters or e-mails . . . which are in Gaelic'; although 'there are many fluent Gaelic speakers amongst NHS Eileanan Siar staff, there is less confidence amongst these speakers in their Gaelic literacy abilities', so 'the likelihood of Gaelic letters or e-mails being dealt with quickly and efficiently is not guaranteed'. The only action that the plan proposes, however, is that all letters should have the bilingual NHS Eileanan Siar logo at the top, and that strap lines and slogans 'should' be bilingual (2.3(a), p. 20), which is again a commitment that falls below the commitment to respond in Gaelic to written communications in Gaelic, something that is found in many Gaelic language plans of authorities that would not be included in category one. The NHS Eileanan Siar plan notes that '[f]ortunately, the receipt of Gaelic letters or e-mails from members of the public is a very rare occurrence' (2.3, p. 20); given that there is no commitment to respond in Gaelic, this is hardly surprising, and it is worrying that this situation could be described as 'fortunate' in a Gaelic language plan whose very raison d'être is to increase Gaelic language use.

Perhaps the most important area of the NHS Eileanan Siar Gaelic language plan relates to front-line patient services. The plan notes that many nurses in the service are fluent Gaelic speakers, as are a large number of staff involved in family health and community services and in chaplaincy services (2.6, p. 21). Here, the commitments are stronger. With regard to Gaelic in clinical services, the commitment is to 'ensure that patients who would prefer, or feel more comfortable, being attended to by staff primarily through the medium of Gaelic are catered for in this regard', although the plan notes (for no obvious purpose, if the commitment is an unqualified one) that this 'would primarily concern patients such as the elderly, those in long-stay wards, those requiring speech and language therapy, patients with dementia and psychiatric patients' (2.6(a), p. 22). An issue here, though, is not the commitment itself, but making it a practical possibility. While the plan mentions nursing and other staff, it makes no mention of other types of medical professionals, including doctors. Furthermore, it merely provides that where Gaelic-speaking staff are on duty, 'they should be encouraged to provide an active offer for patients to use Gaelic'; it is difficult to see how the commitment to provide such service could be guaranteed if staff are only 'encouraged', rather than required (as, perhaps, a term of employment), to provide such services. In terms of recruitment, however (4.2, p. 33), the plan only commits human resources to undertake a review of the categories of posts to establish which can be designated 'Gaelic Essential' or 'Gaelic Desirable', and there is no firm commitment to a completion date for this review; furthermore, the plan does not actually commit the authority to designating posts in such a way.

With regard to publications (section 3, p. 25), the commitments are very general. With regard to 'public information', the plan commits NHS Eileanan Siar to 'continue to extend the range of the inclusion of Gaelic content in public information leaflets, booklets or posters', and to this end will carry out an audit of resources currently available and produce guidance (3.1(a), p. 26). A similar commitment is made in relation to NHS Eileanan Siar magazines, newsletters and circulars (3.1(c), p. 27). The use of the word 'increase' in relation to such provision is highly problematic: it is unclear what the baseline is by which to measure it, and even a tiny incremental change to that baseline might be considered an 'increase' which satisfies the commitment. Crucially, users are left unclear as to what level of service they can actually expect. Yet, such commitments are quite common in Gaelic language plans.

A final example of the highly problematic nature of many of the commitments in the NHS Eileanan Siar Gaelic language plan is in relation to its website (3.4, p. 28). The authority acknowledged on publication of its plan, in 2012, that there is virtually no Gaelic content on its website and committed itself to developing the Gaelic content of the website 'where suitable, with attention given to appropriate content, commensurate with the bilingual character of the NHS Eileanan Siar's corporate identity' (3.4(a), p. 28). In spite of this commitment, a thorough examination of the authority's website in August 2018 (http://www.wihb.scot.nhs.uk/) indicated that little has changed: there appear to be no Gaelic web pages, and a search of the website using the search term 'Gàidhlig' revealed no hits.

While, as noted, there is very little data or research on implementation, a recent controversy involving the National Museum of Scotland's Gaelic language plan provides another illustration of the problems that can occur in the transition from policy on paper to practice within an institution. The National Museum of Scotland (NMS) opened a much-anticipated special exhibition on the Jacobites in June 2017, which was greeted with protests from Gaelic activists concerning the lack of Gaelic signage and the general marginalisation of the language in the exhibit.[22] The webpages dedicated to the exhibition appeared to be in English alone, there did not appear to be a Gaelic version of the exhibition guide, and the interpretative materials in the exhibit were also in English only, although Gaelic translations of the main panels of the exhibition could later be downloaded from the primary webpage for the exhibit.[23] At the time, the NMS Gaelic language plan covered the period 2012 to 2015 (National Museums Scotland 2012), although a second plan for the period 2017–22 was approved after this controversy. Section 3.2.2, in the 'Core Commitments' section of the first NMS Gaelic language plan provides that the NMS will '[c]ontinue to provide side by side English and Gaelic interpretation for exhibitions that tour to Gaelic-speaking areas or that have a Gaelic related theme or connection'. Section 3.5.2 of the first plan provides that the NMS will '[c]ontinue to produce dual English and Gaelic guides for relevant exhibitions'.

The NMS has offered in justification for its treatment of Gaelic in the exhibition that the museum does not think it is appropriate for this exhibition to be bilingual since its approach 'is to explore the Jacobite cause in its full pan-European historical context', and that '[t]here is a common misconception that the story of the Jacobites is solely a Highlands story when . . . the Jacobite movement had supporters in England, Ireland, France and other continental countries as well as both the Lowlands and Highlands of Scotland'.[24] However, the first NMS Gaelic language plan did not require that bilingual provision is required only when an exhibition is 'solely a Highlands story', but when the exhibition has 'a Gaelic related theme or connection', and it would be difficult to conceive of a topic that has a stronger or more obvious 'Gaelic related theme or connection' than the Jacobites. In response to the controversy, the Bòrd issued a press release in which it stopped short of directly criticising the NMS, and it appears that no further steps, including using its powers under section 6 of the Act, have been taken by the Bòrd in relation to what appears to be a fairly clear breach of an important commitment of a significant national cultural institution.

To conclude, it is important to reiterate that a full assessment of the content of over fifty approved Gaelic language plans was not possible in the space available, and that relatively little can yet be said about implementation or the impact of the plans on language use and attitudes. The plans have produced some positive changes, at least in terms of policy. For example, virtually all public authorities with Gaelic language plans have agreed to some form of bilingual logo (although there appears to be considerable variation in the approach taken: McLeod 2011b), and many authorities' plans provide for the use of bilingual letterheads, straplines and so forth. There is frequently a commitment to using at least some Gaelic in external signage, and in the stronger plans the commitment approaches full bilingual provision. In other areas, though, particularly in relation to communication with the public, the record is decidedly mixed; frequently commitments are phrased as aspirations rather than hard obligations, or are subject to a variety of conditions relating, for example, to sufficiency of human or other resources; sometimes the commitment is nothing more than an agreement to form a policy of some sort at some point in the future. In all such cases, users are not provided with a clear idea of what they can expect in terms of Gaelic-medium service provision. Although the Bòrd fully expects that commitments will be strengthened in subsequent Gaelic language plans, changes have frequently not been dramatic. There is also not much evidence of a coordinated approach to Gaelic language plans; often, the commitments of authorities which serve the same public differ in significant ways, and in these circumstances it is unlikely that members of the public could be expected to know what to expect in terms of basic service provision in their area. The problem is compounded by the fact that many public authorities operating in particular locations have still not prepared plans. Thus there remains a range of serious concerns about the content of the plans.

As noted, there are very little data and almost no research on implementation of plans, nor is much yet known about any behavioural and attitudinal changes which the plans have effected. There are, however, reasons to be concerned about implementation, and the recent controversy concerning the NMS's Jacobites exhibition illustrates that the mechanisms for dealing with perceived failures in implementation are not particularly robust. While activists could demonstrate against the authority, there was no obvious avenue for them to seek redress, in stark contrast to the situation in Ireland and Wales. After ten years of operation, it does appear that the time is now ripe for a more systematic evaluation of the operation and effectiveness of the Gaelic language plan mechanism. Ultimately, the mechanism was meant to increase use of Gaelic and to promote the status and acquisition of Gaelic more generally, and if it is failing to deliver such benefits, content, implementation and enforcement of the plan mechanism needs to be reconsidered, and alternatives, including, perhaps, a regime based on clear language rights and a language commissioner rather than administrative mechanisms such as Gaelic language plans, need to be examined.

Notes

1. 2005 asp 7. Available online at http://www.legislation.gov.uk/asp/2005/7/contents (last accessed 15 August 2018).
2. The Gaelic Language (Scotland) Act 2005 Commencement Order 2006, SSI 2006/31 (C.3), 25 January 2006. Available online at http://www.legislation.gov.uk/ssi/2006/31/pdfs/ssi_20060031_en.pdf (last accessed 15 August 2018).
3. CNES, known as Comhairle nan Eilean at the time, had adopted a bilingual policy in 1975 which it occasionally updated.

4. This was an important factor in the passage of Canada's Official Languages Act 1969 and its Constitution Act 1982, with its guarantees for the rights of 'official language minorities' (French and English). The Preamble to the Council of Europe's Framework Convention for the Protection of National Minorities asserts that 'the protection of national minorities is essential to stability, democratic security and peace in this continent': Council of Europe, Strasbourg, February 1995, Council of Europe Document H (95) 10, ETS No. 157. Available online at http://www.coe.int/en/web/conventions/search-on-treaties/-/conventions/treaty/157 (last accessed 15 August 2018). The Preamble to the European Charter for Regional or Minority Languages expresses similar ideas: Council of Europe, Strasbourg, November 1992, ETS No. 148. Available online at http://www.coe.int/en/web/conventions/search-on-treaties/-/conventions/treaty/148 (last accessed 15 August 2018).
5. This is also a key aim of Canada's official language laws and policies.
6. This is certainly the overriding aim of the European Charter for Regional or Minority Languages, supra, note 4, which the UK ratified in 2001 and under which Gaelic is given protection.
7. Defined in subsection 10(2) of the Act to include Scottish public authorities, cross-border public authorities (but only in relation to functions they exercise in or as regards Scotland which do not relate to reserved matters under the Scotland Act 1998) and the Scottish Parliamentary Corporate Body (the body created under section 21 of the Scotland Act 1998 to manage the staffing, property and services of the parliament).
8. Subsection 3(1).
9. Paragraph 3(4)(a) and subsection 10(4).
10. Paragraph 3(4)(b). Plans must also contain any further information that may be prescribed by the Scottish Government, in consultation with the Bòrd, as set out in regulations made by the Scottish Government (paragraph 3(4)(c) and subsection 3(7)), but thus far no such regulations have been made.
11. Subsection 3(6).
12. Subsection 5(1).
13. Section 7.
14. The Bòrd is empowered to issue such guidance under section 8 of the Act, and the guidance must be approved by the Scottish Government. The Scottish Government has not yet issued any guidance, but has approved the Bòrd's guidance.
15. Strubell has produced different versions – and he himself and others have noted that there are many factors which might impair the operation of the model (see Walsh and McLeod 2008, at 24).
16. Dr Timothy Armstrong has prepared a paper on best practice in collecting data on language use and ability in an organisation, which the Bòrd makes available on its website, available at http://www.gaidhlig.scot/bord/gaelic-you/tools-and-resources/development/ (last accessed 15 August 2018).
17. Available online at http://www.gaidhlig.scot/bord/gaelic-you/tools-and-resources/development/ (last accessed 15 August 2018).

18. In Glasgow City Council area, for example, in 2011 there were 9,469 people with Gaelic language skills, but they made up only 1.7 per cent of the population. In Edinburgh City Council area, there were 5,935 people with such skills, but they made up only 1.3 per cent of the population (National Records of Scotland 2015: supporting spreadsheet, figure 1).
19. Section 6.
20. There has been some very useful research done on the 'Gaelic labour market', but it is not particularly recent and will not fully reflect any changes in jobs in which Gaelic is an essential or desirable skill that have been effected by Gaelic language plans. See, for example, HECLA Consulting et al. (2008); Marsaili MacLeod (2009a, 2009b). It is understood that further research is being undertaken at present for the Bòrd on the present state of the Gaelic labour market.
21. Available online at http://www.nhs24/scot/get-in-touch/language-line/ (last accessed 15 August 2018).
22. See, for example, http://www.scotsman.com/regions/edinburgh-fife-lothians/ national-museum-facing-protests-over-lack-of-gaelic-in-jacobites-exhibition-1- 4485300, http://www.heraldscotland.com/news/15368799.Protests_over_lack_ of_Gaelic_in_exhibition_on_Jacobite_uprisings/ (last accessed 15 August 2018).
23. Available online at https://www.nms.ac.uk/national-museum-of-scotland/ things-to-see-and-do/past-exhibitions/bonnie-prince-charlie-and-the-jacobites/.
24. Personal communication by email from NMS, Monday 17 July 2017.

References

Bòrd na Gàidhlig. 2007a. *The National Plan for Gaelic 2007–2012/Plana Nàiseanta na Gàidhlig 2007–2012*. Inbhir Nis/Inverness: Bòrd na Gàidhlig.

Bòrd na Gàidhlig. 2007b. *Guidance on the Development of Gaelic Language Plans/ Stiùireadh air Deasachadh Phlanaichean Gàidhlig*. Inverness/Inbhir Nis: Bòrd na Gàidhlig.

Bòrd na Gàidhlig. 2012. *National Gaelic Language Plan 2012–2017: Growth and Improvement/Plana Cànain Nàiseanta Gàidhlig 2012–2017: Fàs and Feabhas*. Inverness/Inbhir Nis: Bòrd na Gàidhlig.

Bòrd na Gàidhlig. 2014. *Dreachd dhen stiùireadh airson a bhith dealbh phlanaichean cànain Gàidhlig/Draft Guidance on the Development of Gaelic Language Plans*. Inverness/Inbhir Nis: Bòrd na Gaidhlig.

Bòrd na Gàidhlig. 2018. *National Gaelic Language Plan 2018–2023 / Am Plana Cànain Nàiseanta Gàidhlig 2018–2023*. Inbhir Nis/Inverness: Bòrd na Gàidhlig.

Cooper, Robert L. 1989. *Language Planning and Social Change*. Cambridge: Cambridge University Press.

Dunbar, Robert. 2010. Language Planning. In Moray Watson and Michelle Macleod (eds), *The Edinburgh Companion to the Gaelic Language*, 146–171. Edinburgh: Edinburgh University Press.

HECLA Consulting, Marsaili MacLeod, Mike Danson and Douglas Chalmers. 2008. *Measuring the Gaelic Labour Market: Current and Future Potential – Final Report, Stage 2*. Inverness: HECLA Consulting.

MacCaluim, Alasdair. 2011a. 'From Politics to Practice': A' Cruthachadh Plana Gàidhlig do Phàrlamaid na h-Alba. In John M. Kirk and Dónall P. Ó Baoill (eds), *Sustaining Minority Language Communities: Northern Ireland, the Republic of Ireland, and Scotland*, 187–191. Belfast: Cló Ollscoil na Banríona, Queen's University Belfast.

MacCaluim, Alasdair. 2011b. 'From Politics to Practice': Creating the Scottish Parliament's Gaelic Language Plan. In John M. Kirk and Dónall P. Ó Baoill (eds), *Sustaining Minority Language Communities: Northern Ireland, the Republic of Ireland, and Scotland*, 192–195. Belfast: Cló Ollscoil na Banríona, Queen's University Belfast.

MacLeod, Marsaili. 2009a. The Meaning of Work in the Gaelic Labour Market in the Highlands and Islands of Scotland. Aberdeen: University of Aberdeen, unpublished PhD thesis.

MacLeod, Marsaili. 2009b. Gaelic Language Skills in the Workplace. In John M. Kirk and Dónall P. Ó Baoill (eds), *Language and Economic Development: Northern Ireland, the Republic of Ireland, and Scotland*, 134–152. Belfast: Cló Ollscoil na Banríona, Queen's University Belfast.

McLeod, Wilson. 2006. Leasachadh solarachadh sheirbhisean poblach tro mheadhan na Gàidhlig: duilgheadasan idè-eòlach agus pragtaigeach. In Wilson McLeod (ed.), *Revitalising Gaelic in Scotland: Policy, Planning and Public Discourse*, 25–47. Edinburgh: Dunedin Academic Press.

McLeod, Wilson. 2011a. Planaichean Reachdail Gàidhlig: cothroman is cnapan-starra. In Richard A. V. Cox and Timothy Currie Armstrong (eds), *A' Cleachdadh na Gàidhlig: slatan-tomhais ann an dìon cànain sa choimhearsnachd*, 227–248. Clò Ostaig: Sabhal Mòr Ostaig, Slèite, An t-Eilean Sgitheanach.

McLeod, Wilson. 2011b. Gaelic Language Plans and the Issue of Bilingual Signs. In John M. Kirk and Dónall P. Ó Baoill (eds), *Sustaining Minority Language Communities: Northern Ireland, the Republic of Ireland, and Scotland*, 203–211. Belfast: Cló Ollscoil na Banríona, Queen's University Belfast.

Milligan, Lindsay, Douglas Chalmers and Hugh O'Donnell. 2010. Gaelic Language Plans in Context: Issues of Application and Tokenism. In Kenneth E. Nilsen (ed.), *Rannsachadh na Gàidhlig 5: Fifth Scottish Gaelic Research Conference*, 322–338. Sydney, CB: Cape Breton University Press.

National Museums Scotland/Taighean-tasgaidh Nàiseanta Alba. 2012. *Gaelic Language Plan 2012–2015/Plana Gàidhlig 2012–2015*. Edinburgh/Dùn Èideann.

National Records of Scotland. 2015. *Scotland's Census 2011: Gaelic Report (Part 1)*. Edinburgh: National Records of Scotland.

NHS Eileanan Siar/NHS Western Isles. 2012. *Gaelic Language Plan/Plàna Cànan Gàidhlig 2014–17*. Steòrnabhagh/Stornoway.

Ó Flatharta, Peadar, Siv Sandberg and Colin H. Williams. 2014. *From Act to Action: Implementing Language Legislation in Finland, Ireland, and Wales*. Baile Átha Cliath: Fiontar, Ollscoil Chathair Bhaile Átha Cliath.

Scottish Executive/Riaghaltas na h-Alba. 2003. *The Gaelic Language Bill Consultation Paper/Bile na Gàidhlig: Pàipear Comhaireleachaidh*. Edinburgh/Dùn Èideann: Scottish Government/Riaghaltas na h-Alba.

Walsh, John and Wilson McLeod. 2008. An Overcoat Wrapped Around an Invisible
    Man? Language Legislation and Language Revitalisation in Ireland and Scotland.
    Language Policy 7, 21–46.
Walsh, John and McLeod, Wilson. 2011. The Implementation of Language
    Legislation in Dublin and Glasgow. In John M. Kirk and Dónall P. Ó Baoill
    (eds), *Sustaining Minority Language Communities: Northern Ireland, the Republic
    of Ireland, and Scotland*, 156–175. Belfast: Cló Ollscoil na Banríona, Queen's
    University Belfast.

12

The Future of Gaelic Language Revitalisation in Scotland

Marsaili MacLeod and Cassie Smith-Christmas

Introduction

Individually and collectively, the chapters in this collection offer empirically rich and compelling insights into the modern Gaelic community and language planning initiatives. The cases examined here have shed light on the complex processes and patterns of Gaelic language acquisition, use and management across a range of spaces of interactions: in the community, in public organisations and in educational settings. Gaelic continues to be classified as 'definitely endangered' in the UNESCO Atlas of the World's Languages in Danger (Moseley 2010) on account of weak intergenerational transmission of Gaelic in the home. The contributions here clearly illustrate, however, that the decline of Gaelic as a 'mother tongue' is not necessarily incompatible with Gaelic's maintenance as an additional language used by an expanding bilingual population in private and social domains.

The socio-political status of Gaelic as a minority language plays a fundamental role in the degree of language acquisition, maintenance and use of Gaelic throughout an individual's lifespan, as well as at different geographical scales within Scotland. Central to the findings presented here, therefore, is the national policy for Gaelic, as enshrined in the Gaelic Language (Scotland) Act 2005 and implemented through Gaelic language plans and initiatives. As Dunbar explains, the overriding purpose of the Act and the National Gaelic Language Plan is the revitalisation of the Gaelic language. Yet the authors in this collection show that, some thirteen years after the ratification of the Act, it is unclear whether this framework is effecting the attitudinal and behavioural change it aims to produce. In this final and concluding chapter we synthesise the main themes which arise from our findings and elaborate the implications for theoretical claims about minority language revitalisation, for language planning and policy, and for future research.

Revitalising Gaelic in Scotland: issues and obstacles

Three cross-cutting issues can be elaborated from the authors' examinations. The first emergent theme is one of ambiguity: ambiguity over what it means to be a 'Gael' in modern Scotland; ambiguity over what revitalisation means in a national context today; and ambiguity over the policy and planning mechanisms best-suited to support the maintenance of a community of Gaelic bilinguals. The second and related unifying theme is one of new speakerhood, which connects with a burgeoning theoretical debate over the possibilities for first and second language acquisition of minority languages in so-called 'post-traditional' communities (cf. Nic Fhlannchadha and Hickey 2018). A third and final recurring theme is one of capacity: capacity within institutions and organisations which are committed to Gaelic language planning through statutory language plans or through their role in providing Gaelic materials and services.

Ideological ambiguities

McLeod's socio-historical review of 'new speakers' in Gaelic policy highlights an ambiguity over the policy response to continued language shift in Gaelic-speaking families and the role of intergenerational transmission in Gaelic's revitalisation. Increasing the number of mother tongue speakers was a goal of the first National Plan for Gaelic (Bòrd na Gàidhlig 2007), but the subsequent National Gaelic Language Plan (Bòrd na Gàidhlig 2012) treats Gaelic speakers as a unified community, singular rather than plural, with the revival of absolute numbers of Gaelic speakers the overarching policy goal. As such, there is a lack of clarity over what support might be appropriate for the reproduction of 'traditional' or first language (L1) Gaelic speakers, who acquire Gaelic in the home and community – and usually in conjunction with formal education – as distinct from 'new speakers', who have little or no home or community exposure to the language and typically acquire it through Gaelic immersion education or in the classroom in adulthood (cf. O'Rourke et al. 2015).

Although there has been long-term ethnographic research into Gaelic language maintenance efforts *within* the family (see Smith-Christmas 2016, 2018), the absence of chapters on targeted initiatives for family language planning reflects a lacuna in this area of wider language policy. In contrast to family language planning initiatives which exist/have existed for Irish (Tús Maith) or Welsh (Twf), for example, there are no national initiatives whose primary aim is supporting Gaelic language use in the family. Rather, parent and toddler groups, as described by Kirstie MacLeod, are the primary strategic policy vehicle for supporting any caregiver with an interest in early years Gaelic acquisition. Yet in her ethnographic study of such a group, Kirstie MacLeod notes the ideological misalignment between language-in-education policy for Gaelic, with its 'narrow focus on primary enrolment', and the lived realities of parents and carers, whose primary concern is often the quality and convenience of the early years learning environment.

Timothy C. Armstrong and Stuart Dunmore both engage with the role of schools in Gaelic's revitalisation, and, more importantly, with the responsibility of state-level education institutions to create the next generation of Gaelic speakers. Armstrong questions the ideological basis for Gaelic immersion education, arguing that a revivalist ideology, which links language and identity, is necessary. Yet his ethnography of the construction of a language policy for a new Gaelic school in Edinburgh shows how a revivalist ideology can be resisted and contested in the public domain. His claim that, 'We still do not have clear vision among activists, policy-makers or educationalists of exactly what a "Gaelic school" means', is brought into sharp focus in light of Dunmore's findings. The dataset analysed by Dunmore underlines the impact of a weak model of Gaelic immersion in secondary school education on longer term identification with the language. As we learn, Gaelic-medium educated children are not necessarily going to become active bilinguals in adulthood. In a similar vein, Marsaili MacLeod relates the mismatch too between the policy aspiration to create a new generation of fluent speakers through a national adult Gaelic language learning programme which offers only 216 hours of language tuition, and the protracted and frustrated process of learning Gaelic for even the most motivated of adult learners, many of whom will never reach fluency.

Intergenerational change and new speakerhood

These observations suggest a second key theme of *new speakerhood*. As has been emphasised throughout these chapters, there is a recursive relationship between the family, the community and education as sites for creating new Gaelic-speaking identities. Dunmore stresses, 'it is clear that the goal of strengthening Gaelic language socialisation in the home and community needs to be prioritised alongside developing GME as a policy objective'. Conversely, elsewhere Smith-Christmas' diachronic study of Gaelic family language practice concludes 'while the caregivers' use of the minority language in the home is extremely important to achieving intergenerational transmission, it is only part of the process, so to speak, in ultimately achieving this important stage' (2016: 113). The extent of what MacKinnon (2011) refers to as 'runaway language shift' in Scotland means the scale of the challenge of restoring intergenerational transmission cannot be underestimated, even in families and households which are committed to using Gaelic as a daily language.

The contributions from Armstrong and Marsaili MacLeod illuminate the common challenge for the cultivation of new speakers, irrespective of age: the creation of naturalistic contexts for new speakers, which can enable them to undergo the identity transformations necessary for active speakerhood. Yet we learn of the social realities of would-be adult new speakers, such as Mac, who deliberately 'seek out conversations', but often to no avail. The plausibility of becoming an active Gaelic speaker through a transformation in linguistic practice, or *muda* (cf. Pujolar and Puigdevall 2015; Puigdevall et al. 2018), is often circumscribed by a lack of opportunities to use Gaelic in the community context, which can, as a result, undermine the typical adult learners' confidence of ever becoming a fluent or legitimate (cf. Sallabank and Marquis 2018) speaker. The policy goal to achieve 'out of classroom' use by second language (L2) adult learners of Gaelic mirrors the public discourse over the 'language of the playground' amongst younger speakers, which is construed as a 'benchmark' of success in language acquisition policy.

Such new institutional contexts for language acquisition, and the advent of habitual new uses and users of Gaelic, prompts reflection on contemporary speech as the linguistic and social boundaries between 'learners' and 'natives' weaken. McLeod points out that young 'native' speakers can also depend on school-based input, and that most are English-dominant (see also Dunbar 2011), leading to the concerns articulated by participants of Susan Bell and Mark McConville's study. Here, the dominant language ideology among adult Gaelic speakers is found to be a form of 'retrophilia'. Bell and McConville's participants attach the highest value to 'good traditional Gaelic', the vernacular language still used by the typical older, native speaker, as compared to 'Gaelic which is just like a thin porridge', as one participant said of contemporary Gaelic learnt through schooling.

The perceived markers of 'good traditional Gaelic', according to Bell and McConville's participants, include the use of 'natural idioms', which form the focus of Sìleas L. NicLeòid's study of children's Gaelic. NicLeòid offers children's perspectives on their own language, relating how older children establish their own personal paradigms for speaking Gaelic, and claim their Gaelic as 'modern', as distinct from vernacular Gaelic characterised by idiomatic expressions. Here the agency of children themselves is exercised as they unselfconsciously use a form of institutional Gaelic which they acknowledge differs from the Gaelic of older speakers. '[T]hey speak Gaelic in a way we don't speak now' said one, and as such, said another, 'it's not cool'. This stance constructs traditional language as 'old-fashioned', and renders 'school Gaelic' as 'modern'. The situation of the schoolchildren interviewed by NicLeòid, who by virtue of Gaelic immersion education seemingly occupy a stable and unproblematic identity position, contrasts with the experiences of Gaelic-medium educated adults reported by Dunmore, whose Gaelic-speaking identities are fluid and dependent upon social networks outside of the home and family, in particular in post-secondary education and employment.

In Ireland, a body of work (cf. Ó Murchadha 2013; Ó Murchadha and Ó hIfearnáin 2018; Nic Fhlannchadha and Hickey 2018) demonstrates that a new non-traditional variety of Irish is being accommodated while access to conservative native speaker models diminishes, raising concerns over 'what is sustainable in a minority language context, and what is desirable from the perspective of the people who speak the language' (Nic Fhlannchadha and Hickey 2018: 50). This question is tackled in Bell and McConville's case study. In the *Dlùth is Inneach* consensus-building process, the concerns held by Gaelic speakers over perceived linguistic accommodation and hybridisation emerge, although there is a lacuna of linguistic evidence on the extent of either process. As McLeod (2017) notes, dialectal diversity has not been problematised or prioritised in acquisition or in corpus planning. Yet the findings here suggest that the tension arises not from concerns over a loss of dialectical diversity or from an ideological leaning to language purism, but from a concern that fluency levels are being eroded through what NicLeòid describes as 'a process of simplification'.

The observations in these studies have important links with reclamation efforts in other small language contexts, where academic debates over the meaning of a transition to 'post-traditional' language reflect tensions in policy and praxis. On the one hand, a body of research on new speakerhood (cf. O'Rourke and Walsh 2018) argues for a non-preservationist stance which accepts linguistic innovation and hybridisation, while others theorise new linguistic features amongst younger bilingual speakers as symptomatic of language attrition due to the dominance of the majority language in the community, despite schooling in the minority language (see, for example, for Irish the work of Péteráry et al. 2014, and for Welsh, Thomas and Roberts 2011).

The professionalisation of Gaelic revitalisation

The national commitment to Gaelic's revitalisation in Scotland and the legislative framework for securing it as an official language of Scotland places Gaelic in an enviable position relative to a number of other small language communities in Western Europe which are still vying for official recognition and/or support. Indeed, as a social movement Gaelic revivalism has been an undoubtable success: scholars researching Gaelic language shift in the 1970s (cf. MacKinnon 1977; Dorian 1981) could not have predicted a confident generation of young speakers refashioning Gaelic identity in the way they are today. The achievements in Gaelic broadcasting, in Gaelic education and in public life reflect the remarkable resilience and tenacity of Gaelic speakers in Scotland and the work of organisations and individuals who were instrumental in initiating this process of state-led legitimation. Notwithstanding, there are some inherent challenges in the professionalisation of language planning endeavours. On the one hand it has raised the status of Gaelic in Scotland and facilitated an expansion in Gaelic education, in broadcasting and in language management initiatives. On the other hand, the research here shows that the sector is confounded by the scale of the challenge, which requires professional resources and a workforce equipped with the necessary language and professional skills. This gives rise to the third cross-cutting theme of *capacity*.

Creating opportunities for the habitual use of Gaelic in public life has required the reclamation of community and public domains which have historically undergone language shift to English. Given that a considerable proportion of Gaelic speakers do not use Gaelic at home, and reflecting the mixed sociolinguistic composition of most bilinguals' households, these domains of use are instrumental to reversing language shift.[1] The studies here highlight how the professionalisation of Gaelic language planning has given rise to a type of professional work which offers new symbolic and material spaces for Gaelic use (cf. McEwan-Fujita 2008; MacLeod 2008). Macleod et al.'s study (this volume) of the language planning workforce represents strong objective evidence that language planning is, however, a marginal concern of public sector organisations. They draw attention to a shortage of Gaelic skills within organisations which in turn weakens their capacity to effect change in linguistic practice when interacting with the public. The authors allude to the potentially negative impact this working collective has on Gaelic practice and behaviours, particularly in local authorities, where only a minority involved in Gaelic language service activities work through the medium of Gaelic. Increasing the capacity of organisations to extend Gaelic language plan commitments beyond the symbolic measures described by Dunbar requires high-level language skills training, for both oral and written skills, which the national Úlpan course described by Marsaili MacLeod does not offer. The case studies presented by Dunbar highlight how issues of capacity can affect implementation of GLPs: the emphasis on symbolic measures to raise the status of Gaelic will seldom effect a change in the level of interactional use of Gaelic between staff and the public.

Ingeborg Birnie's case study addresses this very issue, through analysis of *in situ* bilingual practices in the community of Stornoway, the main settlement in the Gaelic heartland. Birnie's analysis of the language of interaction in public spaces demonstrates that the level of Gaelic is not correlated with the presence or absence of statutory organisational GLPs. Aligning with the growing interest in the ethnography of language as a means to investigating language policy (cf. McCarty 2011), this study adopts Shohamy's (2006) approach to the micro-study of 'real' language policy as enacted by speakers rather than penned by organisations. Norms and beliefs about appropriate language use explain why Gaelic is used only for speaking 'to who they know about what they know'. As Dunbar notes, the GLP mechanism is meant to increase the use of Gaelic – which, Birnie's results suggest, it does between front-of-house staff with Gaelic skills. But convincing the public to uphold and assert their language preference for Gaelic or to negotiate its use with strangers involves transgression of the use of the common language as a 'mode of social alignment' (Clayton 2009: 486). It seems the Gaelic-speaking public has not yet bought into the 'new sociolinguistic order' (cf. O'Rourke et al. 2015) that the language management initiatives seek to bring about.

The cases thus call into question the organisations best-placed to revitalise Gaelic at a local level. Changing grass-roots societal norms, Armstrong suggests, requires leadership on controversial ideological questions which government agencies, he argues, are not necessarily in a position to undertake. Armstrong posits that 'on-the-ground language activists' could be the most effective actors to develop the 'ideological clarification' required at a local level, in order to bring about changes in local institutions, including schools. Certainly, Kirstie MacLeod's example of a national resource pack for early years Gaelic providers demonstrates how a top-down approach to language planning can be misaligned with localised beliefs and practices. One way to give agency to Gaelic speakers is through a language-rights regime, as articulated by Dunbar, yet there is little political appetite among Gaelic speakers to agitate for such change.

Taken together, these findings suggest that multiple agendas, negotiations and ideological stances characterise relationships between Bòrd na Gàidhlig, public authorities and diverse community groups who hold a stake in Gaelic language revitalisation. Through the study of the practices and ideologies of speakers in a range of contexts, the findings presented here force us to reconsider the very meaning of Gaelic 'revitalisation' and cause us to rethink what would constitute a success in Gaelic revitalisation in Scotland. The national goal, as set out in the 2012–2017 National Plan for Gaelic, is to increase the total number of Gaelic speakers to 65,000 by 2021. The observations of Williams (2017: n.p.) in relation to Welsh language planning might equally apply to Gaelic in Scotland: 'the somewhat arbitrary target does not necessarily serve the goals of revitalization: a putative set of skills among a politically symbolic target population matters less than actual usage of Welsh in a wide range of domains in daily life'. As the authors in this volume show, the challenges and opportunities for revitalising Gaelic in Scotland are variegated and complex, and their implications for the future of the Gaelic community are unclear.

Future research directions

We close with some observations on areas of Gaelic language management, beliefs and practices which deserve more attention in future research. In order to better understand language development in a bilingual context, the characterisation of the linguistic profiles of young speakers and the types of language ability they possess is needed. Macleod et al.'s (2014) pilot study of children's GME classroom speech performance offers a starting point for exploring aspects of grammatical competence, while Nance (2015, 2018) has conducted analysis into phonological variation among children. In the last five years, there has been a considerable body of research on the social characteristics of adult L2 users of Gaelic, but less so on their linguistic characteristics (see Cole 2015 for an investigation of structural variation as a result of language shift). Understanding how domain-specific input and use interact with age effects over the life cycle could usefully inform the development of pedagogical materials and assessment tools for the teaching and learning of Gaelic.

The impact of organisational and structural changes on people's language attitudes and behaviour towards Gaelic is a long-term process, and one in which policy cannot *directly* intervene. However, the success of organisational Gaelic language plans, suggests Dunbar, should be judged upon the impact of plans on the internal workings of an organisation and the use of bilingual services by Gaelic users. The need for a 'systematic evaluation of the operation and effectiveness' of the Gaelic language plan mechanism is clearly needed in order to reveal any mismatches between the intended impact and outcomes and the aspirations of the Gaelic communities that they serve. Such research might focus on organisations and departments with daily interactions with Gaelic speakers, such as in health care, education and public administration, where any potential impacts are likely to be greatest. Comparative research with other minority language contexts and language planning models could identify alternative or complementary approaches to language revitalisation, which could be adapted to the Gaelic context.

The authors in this volume bring a range of methodological approaches to bear on both rural and urban sociolinguistic contexts, yet there are important omissions. There remains a lacuna in research over the material aspects of language revitalisation, including literary texts, online resources and corpus-building materials. A critical analysis of the material, and its production and application, could usefully inform the authorship of new materials to support language revitalisation, and identify gaps that the academic community's expertise could inform. A second research gap pertains to studies which examine performative and interactional aspects of language use in traditional and non-traditional contexts, including digital media, occupational settings and online communities. It is within these settings where much of the daily life of Gaelic speakers is likely to be situated in an increasingly networked and digitised society. A closer reading of language practices, including code-switching, translanguaging and other novel forms of interaction, would shed conceptual and empirical light on what it means to be(come) a Gaelic speaker in twenty-first-century Scotland.

Note

1. In 2011, 58.8 per cent of all Gaelic speakers reported they used no Gaelic at home (2011 Census, National Records of Scotland 2015).

References

Bòrd na Gàidhlig. 2007. *The National Plan for Gaelic 2007–2012/Plana Nàiseanta na Gàidhlig 2007–2012.* Inbhir Nis/Inverness: Bòrd na Gàidhlig.

Bòrd na Gàidhlig. 2012. *National Gaelic Language Plan 2012–2017: Growth and Improvement/Plana Cànain Nàiseanta Gàidhlig 2012–2017: Fàs and Feabhas.* Inverness/Inbhir Nis: Bòrd na Gàidhlig.

Clayton, John. 2009. Thinking Spatially: Towards an Everyday Understanding of Inter-ethnic Relations. *Social and Cultural Geography* 10(4), 481–498.

Cole, Beth. 2015. Morphosyntactic Variation in Uist Gaelic: A Case of Language Shift? Aberdeen: University of Aberdeen unpublished PhD thesis.

Dorian, Nancy C. 1981. *Language Death: The Life Cycle of a Scottish Gaelic Dialect.* Philadelphia: University of Pennsylvania Press.

Dunbar, Robert. 2011. Bilingualism: Conceptual Difficulties and Practical Challenges. In John M. Kirk and Dónall P. Ó Baoill (eds), *Strategies for Minority Languages: Northern Ireland, the Republic of Ireland, and Scotland*, 150–163. Beul Feirste: Cló Ollscoil na Banríona.

McCarty, Teresa L. (ed.). 2011. *Ethnography and Language Policy.* New York: Routledge.

McEwan-Fujita, Emily. 2008. '9 to 5' Gaelic: Speakers, Context, and Ideology of an Emerging Minority Language Register. In Kendall A. King, Natalie Schilling-Estes, Lyn Fogle, Jia Jackie Lou and Barbara Soukup (eds), *Sustaining Linguistic Diversity: Endangered and Minority Languages and Language Varieties*, 81–93. Washington, DC: Georgetown University Press.

MacKinnon, Kenneth. 1977. *Language, Education and Social Processes in a Gaelic Community.* London: Routledge.

MacKinnon, Kenneth. 2011. Runaway Language Shift: Gaelic Usage in Home, Community and Media in the Isle of Skye and Western Isles, 1986/8, 1994/5 and 2004/5 – Any Prospects for Reversal? In Richard A. V. Cox and Timothy C. Armstrong (eds), *A' Cleachdadh na Gàidhlig; slatan-tomhais ann an dìon cànain sa choimhearsnachd*, 201–226. Slèite: Clò Ostaig.

MacLeod, Marsaili. 2008. Revitalising Rural Europe's Indigenous Languages: 'Technologisation' and the Gaelic Language. In Grete Rusten and Sarah Skerratt (eds), *Information and Communication Technologies in Rural Society: Being Rural in a Digital Age*, 125–151. Oxon, UK: Routledge.

Macleod, Michelle, Marsaili MacLeod, Anne Thirkell and Do Coyle. 2014. *Young Speakers' Use of Gaelic in the Primary Classroom: A Multi-perspectival Pilot Study.* Soillse Research Report. Sleat, Isle of Skye: Soillse.

McLeod, Wilson. 2017. Dialectal Diversity in Contemporary Gaelic: Perceptions, Discourses and Responses. In Janet Cruickshank and Robert McColl Millar (eds),

Before the Storm: Papers from the Forum for Research on the Languages of Scotland and Ulster Triennial Meeting, Ayr 2015, 183–211. Aberdeen: Forum for Research on the Languages of Scotland and Ireland.

Moseley, Christopher (ed.). 2010. *Atlas of the World's Languages in Danger*, 3rd edition. Paris: UNESCO Publishing. Available online at http://www.unesco.org/languages-atlas/index.php?hl=en&page=atlasmap (last accessed 8 January 2018).

Nance, Claire. 2015. Intonational Variation and Change in Scottish Gaelic. *Lingua* 160, 1–19.

Nance, Claire. 2018. Linguistic Innovation Among Glasgow Gaelic New Speakers. In Cassie Smith-Christmas, Noel P. Ó Murchadha, Michael Hornsby and Máiréad Moriarty (eds), *New Speakers of Minority Languages: Linguistic Ideologies and Practices*, 213–226. Basingstoke: Palgrave Macmillan.

National Records of Scotland. 2015. *Scotland's Census 2011: Gaelic Report (Part 1)*. Available online at http://www.scotlandscensus.gov.uk/documents/analytical_reports/Report_part%201.pdf (last accessed 2 November 2015).

Nic Fhlannchadha, Siobhán and Tina M. Hickey. 2018. Minority Language Ownership and Authority: Perspectives of Native Speakers and New Speakers. *International Journal of Bilingual Education and Bilingualism* 2(1), 38–53. doi:10.1080/13670050.2015.1127888

Ó Murchadha, Noel P. 2013. Authority and Innovation in Language Variation: Teenagers' Perceptions of Variation in Spoken Irish. In Tore Kristiansen and Stefan Grondelaers (eds), *Language (De)Standardisation in Late Modern Europe: Experimental Studies*, 71–96. Oslo: Novus.

Ó Murchadha, Noel and Tadhg Ó hIfearnáin. 2018. Converging and Diverging Stances on Target Revival Varieties in Collateral Languages: The Ideologies of Linguistic Variation in Irish and Manx Gaelic. *Journal of Multilingual and Multicultural Development*. doi:10.1080/01434632.2018.1429450

O'Rourke, Bernadette and John Walsh. 2018. Introduction. *Journal of Multilingual and Multicultural Development*. doi:10.1080/01434632.2018.1429449

O'Rourke, Bernadette, Joan Pujolar and Fernando Ramallo. 2015. New Speakers of Minority Languages: The Challenging Opportunity. *International Journal of the Sociology of Language* 231, 1–20.

Péteráry, Tamás, Brian Ó Curnáin, Conchúr Ó Giollagáin and Jerome Sheahan. 2014. *Iniúchadh ar an gCumas Dátheangach: An Sealbhú Teanga i Measc Ghlúin Óg na Gaeltachta/Analysis of Bilingual Competence: Language Acquisition Among Young People in the Gaeltacht*. Baile Átha Cliath: Partners in Print.

Puigdevall, Maite, John Walsh, Estibaliz Amorrortu and Ane Ortega. 2018. 'I'll be One of Them': Linguistic *Mudes* and New Speakers in Three Minority Language Contexts. *Journal of Multilingual and Multicultural Development*. doi:10.1080/01434632.2018.1429453

Pujolar, Joan and Maite Puigdevall. 2015. Linguistic Mudes: How to Become a New Speaker in Catalonia. *International Journal of the Sociology of Language* 231, 167–187.

Sallabank, Julia and Yan Marquis. 2018. 'We Don't Say it Like That': Language Ownership and (de)Legitimising the New Speaker. In Cassie Smith-Christmas,

Noel Ó Murchadha, Michael Hornsby and Máiréad Moriarty (eds), *New Speakers of Minority Languages: Linguistic Ideologies and Practices*. Basingstoke: Palgrave Macmillan.

Shohamy, Elena. 2006. *Language Policy: Hidden Agendas and New Approaches*. New York: Routledge.

Smith-Christmas, Cassie. 2016. *Family Language Policy: Maintaining an Endangered Language in the Home*. Basingstoke: Palgrave Macmillan.

Smith-Christmas, Cassie. 2018. 'One Cas, Two Cas': Exploring the Affective Dimensions of Family Language Policy. *Multilingua – Journal of Cross-Cultural and Interlanguage Communication* 37(2), 131–152.

Thomas, Enlli Môn and Dylan Bryn Roberts. 2011. Exploring Bilinguals' Social Use of Language Inside and Out of the Minority Language Classroom. *Language and Education* 25(2), 89–108.

Williams, Colin H. 2017. Policy Review: Wake me up in 2050! Formulating Language Policy in Wales. *Language, Society and Policy*. Available online at http://www.meits.org/policy-papers/paper/wake-me-up-in-2050-formulating-language-policy-in-wales (last accessed 1 March 2018).

Index